COMPANIES
WE KEEP

COMPANIES WE KEEP

Employee Ownership and the Business of Community and Place

JOHN ABRAMS

Foreword by William Greider

CHELSEA GREEN PUBLISHING COMPANY

WHITE RIVER JUNCTION, VERMONT

Developmental Editor: Shay Totten
Project Manager: Bill Bokermann
Copy Editor: Laura Jorstad
Proofreader: Helen Walden
Book Designer: Peter Holm
Printed in the United States of America

5 4 3 2 1   08 09 10 11 12

Library of Congress Cataloging-in-Publication Data

Abrams, John.
  Companies we keep : employee ownership and the business of community and place / John Abrams ; foreword by
William Greider. -- 2nd ed.
    p. cm.
  Rev. ed. of: Company we keep. c2005
  Includes bibliographical references and index.
  ISBN 978-1-60358-000-7
  1. South Mountain Company--History. 2. Construction industry--Massachusetts--Martha's Vineyard--Case stud-
ies. 3. Employee ownership--Massachusetts--Martha's Vineyard. 4. House construction--Massachusetts--Martha's
Vineyard--Case studies. 5. Employee ownership. 6. House construction--Environmental aspects. 7. Social
responsibility of business. 8. Industrial management--Environmental aspects. I. Abrams, John. Company we keep.
II. Title.
  HD9715.U54S682 2008
  338.7'69080974494--dc22

                              2008025075

Chelsea Green Publishing Company
Post Office Box 428
White River Junction, VT 05001
(800) 639-4099
www.chelseagreen.com

Companies We Keep is the revised and expanded edition of The Company We Keep by John Abrams,
published by Chelsea Green Publishing in 2005.

The Chelsea Green Publishing Company is committed
to preserving ancient forests and natural resources. We
elected to print this title on 100% postconsumer recycled paper, processed chlorine-free. As a result, for this
printing, we have saved:

53 Trees (40' tall and 6-8" diameter)
19,377 Gallons of Wastewater
38 million BTU's Total Energy
2,488 Pounds of Solid Waste
4,668 Pounds of Greenhouse Gases

Chelsea Green Publishing made this paper choice because
we and our printer, Thomson-Shore, Inc., are members
of the Green Press Initiative, a nonprofit program dedicated to supporting authors, publishers, and suppliers
in their efforts to reduce their use of fiber obtained
from endangered forests. For more information, visit:
www.greenpressinitiative.org.

Environmental impact estimates were made using the Environmental Defense Paper Calculator.
For more information visit: www.papercalculator.org.

Our Commitment to Green Publishing

Chelsea Green sees publishing as a
tool for cultural change and ecological stewardship. We strive to align our
book manufacturing practices with our
editorial mission and to reduce the
impact of our business enterprise in
the environment. We print our books
and catalogs on chlorine-free recycled
paper, using soy-based inks whenever
possible. This book may cost slightly
more because we use recycled paper,
and we hope you'll agree that it's
worth it. Chelsea Green is a member
of the Green Press Initiative (www.
greenpressinitiative.org), a nonprofit
coalition of publishers, manufacturers, and authors working to protect
the world's endangered forests and
conserve natural resources. Companies
We Keep was printed on 55-lb. Rolland
Enviro Natural, a 100-percent postcon-
sumer-waste recycled paper supplied by
Thomson-Shore.

CONTENTS

FOREWORD

What you have in your hands is the memoir of one small residential design and building company, written by the cofounder who has been the devoted steward of the enterprise across some thirty-five years. Improbable as this may sound, you will find his story irresistibly charming. It is also, perhaps, challenging to the usual ways of thinking about businesses (and building contractors). But, above all, it is intellectually provocative, because this book takes the reader from the intimate, pedestrian details of company life to much grander propositions about society and the elements of a sound economy.

In this second edition the author has added a new dimension, and the book has become a manual that leads the reader through the steps that his company, and a growing number of like-minded others, are taking to transform themselves into long-lasting models of social entrepreneurism.

There is a seductive quality in all this. You start with an engagingly modest story about one small place that tried to do things differently. Then you find yourself thinking about the nature of honest work and cooperation, about the deeper meanings of quality and enduring value, about designing and creating self-accountability among the people who share in the life of a firm. Finally, you bear witness to the process of embedding strong principles into the genetic code of the company.

John Abrams is one of those rare souls who set out to find his own way in life, without much of a plan but with strong, distinctive personal and social values. He sounds a trifle naive at first because he seems to think that one can adhere faithfully to such convictions while also pursuing commerce. Yet he has succeeded at this (he would probably say he is still working on it). But the story is not really about him; it's about South Mountain Company and how it found its groove and prospered. The author tells enough about himself that you can locate his unself-conscious humility and optimism as authentic. What he really wants you to understand is the living, evolving organism of this company. The message is about how craftsmanship and dignity can be restored and sustained in a world of industrial complexity and the mass-market degradation of cherished values.

And what begins as a memoir of John's own company quickly turns into what is truly at work here—his passion for telling stories. Good stories, compelling stories, stories that showcase the people who have also taken this brave leap into employee ownership. They challenge our notions of growth, decision making, succession planning, and how our society defines success.

Like the other companies John profiles in this how-to memoir, South Mountain starts with a handful of people and expands gradually. Its co-workers become co-owners and work their way through the usual obstacles and temptations of business life. Little by little, however, they find ways—actually the company's precious cornerstones—to sustain a collegial sense of self-criticism. Managed inclusiveness and mutual respect, one might call it. Because John is relentlessly modest (and compassionate) in his storytelling, many of the false starts or wrong ideas are attributed to him and challenged and corrected by others. The business approaches and undertakings are repeatedly held up to the shared values and tested. The process is not without setbacks and compromises. But, even discounting for his modesty, John convinces us that this culture does exist as everyday reality at South Mountain, and that it works.

The story is extraordinary, but what can we learn from it? After all, the company is small and operates in an exotic marketplace—the island of Martha's Vineyard—where the culture and affluence are unusual, and people are disposed to support high principles in home design and building. I began reading the memoir with that thought foremost in my mind. When I finished, I realized, no, that's mistaken. Their experiences are in microcosm, but the ideas and understandings formed among the human beings seem universal. With goodwill and serious values, they are portable to other places, including larger enterprises, where the people also want to do things differently.

William Greider

BOB GOTHARD

Introduction to the Second Edition

You should never have your best trousers on when
you go out to fight for freedom and truth.
—HENRIK IBSEN

A ship in harbor is safe—but that is not what ships are for.
—JOHN A. SHEDD

There's something I'm worried about. It has to do with me.

Each time I read about the exploding economies of China and India and the resources they may consume to emulate the American Way, I wonder why I don't devote the rest of my life—every waking hour—to working on climate change. Imagining the consequences of this pursuit of global parity is enough to suck the hope from me like a vacuum pulls crumbs from a rug.

I worry, too, that I don't change the way I live more significantly. Change is hard. I loved my old Toyota Land Cruiser and drove it a quarter million miles. But after 9/11 when those bumper stickers with a picture of Osama bin Laden said, THANK YOU FOR DRIVING YOUR SUV, I felt I just had to switch. So I bought a hybrid. Now I only support terrorism when I'm going uphill.

None of us can do it all, but each of us can do something. And maybe it's more than we think. At South Mountain Company, the design/build company I founded in 1975 that is now owned and operated by its employees, one of our goals is to make all operations carbon-neutral in ten years. We have not yet fully defined what that means—for us—but we are moving toward the goal nonetheless. As I write, in March 2008, we heat our building and run our forklifts with biodiesel, some of which we make ourselves. We generate 25 percent of our electricity with a wind turbine. By the time you read this we will have increased that to 90 percent thanks to a new, more productive wind turbine and the addition of a solar-electric system. In our work, we are moving closer to net-zero-energy houses, and even our subsidized affordable housing is built to a standard that will allow it to be "forever affordable."

So what? How does our little drop in the bucket matter?

First, it gives us hope. Vaclav Havel, the former Czech president, says this about hope:

> Hope . . . is not the same as joy that things are going well, or willingness to invest in enterprises that are obviously headed for early success, but, rather, an ability to work for something because it is good, not just because it stands a chance to succeed. Hope is not the conviction that something will turn out well, but the *certainty that something makes sense, regardless of how it turns out.*[1]

This is one of the reasons we do what we do—the conviction that it makes sense, regardless of its modest impact. It may be just a drop in the bucket, but rivers are nothing more than accumulations of drops. Each drop has an impact.

At its core, climate change is not a technical problem. It's about how we live, what we value, and how we organize our economy to serve our lifestyles and values. To change our relationship to the Earth we must change our relationships to one another. We need to change our definition of success, so that it's less about doing and making as much as we can as fast as we can and more about satisfying human needs as elegantly and effectively as we can. We need to think about *enough* rather than *more*. We need to consider new forms of governance and business.

At South Mountain our cooperative ownership structure assigns the wealth we make to those who make it. Our democratic system of decision making offers everyone a voice. Our collaborative culture promotes a healthy, meaningful workplace. These, too, give me hope.

I am finding that—since the original publication of this book in 2005—there is a thirst for hopeful stories that bring out the best in all of us, and a concurrent awakening of interest in the potential of broadly shared ownership. This idea—which still mostly flies beneath the radar—is beginning to surface all over the world, in companies small and large. If a lack of believable models is part of what inhibits change, perhaps the story of South Mountain, and democratic, community-based companies like it, can provide inspiration, or at least information, for those looking for a more attractive approach to business success. I would like to think that our story, and those of others who share this journey, can help us as we try to assemble the components of a restorative future.

That future will depend in part on how we address climate change, perhaps the most vexing issue humankind has ever faced. It will require us to think differently, act differently, and dream differently. It will require us to remodel our economy, one drop at a time. It will require radical political change as well. As author Peter Barnes says in *Climate Solutions*:

> We need to act quickly . . . to fix the market flaw that causes climate change. That means creating a workable and lasting system for limiting our pollution of the atmosphere. Such a system would reflect the fact that the atmosphere is a commons that belongs to everyone. It would cap carbon as it enters the economy, and gradually lower the cap [by 2 percent per year] so that,

by 2050, emissions are at least 80 percent below the current level.

He goes on,

> A leak-proof descending carbon cap will have many positive ripple effects. Higher carbon prices will spur private investments in conservation, efficiency, and non-carbon technologies. Utilities will know what kinds of plants to build. . . . Automakers will know what kinds of cars to build. . . .[2]

And legislators will finally know what to subsidize: mass transit, smart electricity grids, energy efficiency, renewable energy, converting waste to resources, extended producer responsibility, localization, third-party certification of natural resource use, and those endeavors that promote and restore community.

As a culture, we have just begun these transformative tasks. To design and build an entirely new worldwide energy system and ethos, we will need to muster the equivalent of a wartime mobilization. If we commit unprecedented investment and unleash our creativity, we are likely to produce economic opportunity and prosperity in the face of crisis. This great undertaking could create good work, alleviate poverty, and save the planet from ourselves. It will take more than investment; it will require collaboration of a type and scale heretofore unknown. We will need new tools, new abilities, and new ways of working together. All of us will need to own the endeavor. A central requirement for the journey may be the ability to own our workplaces and share responsibility for the outcomes, both good and bad.

That is what this book is about. It's about the recognition that when the people who are making the decisions bear the responsibility for the consequences of those decisions, and also share in the rewards that accrue, better decisions will result. It's about building community within the workplace and connections to the communities where we work and live.

If we learn the skills of collaboration in the workplace, the benefits might spread to civic and social life as well. In the November 2007 issue of *The Journal of Organizational Behavior*, Gretchen Spreitzer, a professor at the University of Michigan's Ross School of Business, says that her research has led to the conclusion that "When employees can partici-pate and have a role in governance issues, they are likely to . . . be further attracted to participatory leadership in other settings."[3] Exposure to egal-itarian methods in the workplace can nourish democratic inclinations in all walks of life. It is my belief that widespread employee ownership of business can play a part in the new human story as it unfolds, by spread-ing the ethics of ownership, responsibility, democratic participation, and ecological stewardship.

Curbing corporate abuse, reining in the global corporate juggernaut, and mobilizing to grapple with climate change are largely dependent on the kind of political change Barnes recommends. But politics is a crapshoot, where the dice may not fall the way we wish and each of us can have only a minor impact on the political process. Meanwhile, however, our democracy offers other choices. While we work toward political solutions, we have the liberty to invent the corporation of the future right now. We can make whatever kinds of companies we want.

Nothing stands in our way.

My earliest memory is an incident that occurred when my family lived in San Francisco from 1949 to 1952. I must have been two. I was still in a crib and I couldn't talk, or only barely, but I could climb in and out of my crib. It seemed like half a mile to the other side of the room, where my sister Nancy's bed was. Three years older than me, she was a mentor and friend. She talked to me a lot. And she had a pillow on her bed.

I had noticed my parents had pillows, too, on their bed. Why didn't

I? It was nearly bedtime. In my one-piece pajama suit, all flannel and containment, I padded out of the room, down the hall, and into my parents' room (they were probably downstairs; Nancy was in the bathroom brushing her teeth). I tugged at a pillow. It slid off the bed easily, and I dragged it down the hallway to my crib.

The pillow was unwieldy, like a sack of grain. I pushed it up against the crib bars, over my head, tussled with it a bit, and then with a final effort tipped it in. I had a pillow. I hoisted myself up and in, squirreled under the covers, and settled my head into this new soft luxury.

My mother came in to read me a book. She pulled up a chair next to the crib. Then she noticed. "Where did that pillow come from?" I wonder how I reacted. Deer in the headlights? Or nonchalant, smug with success? Who knows? She left the room, and when she came back a moment later, she was cooing and apologetic: "Oh, you felt left out? Everyone else had one and you didn't? Oh, well . . . you've got a pillow now."

Oh, the sweetness of being understood!

When I told this story once, my wife, Chris, chuckled and said, "Pretty funny that your first memory is of the discovery of a plot to deny you something and your subversive activities to right the wrong."

Talk about being understood.

That's what the reaction to this book has been like; I feel like I have been understood. When the book was first released I had the opportunity to see the results of my work, just like our designers and carpenters do when they stand back to examine a completed house. At the time, however, I had no idea how people would respond, or if they would at all. It has not been deafening but it has been steady and enthusiastic. I am thrilled to have the opportunity to further develop the book, to reply, having learned enough—from readers, friends and family, people in the company, and events of the three years since its publication— that I have something more to say.

A number of people have asked for a new thread: How can companies make these transitions; what is the road map to employee ownership, and how do we traverse it? As my good friend and faithful critic Jamie Wolf says: Can you make this book be about *my* company as much as it is about yours?

To address that, I have expanded the focus on employee ownership: more depth, more breadth, and more of the practical information necessary for businesses considering a restructuring. The context is important. My fellow baby boomers own several million businesses, and during the next two decades most of these founders will exit. The businesses will either shut down or be passed on. Selling to employees is an option that deserves to be more widely understood, for it offers powerful benefits to all parties. There is a need for more information as employee ownership becomes an important entity of choice. There is new knowledge and there are new practices that make employee ownership more widely applicable.

The first chapter is the beginning of our story. The second chapter examines the idea of employee ownership and its place in our economy. It aims to put the story of South Mountain Company in a broader context. The rest of the book continues our story, traversing the ground we have covered and connecting it, I hope, to the awakenings I see all around me.

In the appendices there is a detailed blueprint of the South Mountain system. There is also an agenda with the steps needed for employee ownership conversions, and resources to guide and assist the effort— the itinerary for safe passage.

I have made revisions and updates throughout the book as well, many of them in response to specific inquiries I have received from readers.

"So . . . ," say some, "why not just write another book?"

Because this one's not done yet, for me at least. Rather, it feels ripe for renovation. The additional information I want to communicate fits neatly into the existing context, and I would like for those who read this second edition to have the full experience of *this* book, not some other one.

There's another thing.

Sometimes—this will ring a bell, I'm sure—we walk away from a completed conversation or emerge from a meeting, and, on the way home, we suddenly realize, *Oh yes, of course,* that's *what I should have said.* That's *what would have moved things forward;* that's *what would have done the trick.*

That's what this feels like. I have an opportunity here to keep the conversation going, to say some things I meant to say, and didn't, or didn't know enough to say at the time. Through the *Companies We Keep* Web site I hope this second edition can nurture an ongoing discussion. Visit www.southmountain.com/companieswekeep after you finish the book, and let's keep talking.

This is all about us, and all about sharing ownership of the future. It's about thinking differently, acting differently, dreaming differently, and encouraging one another along the way. If this book, and the ongoing exchange it may provoke, can help us to learn to work together in healthier, more productive ways, then I'll rest easy. I still may be doing less than I wish, each day, to tackle climate change. I still may not do enough to change the way I live. I may not have the conviction that all things will turn out well. But I will have the hope that, by acting together, our lives and our companies and our time together will make sense, regardless of how it all turns out.

COMPANIES
WE KEEP

BRIAN VANDEN BRINK

· 1 ·

Cornerstones

When I look back on all the crap I learned in high
school, it's a wonder I can think at all.
—PAUL SIMON, FROM THE SONG "KODACHROME"

South Mountain Company, the business I cofounded in 1975 on the island of Martha's Vineyard, makes houses. Big houses, small houses, and neighborhoods, new from scratch and remade from old. Affordable houses and distinctly unaffordable houses. Sweet successes and partial failures. We do all the parts—we plan, develop, design, build, finish, and furnish. In the doing we form lasting relationships with our clients and their land. We maintain the buildings after completion, learn from how they work and age, and alter and add when the time comes. We do other work, too—we design and manufacture lighting and furniture, we do solar and wind installations, we consult with other companies about business and building. Over the past thirty years, working on the Vineyard, we have become, individually and collectively, active participants in the life of our island community and the planning for its future. It has been a remarkable journey of discovery.

Along the way, as we have become a part of this place, we have come to sense that we are only at the beginning, that our endeavors—and our company—may have, or can aspire to have, some of the enduring qualities of the buildings we fashion. We have made a series of commitments to the future of the people within the company, to those who will come after us, and to the island where we all live and work. We are building a community of enterprise that we hope will have the strength to nurture stable relationships, the flexibility to shift with changing times, and the ability to sustain itself for generations.

I am finding out that people mostly don't think of companies this way. Companies are entities that people start, capitalize, run, work for, buy and obtain services from, sell, and disband. But South Mountain has become, for us, as much a community as a company. We build not only houses, but also connections and bonds between people, between people and land, and between commerce and place. We are organized around the idea of maintaining and perpetuating an ongoing business community, and sharing ownership democratically with the people we work with. We think we are crafting a company to keep.

If we are lucky in life, work becomes an expression of who we are and one of our most important anchors of meaning. I was lucky enough to discover this early and quite by accident. The story of my coming of age has now become a familiar one—a 1960s kid, brash and audacious, who set out to make a new world free of greed and conformity, aligned with nature, grounded in justice for all.

When the '60s ended I had just turned twenty. I renounced, for a time, modern consumer culture and technology in favor of the skills and tools of rural self-sufficiency. Like many others, I was more at home in America's agrarian past than in mainstream society's present. The journey was not without contradictions: We went deftly from the suburbs toward Walden like hopping across a creek, thinking we could cross back if necessary. But this inconsistency seemed less important than the value of our dogged attempts to imagine new ways that made sense to us.

It was a passage aligned with the sweeping political and social upheaval of the times. We were contending with war in Vietnam and war in the streets. We had experienced the Cuban missile crisis as teenagers and huddled beneath our desks as schoolchildren.

My wife has a favorite comic strip in which a son says to his father, "Now wait a minute, let me get this straight. You're saying that in the school you went to they used to tell you in the event of nuclear attack you should get under your desk?"

The father says, "That's right."

In the next panel the son asks, "Would that be the same school where you learned everything else you know?"

We had similar questions. The search for answers led us to unexpected places from which the return seemed increasingly unlikely. A new culture was so much in the air that our identification with it was almost like slipping into a pair of comfortable shoes. I don't know the word that would best describe what we were then—network, tribe, clan—but wherever we traveled we felt a shared collective consciousness that was a product of our profound alienation from the values we saw reflected in society combined with exquisite anticipation of the invention of a new way of living, a new kind of economy, and a new approach to democracy.

Crash Course

Immersed in our new surroundings, apart from our suburban roots, we made shelter by fashioning crude tepees and fixing leaky roofs on abandoned farmhouses. I began to have an urge to understand buildings. I marveled at ancient barns, walked on their hewn timbers, studied how the parts were joined, and sometimes dismantled them piece by piece. Old Capes, Colonials, Victorians, and bungalows became at once church and school: places where I could gaze with pleasure through tiny panes of handblown glass, run my hands over undulating horsehair plaster walls, poke around in attics finding the stuff that lay behind lime-mortared chimneys, and learn secrets from those who made these buildings long ago.

Root cellars, woodsheds, corncribs, blacksmith shops, junkyards, stone walls, rusted farm implements, and especially the old-timers who loved a wide-eyed audience—all contributed to our new storehouse of arcane knowledge. We rummaged through bins at farm sales, searching for old tools like broadax and adze for hewing, froe for splitting, peavey and cant hook for wrestling logs around, and beetle for persuading uncooperative timbers to fall into place. Grateful for the remnants of another time, we hauled them home to test them out and learned to use them to live and work in the rural outbacks of Vermont, Northern California, Oregon, and British Columbia. Our lives then were devoted to the basics: growing and preparing food, raising animals, finding water, making and mending clothing, creating shelter, fabricating toys for our young ones, entertaining ourselves. There was no separation between work and play. Building and design gradually became particular passions of mine, and here, too, there was no distinction—each of the two was an integral part of a whole. Our newfound ethic of self-sufficiency dictated that we learn by the seat of our pants, far away from conventional classrooms, no matter how difficult the challenges were and how unattainable the elusive ideal of self-sufficiency.

I was lucky to have begun my work with a partnership that was far more than a business relationship. Mitchell Posin was my closest friend. We not only worked side by side but also traveled and lived together during those years. He came from Brooklyn, and his working-class background, which included repairing furniture with his father and laboring during his teens at a riding stable (yes, there were still horses in Brooklyn), was the perfect complement to my academic upbringing. He had the ability to think like a craftsman and work with his hands, and I brought the ability to research, scheme, and absorb knowledge by reading. We learned from each other.

The first house we built was in Vermont in 1972. We heard through the grapevine that Harry Saxman, who lived up the road, was planning to build a house. We went to see him.

"We hear you're planning to build a house," we said, "and we're wondering if you've got someone to build it."

"Can you guys build a house?" he asked.

"Well . . . sure, yes, we can."

He hired us. He did the contracting and we did the building. We knew some carpentry and something about buildings, but we didn't have the foggiest notion how to build a house. Each day we worked hard at the job site; each night we spread out on the rough living room floor of the farmhouse we were caretaking with a stack of carpentry and building books, desperately trying, by flickering kerosene light, to figure out how to do the next day's work. Talk about seat of the pants; this was a crash course. Somehow the house got built.

One Job

In my youth I had few jobs and never stuck long with any of them. As a kid, I had a paper route that I loved. Flinging papers from my bicycle perch and trying to "porch 'em" just right was a delight. I had few summer jobs in high school. When I was in college I worked one summer in a brick kiln . . . for a few weeks. And in Colorado I had a job at a sawmill . . . for a few more. When I tired of Marlboro College (after one semester), instead of getting a job I opened a hippie store in Brattleboro, Vermont.

We sold artwork and crafts on consignment, drug paraphernalia, and strange clothing, and ours was the only place in town, at the time, to buy records, both new and used. Later, while I was at Wesleyan University in Connecticut, a friend and I started a firewood business. I worked odd jobs from the communes I lived in: dismantling buildings and working for a surveyor in Vermont, clearing brush in British Columbia, making oak firewood and cedar fence posts in Oregon, doing small carpentry jobs wherever I went.

My first real job came in 1973. I was doing some woodwork for my father-in-law and needed some rough oak planks planed. I took them to a nearby woodworking shop, Krager Custom Woodwork, located in a cavernous space in a complex of old mill buildings near the Hudson River in Garnerville, New York. I fell in love with the place the moment I walked in. Sawdust was everywhere; it hung in the air as if suspended in time, its aroma perfumed the space, and a thin coating softened the oversize, antiquated industrial machinery. Each piece of wood in the scattered piles seemed to clamor to be the next one chosen, anxious to become the next cabinet or coffee table. I didn't want to leave. After the foreman had finished planing, I piled the boards into my truck and went back inside, to the office, and introduced myself to Dan Krager.

"I want to come to work here," I announced.

"We really don't have that much work that we need to hire someone else," he replied.

"I'll work cheap and I'll work hard. I'll do whatever you ask. Just give me a shot."

The way I remember it, I told him that if he didn't give me a job, I'd just hang around and be a pain in the neck, so he might as well. I'm not sure it went quite that way, but he did give me a job.

It was thrilling. I'd wake up excited each morning, hop out of bed, throw on my clothes, and tear over to spend another day belt sanding or pushing wood through a table saw. It was hard, boring work, and I loved every minute of it. There were only four of us in the shop, so I got to witness—and mostly be a part of—each step of every process and project. It was a tremendous learning experience until, a few months later, Dan called in the three of us and told us he was going out of business. He wasn't making it.

It was a sad day, but during my time there I had become friendly with the shop foreman, Kingsley Van Wagner. He and I decided to start doing cabinetry on our own. We bought some equipment at the Krager shop auction, and the first iteration of South Mountain Woodwork began. I called Mitchell, who was in western Massachusetts, and asked him to come down to help build a new shop and work with us. He did, and we were soon off and running. It went well for a year or two, but when the opportunity to build a house on Martha's Vineyard came up, Mitchell and I departed. Kingsley stayed behind and continued the cabinet business.

It turns out, now, that aside from that brief interlude at Krager's (the only experience I ever had working for a boss, for a paycheck, for more than a month or two), my only job has been my work at South Mountain Company on the Vineyard. It also turns out that my work has been so completely enmeshed with all the parts of my life that it has never felt different from play. I remain uncertain about the difference.

Stumbling into Business

Mitchell and I did not originally intend to go into business; we stumbled into it by accident while we meant to be learning to practice a craft and explore our passion for building. We didn't mean to be on the island of Martha's Vineyard, either; that, too, happened almost by mistake. We came to the Vineyard in 1975 to make a house for my parents. My mother and father had the impression that we could actually design and build them a house, despite our relative lack of experience. Their generous faith expanded our abilities, but we bit off more than we could chew. We planned to spend six months building and then leave the Vineyard with a pocketful of change, but twelve months later we were still hustling to finish this detailed, timber-framed house with handmade doors, windows, cabinetry, and built-ins. The money had long since run out. While we were struggling through the project, new opportunities came our way.

We had no intention of staying, but in the fall of that year we set up shop in Roger Allen's old barn at Allen Farm. We found ourselves designing and building more houses on the Vineyard, and losing money on each one. Perhaps that provided us with moral justification for what we were doing. Our mission was twofold: to keep working and to build the perfect house. We managed to accomplish the first.

A defining moment for me happened during a visit of a friend and mentor who closely followed our work. We were touring our projects. He admired the work. "It's good," he said. "Beautiful work. Making any money?"

"No way," I laughed.

"Nice idea, Abrams," he said. "Novel, anyway. Subsidized housing for the rich."

His blunt assessment triggered the realization that I needed to learn about business, but I wasn't thrilled with the prospect. *You've gotta be kidding,* I thought. *I'm still learning the basics of design and can't even make a credible set of working drawings yet. And building? Framing an unequal pitch valley is as mysterious as the darkest jungle. Now this?*

But it was clear to me that our design/build stool would not stand without a sturdy business management leg. So I began to learn, in my own random and ragged way, and it would lead to interesting places, unusual findings, and lucky discoveries.

There was plenty to learn: estimating, ordering, contract writing, scheduling, and insurance. There was bookkeeping and banking to do, cash flow and credit to consider. I traversed back and forth through Bernard Kamaroff's classic *Small Time Operator*[1] (now in its tenth edition and still the best—and most irreverent—basic small-business instruction manual). Then there were taxes: income, sales, and excise. Kamaroff has a chapter in his book called "Deep in the Heart of Taxes." I didn't want to visit.

But I came to understand that if our business foundation was level and strong, we could build on it. If not, we were doomed to repeat each mistake. The work continued to fall in our laps as people saw the reasonably good buildings we were making, but we had grown tired of subsidizing. So we shuffled paper, created systems, hired a bookkeeper and an accountant, and gave the same respect to our spreadsheets that we did to our chisels. We learned about the utility of profits. The stool gained balance. Greater business understanding brought new freedoms. I learned that business is a craft just like making a staircase. This simple recognition was fuel for the journey.

Some of our best business lessons came from our clients. Eli Sagan, a great supporter, taught us about profit. When we had completed the design for his family's house and were working on the contract, he said, "I want to be sure you make a profit on this house, because you're in business and you must, but I'm not willing to pay more than I should. So I'm going to teach you how to make a fair profit." He did. He went through our estimate line by line with us and asked us the right questions to make sure we had the bases covered. It was lucky for all of us.

Others came from unexpected places. When we had arrived on the Vineyard to build a house in the town of Chilmark, people we met chuckled when we told them why we were there. "Move right into town, from outside, and build a house? No way. You gotta be Herbert Hancock to do that. He runs the town. He's the main builder. He's the only one who gets a permit."

Along with being the primary builder in town, Herb had already been a selectman for eleven years. He was also an assessor, a member of the board of health, and the building and zoning inspector. Whatever went through town hall went through Herb. Alarmed by what we heard, we prepared our plans carefully before we went to see him. We inquired respectfully about the process for getting a building permit. Contrary to the rumors, he was gracious and welcoming. He made short work of the permit and generously gave us useful advice about the mysteries of horizontal wind-driven rain and the complexity of island soils. Our experience with Herb was an important lesson. It's not uncommon for those without authority to fear or suspect those who have it. But more often than not, municipal officials are simply people who are dedicated to their community. We learned that if we question rather than declare, understand the view from the other side of the table, and search out commonalities, collaboration is more likely than conflict.

Step by step and lesson by lesson our casual, impromptu practice evolved into an organization with a new vantage point. We were used to looking critically at what we designed and how we translated intention to building. Now we could look at ourselves as an entity and examine the kind of business we were designing and building. Our principles, which we had invested in the buildings, began to steer the business as well.

Adventure

In 1984 my partner Mitchell went on to other things—farming especially[2]—but the company endured. My colleagues and I have now been working on this small island for my entire adult life. From the doing

I've learned something about buildings, business, and life in a small community. There are lessons from all three I'd like to forget, and others I wish I could remember, but mostly I've learned that small enterprises, if driven as much by principled practice as by profit, can produce work-place satisfaction, support good lives, and help shape strong commu-nities. This learning has led those of us at South Mountain to adopt a fundamental purpose: to use our business as a tool to help us create these good things. Over time both the community we work in (the island) and the community we have made (the company) have come to matter to us as much as the work we do.

You may think this story is too quixotic to have much meaning for others. Here's my hope: that you will see that South Mountain is, perhaps, a working model for our larger aspirations, and more typical than you might guess. The story—what my colleagues and I learned from one another, the mistakes we made and our accidental discov-eries, and the principles we found to guide us—speaks to the larger struggle many of us are facing today: how to live properly and profit-ably, aligned with our values in a world that sometimes seems devoid of any.

I will focus on eight cornerstone principles we have discovered, and how they indicate the promise of small business as a counterforce to the conventional "Bigger is better, profits come first, and location is incidental" message. For the sake of good work and good community I will question some cherished assumptions about business, argue for broader and deeper measures of success, and tender alternatives that have worked for us—so far—and may work for others.

In *The Soul of Capitalism*, author William Greider proposes that our economic system is most likely to be transformed, over time, by a vari-ety of small-scale reformers working from within, experimenting with new forms of business in which Americans own their work, their voice, and their self-expression. He believes that this change is already under way. I like to think that my colleagues and I are among those sharing this adventure. Our paths follow those of adventurers who took similar routes in earlier times, and from whose journeys we have learned enough to enhance our own. Like my grandfather's.

Morris Abrams Inc.

It was New Year's Eve, 1899, and the vibrant capital of New World commerce and culture was decked out and lit up. As his ship edged into New York's harbor, nine-year-old Russian immigrant Morris Abrams was spellbound by the spectacle before him. Fireworks blazed across the night sky. It felt like it was all for him. He instantly fell in love with America.

The flames of my grandfather's lifelong passion and optimistic embrace of this country were never doused by his hard childhood, two world wars, the Great Depression, and several recessions.

In his early teens Morris went to work for a hardware merchant named Lemkin on Center Street in Lower Manhattan. He learned the business and helped his boss build it. He married, and in the early 1920s he and his wife lived in an apartment in Brooklyn with their three young kids. Lemkin, nearing retirement, refused Morris a partnership and prepared to pass the business on to his own son. It was time for Morris to set up shop for himself.

Just down the street, at 196 Center, Morris Abrams Inc. was established in 1922 to supply hardware, machinery, and equipment to manufacturers, retailers, and contractors. All went well; when my grandfather took in an equal partner named Morris Zippert in the late 1920s, the young company was thriving. The two partners hired friends, family members, and others, and the company grew until the Depression hit. In late 1931 they were hanging on by a thread. They considered their options. With their heads still above water, they could close and walk away owing nothing. If they stayed open and things kept on as they were, they might be forced into bankruptcy, an uncomfortable option because they didn't want others to get hurt. It was a tough call. They decided to hold on for another few months, hoping that Roosevelt's inauguration would make a difference.

It did. As soon as the new president occupied the White House, old customers started returning. Lamp manufacturers, ventilation contractors, woodworking shops, tool-and-die makers—all became active, commerce began to hum, and doors began to open. The business grew slowly over the next decade. The US wartime effort in the 1940s gave it a big boost. By 1950 the payroll had swelled to 110 employees.

They moved to larger quarters at 90 Hudson Street, a solid, dignified seven-story building that occupied most of a city block and was capped by eighteen great arched windows on the top floor. The Morris Abrams Inc. clothbound catalog from 1955 is black with embossed red-and-white lettering. Included in its 569 pages are more than a hundred pages of woodworking and metalworking machinery: lathe grinders, milling machines, punch presses, power shears, benders, the full line of Delta woodworking tools, Crescent planers and band saws, Linley jig boring machines, etchers and engravers, blast furnaces and bench furnaces, and welders of all kinds. Each tool is presented with high-quality photographs supported by carefully worded text and detailed pricing. There's every kind of electric and pneumatic portable tool, followed by cutting tools, abrasives, taps, dies, blades, bits, heads, and reamers. One hundred and ninety-one different varieties of hand files, scrapers, rasps, and rifflers are offered in different sizes, at prices ranging up from $3 a dozen. The sixty-five pages of micrometers, calipers, gauges, dial indicators, and other precision measuring tools are mostly made by Starrett Company and Brown and Sharpe, two venerable New England manufacturers that date back to the nineteenth century and still exist today, their product lines virtually unchanged. There's no sign of Makita, Hitachi, or Bosch—everything in this catalog is made in the USA. Every imaginable hand tool is here—hammers, saws, clamps, pliers, shears, snips, cutters, screwdrivers, and planes. The catalog ends with a hardware section that has toggle bolts, cotter pins, woodruff keys, washers, screws, nuts and bolts, and a miscellaneous equipment section that includes grease, graphite, and gear lubricant mixed with spring winders, belt lacers, and spray painters. From the everyday to the arcane, it's all there.

On page 195, one of the many toolboxes shown is the Union Super-Steel Cantilever tool chest, listed at $5.60. This is the one I'd see beside my grandfather's desk when my father dropped me off at the store when we visited from San Francisco. I'd sit in the office while we talked for a while. Once I had brought my grandfather up to date, he would hand me the brand-new toolbox and tell me, "Go fill it up, have fun, and behave yourself."

As I wandered through the warehouse maze that felt like caves filled with treasure, the workers helped me find the stuff I wanted—braces and bits, block planes, the wonderful ratcheting Yankee screwdrivers, and boxes of fasteners that fit in the neatly divided toolbox trays. Each object on the shelves was wrapped in oilcloth and individually boxed, and when I was through the tool chest was like a bag of presents. I hauled it to the airport when we left, put it on the DC-7 for the long flight home (try that today), and had lost pretty much everything in it by the time we returned two years later for the next round of this ritual.

Morris Zippert's son, Ira, had come into the business after he returned from the war. But none of my grandfather's three children was interested. My aunt became a biologist, my uncle an actor, and my father, the youngest, a physician. No hardware merchants in this bunch. They took to heart their father's message about the value of education, and their motivation carried them to their different fields of interest. How did my grandfather feel about having nobody to carry on the business that bore his name?

During the 1950s the company spawned many others. Senior salespeople left and took lucrative accounts with them. One took the little International Business Machine account and formed Bruckner Supply, which, after some years as a general industrial supplier, began to concentrate on the computer industry. Bruckner succeeded and was recently sold to a larger company for many millions. For Morris Abrams Inc., however, the 1960s brought declining fortunes. The loss of good people, and the business that left with them, took its toll. The company moved to Long Island, closing operations on Hudson Street. They began to specialize, supplying school woodworking and metal-working shops. In the 1960s they sold the company to Power Pipe and Supply, and it continued to spiral downhill. My grandfather kept coming in for years, but there was little for him to do except collect overdue balances. The company was sold several more times, and the final owner let Ira Zippert go, sold the Morris Abrams name, and went bankrupt. The name still exists, like a shadow, and is sometimes used in bidding for New York City municipal contracts.

My memories of the business will always be as I saw it on my child-hood visits, during its heyday on Hudson Street. Built on solid founda-tions of honesty, respect, and loyalty, it seemed to be, at once, stable and magnificent. Did it break my grandfather's heart to see the decay of the institution he built? Nobody seems to know for sure. He died just before his one hundredth birthday (when she heard about his death, my wife said, "That can't be—he's too old to die") without conveying those feelings. He never liked to dwell on the past, but I imagine he must have been hurt by the progression of events. The business could have continued to thrive and endure. But just as Lemkin's legacy plans did not include my grandfather, my grandfather and his partner did not make sufficient provision for the people who'd helped to build their business. Their employees left, each time taking a piece of the business with them and contributing to the disassembly of the enterprise.

The Company as Community

I have come, through my own experiences in life and business, to think that small companies like my grandfather's do not have to die this kind of death. Is such dismantling the inevitable consequence of what economist Joseph Schumpeter termed the "creative destruc-tion"[3] of free-market forces? Or is it a symptom of one of contemporary America's legacies, the frontier mentality (when we are finished with something, we throw it away, we move on, we make a fresh start)? I realize now that the story of the demise of my grandfather's business is, for me at least, a poignant and heartbreaking tale.

When businesses like my grandfather's are cast aside or wither and fade away, we testify neither to inevitable machinations of the marketplace nor to some grand impulse of the pioneering spirit, but only to our own lack of common purpose. The loss is more than economic. Social capital that no catalog or chart of accounts can itemize is squandered. A frame of reference for people's daily lives is gone. When thousands of small businesses die this kind of death in thousands of communities, it may be as damaging to the social fabric as the loss of family farms or the breakdown of marriage.

I recognize that not every company can be the starting point for the establishment of a permanent institution. What I question is the lack of value placed on maintenance of those business communities we create and the communities within which those companies operate. This disregard supports unfettered allegiance to an economy whose rewards have become skewed toward the distant and the global at the expense of the local, and whose system of incentives encourages wage servitude and environmental recklessness.

I come to these conclusions thirty-five years into my business career, as the cofounder of a small company that now has $9 million in annual sales, seventeen owners among its thirty-two employees, and a dedication to the kind of enduring connection to community and place that we hope will survive us and, even, our children. We are still very much a work in progress, but we have set out—briskly, although not unerringly—along a path to a more democratic, more responsible, more permanent kind of company.

The Cornerstones

Our attempt to remake the way we do business pivots on eight essential cornerstones that have emerged as I've looked back over the arc of our collective past. I did not predetermine this number or decide to urge these ideas to be cornerstones; instead, I discovered them during the course of my endeavors, picking through them like a mason building a wall. The stonemason sorts through a pile of material to find just the right stones for the base, the corners, the fillers, the stretchers that lock the wall together, and the capstones to finish it off. He discovers the wall as he builds it, as I found the cornerstones of our business. Each cornerstone revealed itself as I sorted through the pile. Once found, each could be placed, and together they became the foundation of a structure that is perhaps crude, but sturdy.

This book is the story of the development of a particular design for business that is built on these cornerstones:

- Sharing ownership.
- Cultivating workplace democracy.
- Challenging the gospel of growth.
- Balancing multiple bottom lines.
- Celebrating the spirit of craft.
- Practicing community entrepreneurism.
- Thinking like cathedral builders.
- Committing to the business of place.

These principles and practices are embedded in our company. The values I sensed in the way my grandfather did business—honesty, integrity, loyalty, and optimism—are at the core of this new form for business, but they are lodged in a different context. That context—today's complex world, which is experiencing profound change at a blistering pace—is woven into the structure of the book.

Sharing Ownership

In 1987 we restructured South Mountain from a sole proprietorship to an employee-owned cooperative corporation. It was a hinge point in the history of the company. Ownership has become available to all employees, enabling people to own and guide their workplace. The responsibility, the power, and the profits all belong to the group of owners.

In her book *The Divine Right of Capital*, Marjorie Kelly, former publisher of the journal *Business Ethics*, says:

> Thomas Paine's vision was of "every man a proprietor." It's a worthy ideal, to own one's place of work. But in the corporate era, most citizens are necessarily employees, and always will be. We need a new economic vision for a new era: not every man a proprietor, but every employee an owner.[4]

This is not far-fetched, and widespread recognition of the importance of employee ownership may be one of the keys to a restorative future. There must be a dramatic shift in what we do every day, how we do it, and the structures within which we do it. My sense is that the success of South Mountain can be traced back to the lucky findings we made in the 1980s: that employee ownership was the avenue to our best possible future.

Cultivating Workplace Democracy

Shared ownership and control is our method at South Mountain. Every employee as an owner is our intention. More than half of our employees are full owners; each time another joins, each time a new management approach allows more voices to be heard, and each time we distribute more responsibility, we move steadily toward the goals of democracy, fairness, and transparency.

Ownership is the underlying structure that supports a democratic workplace culture. As we learn to clarify the difference between ownership and management, the power of shared ownership becomes ever more apparent. We become better problem solvers, and better dreamers, too.

As we navigate through our fourth decade and begin the transition from Generation One to Generation Two, our purpose becomes clearer: to create an ongoing community of democratic action and strength.

Challenging the Gospel of Growth

A cherished business doctrine is that growth must be a primary business purpose: "Grow or perish" is rarely questioned. At South Mountain we favor certain kinds of growth, but not expansion for its own sake, which author Edward Abbey described as "the ideology of the cancer cell."[5] We embrace growth to achieve specific goals, but always with consideration of the consequences: It may disrupt and endanger treasured qualities. We look for ways to develop and thrive without enlarging, thereby holding to limited growth. When we grow, it is by intention rather than in response to demand. We think about *enough* rather than *more*—enough profits to retain and share, enough compensation for all, enough health and well-being, enough time to give our work the attention it deserves, enough communication, enough to manage, enough troubles, enough headaches.

Balancing Multiple Bottom Lines

We assign priority to a collection of bottom lines while consigning the traditional single bottom line—profit—to its appropriate role as a vital tool that serves the others. We try to satisfy the bottom lines of being glad to come to work, making a good living for our families, meeting the expectations of our clients and business associates, caring for the environment and one another, promoting fairness and health, and improving the world, one house at a time, one neighborhood at a time, one island at a time. We propose cooperation, rather than competition, as the avenue to business success. Metaphorically speaking, these are all bottom lines, even though they cannot necessarily, or easily, be quantified or measured.

Celebrating the Spirit of Craft

When we work as craftspeople, pleasure can soar above the tedium that—at least some of the time—characterizes all work. The Balinese say, "We don't have any art; we do everything as well as we can." They understand craft. A thing well made is a telling of the truth; it reveals how we think and what we admire. Craftsmanship translates well to different scales—everything we make, from a knob to a neighborhood, can be imbued with craft. And it translates to other arenas as well; letters, contracts, drawings, phone calls, schedules, budgets, and relationships can all be as well crafted as a stool or a stairway, and each of these is worth infusing with craft. Work is a chance to enliven everything we do with craft.

Craftsmanship is, for many of our employees and employee-owners, the aspect of our work that evokes the most passion. There is a tremendous sense of accomplishment in making something beautiful, something that employs appropriate materials, tools, and techniques in good proportion and functions with grace and ease.

Practicing Community Entrepreneurism

Making expensive homes in a resort community has many significant returns: freedom to explore craft, opportunities for the pursuit of quality, relationships with interesting people, and financial rewards. By itself, however, it does not directly serve a broad social purpose—beyond providing good jobs to those who do the work and good homes to a fortunate few—no matter how socially purposeful we are in the way we do it. We have attempted to address this reality by using the financial resources and the web of relationships that derive from the work to help solve community problems and to encourage a better future for the place where we live and work. We bring an entrepreneurial approach to these efforts, taking risks and learning from both our public failures and our small successes.

A significant portion of our community efforts has been devoted to affordable housing. The Vineyard has a serious affordable housing crisis. We have worked hard to solve this problem. It is about the heart of community, and we are gratified, after all these years, to see that we are on the cusp of resolution. Now we are turning our attention to renewable energy independence and relocalizing our economy.

Thinking Like Cathedral Builders

At South Mountain, our view of time is squarely at odds with short-term business thinking. Our work will not be finished in our lifetimes; it will continue for generations. British business philosopher Charles Handy gives perspective:

> Cathedrals inspire. It is not only their grandeur or splendor, but the thought that they often took more than fifty years to build. Those who designed them, those who first worked on them, knew for certain that they would never see them finished. They knew only that they were creating something glorious which would stand for centuries, long after their own names had been forgotten. They had their own dream of the sublime and of immortality. We may not need any more cathedrals but we do need cathedral thinkers, people who can think beyond their own lifetimes.[6]

We try to think about our work as the cathedral builders thought about theirs. We try to think for generations, as we try to build for generations. We recognize that any wealth that has accrued to us has been provided in significant measure from the capital of this community, and it is our obligation to ensure that our business becomes an enduring part of the community fabric. To make a durable, robust, and flexible business entity that outlasts its original owners, we plan for succession, so that as we age we can gracefully depart and leave the company—vibrant, stable, learning—in the hands of others.

Committing to the Business of Place

We have a long-term investment in the small island community where we work. All our eggs are in this one geographic basket. People often ask why we would devote such effort to a place that is widely perceived to be just a playground for the wealthy. It surely is that, but it is many other things as well. With all its strengths and weaknesses, assets and problems—its status as a world-famous resort; the vast socioeconomic diversity and discrepancies in its population; the dwindling of its community of fishermen and farmers; the growth of a new, sometimes fragile community of islander and washashore craftspeople and artisans—this is the place that we know best, the place that must serve as a laboratory for our experiments with small business. It's a good place to model new solutions, because it's socially complex and it's still in fair condition. There's hope for it. We have committed to limiting our work to Martha's Vineyard, with the exception of educational work beyond our shores, and to doing everything that we can to make a difference in the quality of our community and our economy.

The Chemistry of Our Culture

Each of the cornerstones will be discussed in detail in its own chapter, but the principles are interdependent and often intersect, and they are therefore woven into the fabric of the whole. I will tell how we came to our beliefs and practices, how we transitioned to employee ownership, how the tenets of our practice emerged, and how we came, with our share of fumbling and bumbling, but with growing confidence, to be who we are today. I will examine the significance and meaning of our journey and consider where these efforts might lead and what new endeavors they may support.

Here, then, is one small business on one small island. Its lessons emerge from its story, but it is only one of many stories of small-business experimentation that are unfolding today in the wealthiest nation the world has ever known. The simultaneous development of countless such stories, rich with intersecting themes—like so many shingles on a steeply pitched roof that provide shelter only because they are woven together—is what gives added meaning to any one account. Recognizing this, I offer our story so that it may take its place among the others; perhaps combined they might together alter, in some small way, the chemistry of our culture.

RANDI BAIRD

▪ 2 ▪

Sharing Ownership

When we all do better, we all do better.
—Paul Wellstone

Don't be afraid to take a big step when one is indicated.
You can't cross a chasm in two small steps.
—David Lloyd George

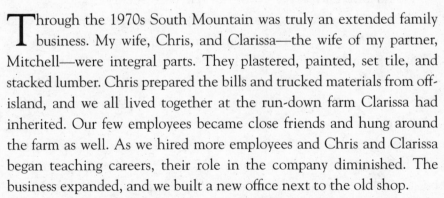

Through the 1970s South Mountain was truly an extended family business. My wife, Chris, and Clarissa—the wife of my partner, Mitchell—were integral parts. They plastered, painted, set tile, and stacked lumber. Chris prepared the bills and trucked materials from off-island, and we all lived together at the run-down farm Clarissa had inherited. Our few employees became close friends and hung around the farm as well. As we hired more employees and Chris and Clarissa began teaching careers, their role in the company diminished. The business expanded, and we built a new office next to the old shop.

By the early 1980s Mitchell had developed a strong appetite for farming; he gradually distanced himself from the business and we formally disbanded our partnership. Chris and I built a house on an adjacent piece of land that Clarissa generously carved off for us, but the business remained in its old quarters at the farm.

One night in 1984 a devastating fire burned the shop to the ground.

We regrouped soon after. Chris and I mortgaged our house, and the people in the company began building a new facility on our property. Some months later South Mountain moved into a well-equipped shop with spacious offices above. The newness was strange, but the space felt good. We were back on track. The dissolution of the partnership with Mitchell was complete. I was left as the sole proprietor of our common creation, which was now ten years old.

I felt uncertain in this new place, but curious and engaged.

The Apples in a Seed

Long before this, we had become committed to both designing and building the projects we took on. Our cues came from accounts of the old master builders of the Middle Ages, the pioneers of early America, the Arts and Crafts movement, and the Shakers. Our abilities were rudimentary and our aspirations high. We were devoted to fine wood-work and alternatives to conventional construction practices. We combined timber framing, passive solar, and an eclectic, unschooled design sense to make learn-by-doing buildings. We had mixed success. With no formal training and little experience, we were unconstrained by knowing what couldn't be done (and conversely unaware of much that could) and equally unencumbered by skill. We reinvented the wheel regularly.

But we were learning at breakneck speed and for a time that was all that mattered. At the tail end of the 1970s a series of important projects began to shape our future. We built two projects that we didn't design, which confirmed our dedication to the design/build integration. (Since then we have rarely deviated from that course; although we have occasionally designed projects that we didn't build, and although we now do some consulting work, for nearly thirty years we have not built anything designed by others.) Finally, in association with the nonprofit Energy Resource Group (which we, with others, had helped to form in order to promote renewable energy), we orchestrated the research, design, and construction of a solar greenhouse attached to the Edgartown School. Teachers, students, and members of the public participated in the barn-raising-style event. It was our first significant venture into community demonstration work—a harbinger of things to come.

We had ten employees, including two who had been there from the beginning. I loved the work and I loved the people. We began to think about the company as an entity and to consider our role in the community. We accumulated expertise in ecological land-use and building techniques. We developed small affordable housing projects as contrast with our high-end work. I had a vague sense that we were developing something of value, but I couldn't yet articulate what our successes might suggest. Author Ken Kesey once said, "You can count the seeds in an apple, but you can't count the apples in a seed." That's how it felt to us; the seeds were germinating.

But while the philosophical underpinnings were evolving, we were also experiencing unexpected growth, which seemed to diminish the sense of intimacy within the company. We were flat-out busy—a perpetual motion machine—but our core became uncertain. Our identity as a family business working out of Allen Farm was gone. So who were we now? I had no idea.

A Democratic Workplace

Our growth, although hardly explosive, had nevertheless brought us to an unsettling perch, as if we were leaning against a wobbly railing on a second-floor balcony. No longer could we run solely on intuition and gut; the business had become too complex. How could the familial qualities we cherished be maintained in a larger context?

Issues that had not been evident became visible and urgent. The two employees who had been with us almost from the beginning, Steve Sinnett and Pete Ives, came to me and said they wanted to stay with

South Mountain, that they wanted to make their careers here, but they needed a greater stake and more than an hourly wage. It was time to do more than reinforce the railing.

Steve had been our first employee and had become a close friend. Attracted by the waterfront scene, he migrated to the Vineyard after college. After a stint as a crew member on the schooner *Shenandoah*, he came to work with us and soon became a fixture. His personal qualities—a restless desire for all things to be better for all people, intense loyalty, unflagging team spirit, and a pitch-in-when-the-going-gets-rough approach—combined to make him indispensable.

In 1978 Pete Ives had come to work. An accomplished mason, painter, drywaller, floor sander, tile setter (and surfer), he had never done a lick of carpentry. He was hungry to learn. Once he said to me, "Just tell me what to do. I'll do anything you ask, as long as I don't have to tell anyone else what to do." He was dedicated, versatile, talented, and convinced that he had no leadership qualities. He became a superb carpenter in a very short time. He began to find confidence in his work. He learned to be a foreman, first reluctantly, then with pride.

The three of us put our heads together and decided that their situation—the desire for a greater stake—was not likely to be unique; it would come up again and again if the company continued to succeed. How could we both remedy the current circumstance and welcome others, in the future, to a new status that offered more participation in decision making, greater responsibility, and opportunities to share profits? The journey of inquiry and experimentation that followed led to our discovery of the first cornerstone of our business: sharing the ownership and control.

Adjusting the Model

Our national wealth has come at considerable social and environmental cost. Unless we provide a greater stake in economic decision making for more people, these costs are likely to continue to increase. Author William Greider is convinced that most Americans think something is wrong "in the contours of their supposed prosperity."

In *The Soul of Capitalism*, he writes:

> I do not find these complaints restricted to the poor or struggling working-class, though their struggles are obviously more stark and often desperate. . . . I have heard people from nearly every income level express an oddly similar sense of confinement, as if their lives were trapped by the "good times" rather than liberated. . . . Think of the paradox as enormous and without precedent in history: a fabulously wealthy nation in which plentiful abundance may also impoverish our lives.[1]

There are significant opportunities to make our economic system more democratic. In *The Divine Right of Capital*, Marjorie Kelly says this may seem daunting when we consider the power of the financial elite, but

> we should remember that the power of kings was once as great. The very idea of monarchy once seemed eternal and divine, until a tiny band of revolutionaries in America dared to stand up and speak of equality. They created an unlikely and visionary new form of government, which today has spread around the world. And the power of kings can now be measured in a thimble.[2]

She makes the point that democracy has been an unstoppable historical force, and that if it "hasn't stopped at the doors of kings, it is not likely to stop at the door of financial aristocracy."[3]

I was thinking along these lines—crudely, however, without the rich historical sense of Greider and Kelly—as I considered my business options in 1986. I wanted the people in our company to feel prosperous and fulfilled in their work, and to share the bounty. We decided to investigate structures that would distribute both ownership and control.

This was surely a hinge point for South Mountain. For a while I was unhinged—alternately frightened and excited by our deliberations. I had the power, and the greatest financial and emotional investment; therefore, I had the most to lose. Under my ownership the company had become a viable, profitable entity with a strong reputation and a backlog of work. Sometimes, during those sessions, it felt like control was slipping away, like I was tugging on the reins of a runaway horse. Then it occurred to me that perhaps I had the most to gain: aside from the lure of clearing this new path and seeing where it led, the possibility of shared responsibility and ownership promised new freedom for me and new potential for the company. It seemed like a potent mix.

We were beginning to tamper with fundamental elements of our work lives. Greider, again, in the foreword to John Logue and Jacquelyn Yates's book *The Real World of Employee Ownership,* says

> Most people go to work for someone else and, unless they happen to be highly skilled professionals or independently wealthy, they consign a major portion of their lifetimes to the direction of others, forfeiting basic rights and autonomy in the process of making a living. With few exceptions, the system works like this: capital hires labor and capital claims ownership of the final product. Can one imagine an economy in which labor hires capital? Where workers have a legal right to the profits and legal responsibility for the liabilities because they are the owners, where workers jointly manage the firm and themselves in a democratic fashion?[4]

We were trying to imagine such an anomaly in our own quiet little corner of the economy.

Our inquiries led us to the concept of a worker-owned cooperative corporation. It seemed radical and uncommon, to be sure, but also practical, especially if we could make the shift to employee ownership and control in a gradual, carefully measured way that would not shake the foundations all at once. Expressions from the participants—excerpted from the notes of those early meetings—evoke the tone of the discourse:

> Our structure should guarantee that anyone who makes a career here be extended the privileges, responsibilities, rewards, and headaches of ownership.
>
> The underlying premise for any change we make must be mutual respect and trust. To lose what we've created in that regard would be tragic.
>
> Very little about our governance and performance systems is defined except by habit, experience, and our various quirky personalities.
>
> Pete and Steve have put a lot into the company; the restructuring should reward them (and others over time) without taking from John, who has led us this far.[5]

With some trepidation on my part, we hired Peter Pitegoff, an attorney at the Industrial Cooperatives Association, now known as the ICA Group, to advise us. I worried that hiring ICA would mean no turning back. The safety and insularity of sole proprietorship, which I had only recently earned, was about to be cast off. Engaging Peter was a semi-public announcement of intention. As a lifelong skier, I compare the feeling to summoning the nerve to drop into a steep couloir when you can't see below the crest and you know your skiing buddies are down below, waiting for you to come. With tips pointed down, I pushed off gingerly.

At a meeting in May 1986 I expressed the view that Chris and I—who owned and lived on the land on which the South Mountain Company premises were located at that time—needed to retain control of the property. I was also concerned that my customary freedom to act solo might become so constrained by shared ownership that I would no longer be comfortable in the business. It was the first ringing of the bell that all who make the shift from sole proprietors to employee-owners must hear. To say it another way, what if the thing we've built with painstaking care and love evolves into something we no longer like? It's a serious risk.

Meanwhile, it was suggested at the same meeting that "at the beginning John could have veto power over new owners, jobs we take, hiring and firing, and wages." By that arrangement I would essentially have been keeping most of the control. The idea was to spread that control widely, so the voices of all the owners had meaning. You can't steal second without taking your foot off first, and we came to agree that the only protection needed was veto power over issues directly related to the property, and that I should have a contract to manage the business until my preferred shares (the buyout of my sole interest) were paid off in full by the company, which would take five years. The payout and contract ended sixteen years ago and I still have the same job although, as you will see, it has changed significantly.

There are infinite variations on the theme of employee ownership. We will examine some of them later in this chapter. But there is one universal requirement: First the owner(s), and then the employees, have to see the value and want to pursue it. If the desire is not present, there's (1) no point in commencing the difficult and complicated journey it will surely be, and (2) no basis for identifying and developing the unique set of principles and doctrine that is going to be right for this owner and these employees. Rule number one for employee ownership transitions: You've got to want it.

In many cases an owner will see the value before the employees, and it requires a process of education and acculturation to get everyone on the same page. Sometimes the employees are threatened by the idea because they think it's an exit strategy for the owner, and they worry that they will lose the security of that expertise and leadership. This bridge must be crossed.

Although trepidatious, we were all on the same page. At Peter's suggestion we adopted a democratic ownership structure patterned after that of Mondragon, a remarkably successful network of worker-owned cooperatives in the Basque region of Spain. Mondragon has operated for more than fifty years on the principles of employees as owners, labor controlling the enterprise and sharing the wealth, members participating in business management and decision making, a limited ratio between top and bottom pay, and education as the key to career development and progress. We made adjustments to this model to fit our own idiosyncratic needs as an organization converting to, rather than starting with, employee ownership. Particularly important was the institution of a lengthy five-year trial period before ownership. This ensured a gradual transition, allowed time to evaluate commitment and suitability before employees became owners, and provided room for training and building understanding before they were thrust into policy decision making.

We established an ownership buy-in fee. We decided this needed to be significant but affordable. If it was too steep it would discourage participation, so we set it at the price of a good used car, an expense everyone seems to be able to manage when necessary. The fee has increased slowly; at this point it's an uncommonly good investment for new owners, and it's still equivalent to the price of a good used car.

Peter conducted a valuation analysis of the company, drafted a set of bylaws, and developed a legal agenda for reorganization that laid out the process coherently. Pitegoff's help was invaluable; we were lucky to find him. His nondoctrinaire attitude was particularly reassuring. He'd never heard of such a long waiting period, for example, but he endorsed it because he understood that we were, essentially, designing a house for ourselves that we had to be comfortable living in. We could always remodel later.

The structure has stood the test of time. The five-year waiting period has turned out to be none too long. We were fortunate, too, to have a smart and open-minded accountant, Gerry Tulis of Tulis Miller in Boston. He had never done accounting for employee-owned cooperatives, but he took it upon himself to become an expert. These days he is able to advise companies that are seeking to make the transition.

Restructuring South Mountain Company

On January 1, 1987, I transferred the ownership of South Mountain Company to a new worker-owned cooperative corporation. Steve, Pete, and I were the original three owners. My compensation was the preferred shares, which were converted to cash over a period of five years from the company profits, and a full ownership share (a more detailed explanation of the mechanics of our structure can be found in appendix 1). The first meeting of the board of directors of the newly reorganized company convened on January 9, 1987. Attending were Steve, Pete, Peter Rodegast (soon to be the fourth owner), and myself. There were seven other employees at the time of the restructuring; they were all on a track toward ownership. This was a critical transformation in the life of the company, the setting of that first cornerstone of our developing business model. The full implications of what we were doing were not yet clear to us.

That was more than twenty years ago. It was a giant step in our journey toward democracy. I'll describe, in the chapters to come, what happened. But I want to detour for a moment to put the idea of employee ownership into context. First, some basics and background about employee ownership; then some brief case studies of employee-owned companies of different scales and structure; and finally, some analysis and discussion of the implications. In the next chapter I will continue the story of South Mountain's march to workplace democracy—how it has developed, and how it works.

Employee Ownership Basics

Peter Pitegoff, in a recent article titled "Worker Ownership in Enron's Wake—Revisiting a Community Development Tactic,"[6] suggests that the concept of employee ownership was tarnished when Enron failed and thousands of employees lost the $1.3 billion that they had, together, invested in company stock. Worker ownership at Enron, which gave only a very few employees any meaningful say in corporate affairs, was characterized by overstated earnings and the ability of top executives to sell their stock while others couldn't. This high-profile tragedy contributed to public perception about abuse of employee stock ownership.

But the Enron debacle and others like it are only the terrible perversion of a good thing, like rape is to sex. They have nothing in common with the kind of employee ownership we will be discussing here, which involves broad distribution of assets to employees combined with some degree of worker control.

Although author Wendell Berry says that we have gone from being a country owned by many to a country owned by a few, this is still a nation of entrepreneurs. Small business remains the backbone of the economy. But what happens to the businesses that result from decades of entrepreneurial sweat and love? They used to get handed down to children. Some still do. But many owners don't know what to do with their business. If there are no family members who want to take it on, and they don't want to close the doors (thereby ending a legacy, leaving people jobless, and losing the embedded value), the only other apparent option is to sell to outsiders. There are, however, other, less obvious options.

For many reasons business owners, or those starting a business, may consider an employee ownership structure. For some it is a succession strategy: a way to retire, receive compensation for some or all of their accumulated equity, and leave the business in the hands of those who have helped to create it. The desire to see the business we have lovingly built sustain itself beyond our tenure can be strong. For some it derives from the belief that the people who create the wealth should share the wealth. Some take this farther and become advocates of a democratic workplace. Some are attracted to the possibility of greater commitment and productivity that employees who share ownership may bring. Some are driven by the objective of keeping key employees from moving on and starting their own businesses. Some are excited by the thrill of shared responsibility within the enterprise. For some, like myself, it's all of those reasons; for many it's one or more. But for others it is simply a practical financial mechanism, an exit strategy with specific tax advantages, and in those cases it may have nothing at all to do with the employees.

Sharing ownership has become widespread in the United States; all indications are that it is likely to become more so. There are two primary forms of employee ownership: the employee stock ownership plan (ESOP) and the cooperative (co-op). The most common form by far is the ESOP, which is well known to business advisers and owners.

There are roughly eleven thousand ESOPs with close to nine million employees in the United States.[7] An ESOP is, in fact, a pension plan, but it differs from conventional pension plans in several ways that make it a useful device with which employees can purchase all or part of the company that employs them. ESOPs invest in the company itself, rather than in outside firms, and they have the ability to borrow. In a sale to an ESOP, an ESOP trust is established that borrows money to buy stock from the owner, usually a portion of the total to start. Each year a part of the company profits are used to pay down the loan; as the loan is repaid, shares in the trust are allocated to the employees, and when the loan is repaid in full, financing begins for the next portion of the stock. When employees leave or retire, the trust buys back their stock.

As qualified pension plans regulated by the IRS, ESOPs are tax-exempt and confer tax advantages to the owners when they sell to employees. Once the employees purchase part or all of the company, they share in part or all of the profits. But they do not necessarily receive a voice in the governance and management of the company. In fact, says Corey Rosen, the director of the National Center for Employee Ownership, in his book *Equity*,

> Treating employee shareholders as true partners in enterprise, and operating the business in a way that reflects it, is [uncommon]. Companies that offer stock to their employees often fail to challenge traditional assumptions and practices. They do little to change their culture. They make no effort to help employees think and act like businesspeople.[8]

In this book, I am talking about those that do, ESOPs and co-ops alike. Rosen goes on to say,

> The research on employee ownership is unusually consistent and unusually clear: employee ownership boosts a company's performance, but only when it is combined with changes in culture and managerial style.[9]

A recent study of 165 ESOPs conducted by the Ohio Employee Ownership Center reported that

> Almost three quarters of ESOPs actually do take some steps to broaden participation in firm management. The changes made in most of these firms are quite modest, however, and a quarter of firms make no changes at all.[10]

Some ESOPs, like United Airlines, Andersen Windows, Procter & Gamble, and Publix Supermarkets, are familiar names. Most are smaller and less visible. Some ESOPs have a commitment to workplace democracy, but these are few. Some of the more exemplary are Carris Reels in Vermont, Johnny's Selected Seeds in Maine, W. L. Gore in New Jersey, Marland Mold in Massachusetts, Antioch Publishing in Ohio, Chroma Technology in Vermont, and Cirtronics in New Hampshire.

Canada has a lively employee ownership movement, too. Wellington West, a Winnipeg-based financial services company with 550 employees at thirty-five locations across Canada, all of whom now collectively own more than 98 percent of the company, was selected number one in a 2006 survey to determine the fifty best-managed companies in the country. A Canadian book called *Employee Ownership: The New Source of Competitive Advantage*, by Carol Beatty and Harvey Schachter,[11] is a warts-and-all study of the successes and struggles of ten employee-owned companies.

In both countries a small portion of employee-owned businesses are worker cooperatives, which are democratic organizations owned and controlled by their workers. A simpler and more direct form of worker ownership than the ESOP, the worker cooperative form predates the ESOP by more than a century and explicitly embodies principles of equitable ownership and control.

Like an ESOP, a worker cooperative resembles a typical corporation, and usually uses the "'C' corporation" or "limited liability company" (LLC) legal framework. It has a corporate shield against liability, earns profits, is governed by board of directors, and in most cases is managed by one or more officers. Three characteristics, however, distinguish it.

First, a worker cooperative is a membership organization, and membership is limited to employees who complete a trial period and invest a membership fee. Second, a worker cooperative is governed democratically by its members, who elect the board of directors (at least a majority) and vote on policy matters on a one-person/one-vote basis, rather than the usual one-vote/one-share governance of an ESOP. Third, a portion of corporate earnings is allocated to members on the basis of their work investment rather than on capital investment. These "patronage allocations" are in addition to normal wages, can be in cash or in a portion retained by the company in "internal capital accounts," and are regulated by Subchapter T of the Internal Revenue Code.

An owner selling to a cooperative sells 100 percent of the company in return for a note from the company that includes the redemption schedule along with terms and conditions that ensure the owner significant control until the note is fully paid off.

An ESOP is far more expensive to form and administer, which usually puts it out of range for companies with less than roughly thirty employees and $5 million in sales. It is subject to regulation by both the IRS and the Department of Labor, which require expensive annual valuations and a variety of other compliance measures.

An employee cooperative is simpler and less costly to establish and maintain, but it is challenging in many ways. The democratic control in a cooperative business is, by its nature, difficult to conduct in an orderly fashion and requires a process of cultural and business education of the employee-owners to understand roles, decision making, risks, and responsibilities. There must be strong bonds of trust between owner(s) and employees, and the owner(s) must be ready to relinquish control over time.

Pitegoff has seen increased activity in worker cooperative development since the 1970s and notes that while they have never been a significant portion of the US economy, cooperatives have had a modest impact in certain industry sectors and regions and in certain historical periods.[12] Over time there have been far more producer co-ops and consumer co-ops than worker co-ops. Producer cooperatives are owned by producers of farm commodities or crafts, who band together to process or market their products; a few well-known examples are Organic Valley and Land O' Lakes. Consumer cooperatives are owned by the people who buy the goods or use the services of the cooperative. REI (Recreational Equipment Inc.) is the largest consumer cooperative in the country.

Arie de Geus, in *The Living Company*, says:

> Co-op fever has recently intensified. Through their
> highly participative governance models (involving both
> members and employees in making decisions), the coop-
> erative system is particularly well suited to combining
> entrepreneurial and social objectives. Because it encour-
> ages internal checks and balances and general transpar-
> ency, cooperative structure also makes it easier to avoid
> the ethical and legal lapses that have brought down the
> management of many investor-owned companies.[13]

In 1984 tax law changes created what's known as IRS's 1042 rollover,
which allows a tax benefit to business owners who sell 30 percent or
more of their company to their employees through an ESOP or a cooperative. They can shelter the capital gains from the sale by putting the
proceeds into qualified domestic securities within twelve months of
the sale. This is often the primary reason why business owners create
ESOPs, but until late 2005 this mechanism had not been used by a
single known cooperative. The Ohio Employee Ownership Center
(OEOC) and attorney Mark Stewart of the firm Shumaker, Loop &
Kendrick in Toledo, Ohio, recently engineered the first use of this for
Select Machine in Brimfield, Ohio.

Select Machine

The company was founded in 1994 by Doug Beavers and Bill Sagaser.
They manufacture, sell, and distribute machined products for construction and demolition equipment. It's a small company, with nine full-
time employees and two part-time. Says Beavers, "Bill and I set up this
company to be the kind of company that we would like to work for
if we were working for someone else." According to observers, they
succeeded.

Doug began his career on the ground floor of a large company, running machines and making parts. He gradually moved up to sales. His partner Bill took the same route, in the same firm, and wound up in purchasing. When the company was bought by a Japanese consortium, Doug wasn't thrilled with the new direction and decided to strike out on his own. He started Select Machine, and a year or so later Bill joined him and became a partner.

But after ten years, and many years before that in the industry, Beavers and Sagaser were ready to slow down. They looked for buyers, but the several potential purchasers they found wanted to take the customer list and some of the equipment and fold the company into underutilized facilities elsewhere. Beavers and Sagaser hadn't built the business to shut the doors and leave the employees out in the cold, so they began to wonder about selling the company to their workforce, and turned to the OEOC for advice.

Director John Logue and the OEOC staff went to work. It immediately became clear that this company was too small to do an ESOP (it would be too expensive), but they thought, *Why not create a cooperative and realize the same benefits for the owners that an ESOP would?* Working with Stewart, one of the nation's leading co-op attorneys, and Eric Britton, an ESOP specialist at the same firm, they invented the tools and legal framework to make it work.

The initial feasibility study was positive. A valuation was completed, and a local bank teamed with a revolving loan fund; together the two were willing to loan money for the initial purchase, which would redeem 49 percent of the owners' stock. Stewart prepared an offering statement, which detailed the proposed transaction, the risks involved, the intent of the owners to sell the rest of the stock over time, the means by which the co-op would redeem the stock, and how the company would be managed.

Once the debt to purchase the 49 percent has been repaid, from company proceeds, Beavers and Sagaser will sell the remaining 51 percent of their shares. Meanwhile, they stay on, as co-op members, and train the other members to run the company successfully.

It's now two and a half years since the co-op was formed. By the end of 2008 the first 49 percent of the buyout should be complete, fully paid off from company net income. Final management plans will be complete and in place. Sometime in 2009 the employees will purchase the other 51 percent and Doug will retire (Bill already has).

Doug Beavers is about the friendliest, most unassuming guy you'd ever want to talk to. He's impressed by the number of firms (about a dozen) who have contacted him since the formation of the co-op, but he is not by nature a crusader. As he puts it, "I'd walk a mile to help anyone, but I'm not looking for pats on the back. We do a lot of charity work, but it's by and large anonymous."

I asked him what he will do after retirement from Select Machine (after all, he's only in his midfifties). "Don't have a clue. This has been a nice ride, but I'm ready for something different. Maybe I'll become a professional poker player (as long as my wife agrees to support me on the down days), maybe I'll be a greeter at Wal-Mart, but I have to tell you this whole co-op thing has really intrigued me." My guess: He'll be doing something in the employee ownership biz.

Select Machine assembled the right team and the job got done. At Johnny's Selected Seeds in Maine it took a longer time, and there were more trials and tribulations on the way to conversion.

Johnny's Selected Seeds

Rob Johnston started Johnny's Seeds in 1973 at the age of twenty-two with $500 in savings and a goal of producing and selling high-quality seeds to home gardeners and specialty commercial growers. He had been working on a communal truck farm in New Hampshire; the produce was sold in Boston and New York. A Japanese distributor in New York City wanted special Oriental varieties. In order to grow these, Johnston first had to find the seeds. "We had to go to Japan to get the seed because no one was offering them," he says on the company's Web site. He became engrossed in his own private seed research project. Other regional growers heard about Johnston, began to contact him for hard-to-find varieties, and he started the seed company.

Several years later he moved the company to Albion, a small town in central Maine. It's still there today, thriving and growing. It was always a mission-driven company; Rob was and remains passionate about high-quality products and customer service. It was organic from the start. Although his business depended on selling seeds, he wrote a book called *Growing Garden Seeds* to educate gardeners about how to save their own.

Today Johnny's has about one hundred full-time employees (and more in the summer) and $20 million in annual sales, and Rob has established an ESOP to sell the company to his employees. They now own 30 percent; a plan is in place to increase their share to 100 percent over time. The ESOP structure is the result of an elaborate and introspective process that goes way back. During the '80s, Rob realized he wouldn't have this company "into eternity"; that he wanted it to keep going and keep growing (it has grown steadily, from 6 to 13 percent per year, for the past twenty-five years); and that he'd better start thinking about what to do with it. He came up with three possibilities: sell it someone else, go public, or sell it to his employees. He also started thinking about what parts of the business he did and did not want to devote himself to. He decided that his strength and his interest was in the products and the customers, not in managing people and numbers, so he hired a general manager, who turned out to be the wrong guy. It took six or seven years to figure that out and get it settled, and they parted company in 1999.

Rob wasn't sure what to do. He met with all the employees and told them that he wanted to find an inspired general manager, but he didn't know how, and he was willing to sell the company if that was the only way. He hired an investment bank and a search firm at the same time. The investment bank came back with three viable offers, but Rob and his wife, Janika Eckert, weren't thrilled with any of them. The search firm recommended Mike Comer, a seasoned manager with an MBA. It was a good match, and Mike was hired to run the company. Rob and Mike have managed the company together since then, with emphasis gradually shifting from Rob to Mike.

In 2004, at Janika's urging ("We're in our midfifties—we've only got so many years to ride our bikes and do other things. Right?"), Rob decided it was time to start exploring the sale of the company to the employees. He and Mike went to an ESOP conference in Boston—the kind of place where, as Rob puts it, "All the third-party types are trying to sell their wares." They were unimpressed. But coincidentally Janika, who had come along to Boston to do some research for a Philadelphia bicycle maker and friend, was impressed by someone she met. She visited Independent Fabrication, the employee-owned custom bike manufacturer in nearby Somerville, Massachusetts. She talked to them about Johnny's, and the quest for information about selling to the employees. They suggested a consultation with the ICA Group in Boston. Ultimately Johnny's hired Jim Megson at ICA to help restructure the company.

The restructuring took several years. Rob wanted senior management to invest money upfront, but they felt it was too risky; Rob finally decided he had to accept that if he wanted to get it done. Now, in 2008, Johnny's Selected Seeds is in the throes of transitioning to an employee-owned company. The stock will be sold to an ESOP in three stages. Funding for the first third was partly money from Johnny's and partly a bank loan. In 2009 the first 30 percent will be paid off, and another chunk will be sold to the employees. This will continue until all is transferred, and Rob will remain as chairman of the board until that time, when he will become a former employee—unless, as he says, "they try to hire me back." And he accepts.

Mike is excited and energized by the process, but staggered by the complexity of it. He expected a shift, but he now sees that this is a long-term evolution. "It's a very complex process," he says. "We have to figure out what democratization means, and to what degree we pursue it." He's sixty-one, and he sees this endeavor—to make the new structure work as it's intended to—as his last big challenge. He says he's learning every day, and the opportunities are greater than he previously thought.

Already he has noticed that there are people within the company—some people—who, he says, always thought of themselves as plain old wage slaves, but are thinking differently now, about themselves and the company. They're stepping back, taking a look, and imagining a career path. He says, "This hasn't been articulated—it's just something you see in their eyes. They're looking up. They get it." At the same time, he's frustrated by others, some in positions of influence, who don't.

As for Rob, he has his own frustrations—primarily that so much of his time these days is occupied with the complexities of the employee ownership transition, all of which is time away from seeds and customers. He wishes it were simpler. But, as Megson points out,

> The complexity is due primarily to the fact that they "want to do it right"—and to do so they must work hard to involve people and prepare them to run the company. They used to have a single shareholder who made all management and policy decisions. Sure, that's simpler. Now they have a real board of directors; that requires a whole new set of policies and procedures.[14]

Rob has concerns, too. He worries that conservatism might come with employee ownership. He describes himself as "hopelessly ambitious"—always looking for new products and new avenues for the business. He's not motivated by financial potential; he's interested in growth and innovation, and he wonders whether the employee owners might become too risk-averse by worrying excessively about protection of their investment.

But mostly he has dreams. He wants to continue to "blur the boundaries between the company and its clientele." He believes that Johnny's does important work, every day, by helping small commercial growers make a living and succeed. When a grower says to him, "You know that new carrot variety you supplied us with? We did very well with it—it was financially successful and our customers really liked it. What else do you have coming up?" it's part of a rich exchange. They are each making the other's business better, and they are each contributing to the health of the small farming industry. Rob hopes to be able to look back, as a wise old "former employee" of Johnny's, and see the seed company as inseparable from American specialty farming.

Sounds like a seed grower who's walking down the same path that he did more than thirty years ago when he wrote a book to help gardeners and farmers save their own seeds.

Carris Reels

Carris Reels, headquartered in Rutland, Vermont, has an even longer history than Johnny's. It was founded by Henry Carris in 1951 to manufacture hardwood and plywood reels (spools) for the wire and cable industry. That's what they do today, almost 60 years later. The only difference is that now some are wood and some are plastic.

Bill Carris, Henry's son, grew up with the company, left Rutland for college and military service, and came back. He took over as CEO from his father in 1980. The company grew and prospered and became a fixture in the Rutland area. Today they have six locations in the United States, one in Mexico, 550 employees, and close to $100 million in annual sales.

Bill is at once a soulful person and a good businessman. He brought management and leadership skills to the company, but he also brought a desire for the Carris employees to become owners and essential participants in the planning of their own future. In 1994, after many years of studying, working with consultants, and assembling his thoughts, Bill completed the Carris Long Term Plan (LTP) and shared it with his employees. It's a remarkable document. I wish I could reprint it here in its entirety, but its thirty-four pages wouldn't fit. Reading it, I experienced profound joy and the desire to stand up and pump my fist at the same time. Written in plain English—conversational, almost—parts of it are heartrending, poignant, and philosophical, but it presents a detailed, pragmatic plan to make Carris Reels a successful, 100 percent employee-owned and -governed company.

The capitalist system suffers from inherent unfairness, according to Carris, while the communist and socialist systems are fundamentally ineffective; he concludes that we need to combine the productivity of the free-market system with better distribution of its wealth, goods, and services. Understanding that to work effectively there must be hierarchy, he nevertheless is absolutely clear about its place: "Equality must be primary, and hierarchy secondary."

> Our goal is to upgrade employees' health, wealth, and happiness as a result of changing from a traditional, privately-held company to an employee-owned and governed organization. Employees are the soul of our corporate community; they deserve to become legal owners. Every attempt will be made to provide opportunities for those who have had the least chance. Personal and spiritual growth will be valued and encouraged for all individuals. There is no organizational success without its individuals succeeding and growing.[15]

The second section of the plan, which is called "Beliefs, Principles, and Values," is broken into three parts: "The Spiritual Company," "The Emotional Company," and "The Physical Company."

And yet, throughout, he recites the mantra of profit, and never loses sight of the fact that "profits = existence." He emphasizes that "although it may seem inconsistent to focus heavily on profit when my mission is to improve one's quality of life, [it] goes hand and hand. Profit is the critical means to achieve our mission."[16] His aspiration is for Carris Reels to be a great provider of all things that a company can provide: employee fulfillment, customer satisfaction, high quality, fair prices, community service, and profit. He doesn't include "changing the world," but that's what they're doing.

Carris knew that he wished to sell the company at a deeply discounted rate to his employees, not to outsiders. He expected to teach the employees to run the business and establish governance based on two basic ideas: One person, one vote; and transparent, accountable decision making using consensus with a one-person, one-vote backup. He didn't expect this to happen overnight, and it hasn't.

The ESOP approach emerged as the most appropriate structure because of the tax advantages, but the system that developed has all the characteristics of a cooperative. Cecile Betit, an independent researcher who has spent more than a decade documenting the Carris journey, says about Bill Carris, "Over the years, material goals had lost importance for him, and he gained satisfaction from being a positive influence in other people's lives." He felt that "liberty and the pursuit of happiness also meant a right to share wealth, to manage our daily work and ultimately to be in control of our lives."[17] Further, he believed that the corporate success stories of the coming decades would be those companies that involved more people in information processing and decision making.

Fifty percent of the stock would be a gift to the employees—Carris felt that this was an essential recognition of their contributions—and the rest would be sold at the predetermined price. Among the thousands of ESOPs in the United States, Carris was unable to find a single ESOP company, to use as a model, that had created 100 percent employee ownership and 100 percent employee governance. He started distributing the stock in 1995; by the end of the year 2000 the employees owned 43.2 percent of the stock. But then, for a while, everything ground to a halt.

The years 2001 through 2003 were the most difficult in the company's history; the dot-com collapse and the telecommunications crisis significantly reduced demand for wire and cable. They had to close a subsidiary company, sell another, resize, and take measures that, for them, felt nearly draconian. Says Betit, "They could easily have put the brakes on their march to employee ownership and control, but they didn't. They just delayed."[18] The management team of Carris, CEO Mike Curran, and CFO Dave Fitzgerald struggled valiantly in the trenches and emerged with their values, and the business, intact. Karin McGrath, the human resources director, has been with the company for thirty years. She told me, "The fact that we survived and we are as strong as we are today was reassuring for all. Everybody was looking for ways to tighten our purse strings. We were open and honest with information. During this time Bill and Barbara Carris went around to all our locations, sat in front of small groups of employees on different shifts, and answered the questions they asked. It meant a lot to the employees—especially those that were not in Rutland."[19]

In 2005 the remaining 6.8 percent of the first 50 percent gift was transferred to the employees, and the first 15 percent (of the second 50 percent) was sold. This was truly the big moment for the company, especially because it came on the heels of such a traumatic time. Says Karin, "Becoming majority owners at 65 percent was huge. It felt like—we are going to make it! There was a lot of excitement."[20]

Betit has devoted a large piece of her life to studying and chronicling the Carris Reels story. In fact, she has been a part of it. Says Karin, "Sometimes we go to Cecile after a meeting and ask for her notes so we can find out what really happened, and who really said what."[21] Cecile says that although Carris's great love for his people and depth of commitment are large factors in the success, it's also come thanks to Curran, Dave Fitzgerald, McGrath, VP of Sales and Marketing David Ferraro, and a host of others. Carris clearly brought the right people on board, and Betit is constantly impressed by how hard they work to stay aligned with their principles. She describes the partnership between Carris (now chairman of the board) and Curran (the CEO) this way: "Bill is the one who relentlessly carries the big vision and Mike is the one that knows how to make things work, the one that always knows just how much heat it will take to raise the temperature."[22]

On January 1, 2008, Carris Reels became 100 percent employee owned and governed. Says Karin about this moment, "Bill's dream was realized. It has been an incredible journey and an incredible gift from Bill and Barb. Employees are proud to work at [and own, and run] Carris Reels."[23]

And how does it feel to Bill? "I would have to say it feels good, but not an end. We still have a lot of work to do . . . to plan for the future success of the business. We have always felt that the success of the business has to trump everything or all the rest of our work will have been for nothing."[24] He adds, "I don't think of it as a transformation but a process of growth that I hope continues. To some extent this is an experiment in change."[25]

Carris Reels has a bright future. How many other bright futures may derive from the extraordinary model they have created, and how much will we be able to learn as this ongoing experiment in change continues? If it's anywhere near as much as we have learned from the storied collection of cooperatives in the Basque region of Spain known as Mondragon, it will not be inconsequential.

Mondragon

In 1941 a young Jesuit priest named Don José Maria Arizmendiarrieta was assigned by the Catholic Church to the town of Mondragon. When he arrived, the area was locked in poverty and still recovering from the devastation of the Spanish Civil War. Don José Maria had narrowly escaped being put to death for his own participation on the Republican side. Convinced that part of his service was to raise the economic fortunes of the people of Mondragon, he founded a technical school. In 1955 five of the graduates, with his assistance, founded a small worker-owned company to manufacture kerosene stoves. More cooperative businesses formed during the remainder of the 1950s, and Arizmendi encouraged the creation of a bank that, when it opened in 1959, became a cooperative credit union dedicated to the establishment of more cooperatives. The association of cooperatives continued to grow; in the 1970s a research institute opened to help with technology development, and in the 1990s Mondragon University, a private university dedicated primarily to the study of business and commerce, was established. Don José died in 1976, but the Mondragon Corporacion Cooperativa (MCC), which binds together all the cooperative enterprises, continues to thrive.

In January 2001, sixty years after Don José's arrival, I visited Mondragon with a small group of Americans for a four-day examination of the culture of both the town and the MCC. Having used a version of the Mondragon principles as the basis for the restructuring of South Mountain Company fourteen years earlier, it was thrilling to get a firsthand look at this system of worker-owned cooperatives that appears to be unparalleled in its dynamism and its impact on a region.

MCC now consists of more than 150 cooperative businesses (and other businesses), in addition to the bank, the research institute, and the university. There are over eighty thousand employees. Roughly half of these are owners. MCC's gross revenues in 2006 were more than $13 billion, making it the largest corporation in the Basque region and the seventh largest in Spain. The co-ops include Spain's largest producer of refrigerators, leading tool-and-die makers, and many other industrial companies. They make forklifts, windmills, bicycles, appliances, nails, wire, boilers, health and exercise equipment, automobile parts, furniture, woodworking and machine tools, specialized electronic products, manufacturing machinery and robots, and dozens of other industrial products. MCC's Eroski is the largest supermarket chain in Spain, and it does catering, dairy farming, greenhouse horticulture, and rabbit breeding as well. Other co-ops provide engineering, market research, and consulting services. Some develop housing in the area. Mondragon has created a total system wherein people can learn, work, shop, and live within a cooperative environment. The town, in its isolated valley, has a vital, prosperous feel—a small bustling city with a comfortable mix of young people from the university, new middle-class families, and those who have been in the valley for generations. The surrounding hills are verdant and productive, dotted with villages and farms. The MCC's influence reaches into every aspect of community life.

We visited Fagor Electronica, a large producer of residential appliances. The sprawling factory looked like any other from the outside. Inside it was clean and bright. The atmosphere was relaxed and not too noisy. People worked in small teams on assembly lines, and they traded places with one another from time to time to relieve tedium, and for each to learn the several jobs on the line. A mezzanine level housed offices, meeting rooms, and a coffee bar. The rooms had glass walls and were highly visible from below. Floor workers freely walked up to conduct business upstairs; managers were comfortable on the floor. There was a sense of camaraderie, teamwork, and integration. We were told that this workplace was highly productive. It felt that way.

Success is an institution at Mondragon. There are several new start-ups each year, and only two have ever failed. In the United States more than 90 percent of business start-ups fail within the first five years. Peter Pitegoff says, "Mondragon stands out as the most successful coordinated complex of worker cooperative enterprises in the world, with demonstrated capacity for economic growth and long-term survival."[26]

The visit, however, produced questions. What drives their recent interest in export and locating new plants overseas? Can they continue dancing on the tightrope between ongoing success in a global business climate and holding true to their core values? Why doesn't their environmental consciousness (which seems higher than normal but not extraordinary) match their concern about social equity and economic democracy?

In response to our questions, our hosts were pragmatic: Their primary purpose is the creation of safe, secure lifelong jobs and prosperity for their employee-owners. Sometimes they must compromise to achieve this. But they continue to attempt to balance their democratic social goals with survival in competitive markets. They are passionately committed to their cooperative principles and always trying to extend democratic values to traditional enterprises they have acquired.

But the biggest question is this: Why is Mondragon such a secret in the United States? It has attracted great attention worldwide, but far less here. Even the US-based socially responsible business movement pays it little mind. Is the idea that capital is a tool, rather than the residence of power, too radical to embrace? Instead of awarding profit and control to capital, Mondragon has succeeded by awarding profit and control to labor in a system of democratic capitalism. It has developed an enduring way to use capital productively and distribute income equitably at the same time.

Select Machine, Johnny's Selected Seeds, Carris Reels, and Mondragon—different scales, different structures, and different locations. They are all part of the leading edge of a movement that is, at present, only a distant blip on the broad cultural and economic horizon. It is, however, gathering steam, generating interest, and provoking questions among many business owners today.

The ESOP or the Co-op: Which Way to Go?

Among small and medium-size businesses considering employee ownership, one of the most common questions is: Which makes more sense, the ESOP or the co-op? Although most employee-owned companies are ESOPs, more companies are exploring and choosing the cooperative alternative.

Jim Megson, the employee ownership consultant with the ICA Group in Boston, has done comparisons for companies to analyze the benefits and drawbacks of each option. These will vary for each company, but here is his summary report for one specific company; I've made minor modifications:

> **Sale to a Worker Cooperative**
> *Advantages*
> • Relatively inexpensive to set up.

- No annual maintenance fees.
- Can use IRS 1042 rollover to defer capital gains under certain conditions.
- Owner can retain oversight until note is paid off.
- Members buy a membership share, which makes ownership "real."
- The democratic structure involves all employees.
- Shares can only be held by employees.

Disadvantages
- Owner sells 100 percent immediately and therefore does not gain from future increases in company value.
- Owner must finance the transaction as cooperatives are not well understood by banks.
- Employees must find the cash to buy a membership share.

Three-Phase Sale to an ESOP
Advantages
- ESOPs are highly regulated and understood by banks.
- Selling the company in stages makes the transaction more manageable for the company.
- Can use IRS 1042 rollover to defer capital gains under certain conditions.
- The value of the stock should increase over time; therefore the price for subsequent portions of the stock would be higher.
- After the first one-third transaction, the owner still retains full control and can see how the system works before turning over control to the employees.
- If things do not work out after the first transaction, there is still the option of selling to a different buyer.

- Employees are not required to invest any of their own money.

Disadvantages

- More expensive to set up ($25,000–50,000).
- Annual maintenance costs of $10,000–20,000 (annual appraisal, plan administrator, etc.).
- Because the first sale is not a controlling interest it will be discounted for "lack of control."
- Owner may be required to provide personal guarantee for bank loan to ESOP.
- Shares can be passed on to heirs, who can vote the shares, potentially diluting the company culture.
- Employees are not required to invest any of their own money.[27]

This is, of course, all very subjective and company-specific. Under "Cooperative," one of the advantages is the democratic structure, but if you don't want a democratic structure, or don't think it will work well in your company compared with the more traditional corporate structure of an ESOP, it doesn't qualify as an advantage. The fact that employees are not required to invest any of their own money is listed as both an advantage and a disadvantage with an ESOP. It's an advantage because employees often do not want to invest; it's a disadvantage because they are therefore less invested.

Each company needs to do its own soul searching and financial analysis. There is no one-size-fits-all in the world of employee ownership. Whether or not an owner is planning to use a tax deferral under IRC Section 1042, the choice between sale to an ESOP or sale to a worker-owned cooperative will yield different tax and cost consequences for the business and a dramatically different employee experience in subsequent operation of the business.

Co-op attorney Mark Stewart and his ESOP attorney partner Eric Britton have written a position paper called "Selling Stock to

Employees Through a Qualified Worker-Owned Cooperative and Sheltering Capital Gain: The IRC § 1042 Rollover." Although the piece was intended to establish the viability of the 1042 rollover for cooperatives, it also includes some detailed comparative analyses of ESOPs and co-ops.

The pair reinforces Megson's assertion that because employee cooperatives, unlike ESOPs, are not employee retirement plans, they are not subject to the numerous restrictions imposed by the Employee Retirement Income Security Act of 1974 (ERISA). As a result, cooperatives avoid such regulatory burdens (and related expenses) as extensive legal and consultant fees to establish the ESOP, hiring a bank trustee or other independent plan fiduciary to represent the employees' interest, an annual independent appraisal, IRS and Department of Labor audits and the possibility of noncompliance findings, and the elaborate nondiscrimination rules imposed on qualified retirement plans.

On the other hand, the advantage conferred on an ESOP because it is a retirement plan is its tax-exempt status, which presents attractive tax-planning opportunities and savings for the company.

An employee cooperative is not a tax-exempt entity, but it can pass profits, losses, and other tax benefits through to its employee members without federal taxation at its corporate level. The employee-recipient is responsible for the tax, and distributions must be made in accordance with Subchapter T of the Internal Revenue Code. The result of this is that the cooperative's income is taxed only once in its journey from the cooperative's business operations to the employee-owner. This single tax treatment is similar to the pass-through of income in a subchapter S corporation or an LLC. In addition, an employee cooperative may establish a qualified retirement plan that is simpler, safer, and more cost-effective than an ESOP to which it can make tax-deductible contributions, as we do at South Mountain.

Regarding the IRS 1042 mechanism, I asked Mark Stewart why it hadn't been done before, given that the provision has been in effect since 1984. He replied,

The professionals involved in employee ownership transitions concentrate on ESOPs; they involve larger companies and there's more money there. There are many co-op attorneys, but their concentration is on consumer co-ops and producer co-ops, like agricultural co-ops, rural electric co-ops, and food co-ops. Very few attorneys understand the potential breadth and scope of worker-owned cooperative businesses in the American economy. But once we started looking at the Select Machine idea, it became clear to us that the articles and bylaws that have been written for decades for these other kinds of cooperatives were easily adaptable.[28]

Stewart and Britton suggest that cooperatives are beginning to take their place as a real option, or "choice of entity," when organizing or reorganizing a business for employee ownership, as some of the advantages become clear. "Many business owners," they say, "would like to take advantage of Section 1042 of the Internal Revenue Code to sell stock in their company without immediate taxation of their capital gains, but are deterred by the complex and potentially onerous rules imposed on Employee Stock Ownership Plans (ESOPs)."[29] But selling to an ESOP, it has become clear, is not the only way. Selling to an eligible worker-owned cooperative can accomplish the same thing while avoiding some of the expenses and legal complications associated with an ESOP.

Is this cooperative approach only applicable to very small companies like Select Machine? The conventional wisdom among most employee ownership experts is that co-ops are best for businesses with twenty-five to thirty employees or less; beyond that, it makes sense to use the ESOP approach. But that may be changing.

Stewart feels that there is no cap on size; if a democratic organization is the goal, a co-op can work at any scale. John Logue of the Ohio Employee Ownership Center thinks the co-op approach is going to take off and become very popular. "There are many people out there,"

he said to me, "besides eccentric businesspeople like yourself and idiosyncratic academics like me, who will find this idea appealing for a
variety of reasons." He described an HVAC company in Oregon he is
working with. They are well above the ESOP financial threshold, yet
the owner doesn't like government regulation, does like his employees,
has some solid workers who will provide adequate succession, and has a
company worth about $650,000 with a total basis of $2,978. There you
have it—ready to become a co-op and use the 1042 rollover.

But all of this, as Megson reminds me, still must be looked at in
terms of size. The "governance difference between running a relatively
small democratic company and a larger one," he says, "is the difference
between direct democracy and representative democracy with all its
implications and complications."

There is normally some adversarial tension between the employees
and management in a company. Employee cooperatives and democratic ESOPs must overcome this conflict and the natural reluctance
of employees to assume responsibility. Democratic companies are most
appropriate when the employees recognize their common interest in
working together to sustain the business and, therefore, their jobs and
careers; when they believe they will create and gain greater value—of
whatever kind—from their work in a collectively owned and managed
workplace; and when they are willing to engage in the process of decision making and learning the skills of business ownership. The hope
is that with equity comes trust, and adversarial tensions succumb to
collaborative bonds. When the employee owners share both profits
and control, there's no separation. The group is vested with both the
benefits and the burdens of distributed power.

The Promise of Employee Ownership

I often wonder why the socially responsible business movement in
the United States has not embraced employee ownership more fully.

This movement has popularized ideas about commerce as a means of implementing people-centered human resources programs, pursuing environmental sustainability, encouraging participation in local community life, and promoting social and economic justice. As far as I can tell, though, there's only a faint murmur (albeit gradually increasing in volume) about distribution of ownership. Entrepreneurs are risk takers, but perhaps—and I am only speculating here—giving up control seems like too great a risk to these pioneers who have already risked so much to build businesses that embody their personal values.

I've come to believe, however, that giving up control is the business risk that has the greatest potential to generate positive returns. It's not unlike choosing to have a baby. There can't be anything we do in life more risky than having children, but for most people the perils are apparently outweighed by the potential pleasures and fulfillments. That's how it felt to me—a worthy gamble. Not to mention that offering ownership without control seems like selling someone a car without turning over the keys.

One of the limitations of employee ownership that may account for some of its lack of attention is the difficulty of raising capital. Investors have little interest. The Mondragon model solved this problem by requiring 50 percent of retained earnings to be reinvested in the company. In this way, Mondragon avoids having to go to capital markets. The workers commit to reinvestment in the company, and capital remains tied to the community. Our system works the same way. Equity is assigned to each owner and we gradually build a reserve fund to buy out owners' equity shares when they retire, thus keeping the shares within the company.

This system also cures another serious structural flaw that inhibited the growth of worker cooperatives for many years. Logue et al. point out in their book *Participatory Employee Ownership* that, as with all forms of business, there have been some failures. The problem, however, was with those that succeeded. Each member of the co-op owned an equal share; if the co-op was successful, all the shares appreciated. When founding members wanted to retire, new workers couldn't afford the share price, so, the authors say, "Success was as fatal as failure: retiring members sold to outside buyers," and gradually the cooperatives became conventional corporations. This, too, was solved by the Mondragon system, where shares must be sold back to the cooperative, and further developed by the Industrial Cooperatives Association (now the ICA Group) into the internal capital account system that employee-owned cooperative businesses use today (see appendix 1 for a detailed explanation).

In the autumn 2007 issue of *Strategy + Business* magazine, an article called "A Cooperative Solution," by Ricardo Lotti, Peter Mensing, and Davide Valenti, discusses Rabobank, the cooperative Dutch financial institution that is among the twenty-five largest banks in the world, and COOP, a consortium of Italian regional retail cooperatives, whose advertising slogan "La coop sei tu" (the co-op is you) has become a national catchphrase. The authors ask, "How well can cooperatives compete with fiercely entrepreneurial companies emerging in a globalizing world?" Whereas to many observers, cooperatives appear to be burdened with features that are liabilities in conventional business models, the authors point out in several ways how cooperative leaders have learned to make them into assets. To give just one example, in terms of long-range planning and experimentation, Rabobank's CEO Bert Heemskerk says, "You can take your time. There's not such an immediate pressure of quarterly results. Obviously, we have to perform well financially and remain solvent. But we don't feel the pressure of showing a 20 percent return this year. If we have 10 or 12 percent, it's acceptable."[30] This means that they, as a private cooperative corporation, do not need to submit to the pressures and demands of Wall Street.

Employee ownership is clearly coming into its own. Corey Rosen says in his book *Equity*,

> What's interesting about employee ownership isn't only that it's widespread. It also turns up in a disproportion-

ate number of influential and innovative companies. Nearly 80 percent of the corporations on *Fortune's* "100 Best Companies to Work For" list had some kind of broad-based ownership plan.[31]

And he continues:

> The extent to which high-tech firms that are focused on the Internet have granted ownership to their employees has no precedent in modern American history. No other industry has ever attempted, much less achieved, the depth, breadth, and extent of wealth sharing found among these firms.[32]

It sounds like we're learning something—that companies offering ownership and control to their entire workforce have the potential to unleash an explosion of entrepreneurial activity. They are offering a share in capitalism itself.

Steve Magowan, a Vermont employee ownership attorney with Steiker, Fischer, Edwards & Greenapple—a firm with offices in four cities—said to me recently, "We feel like employee ownership is expanding for two reasons: (1) baby boomers reaching retirement age, and (2) bad experience with private equity firms." Many business owners have had the experience that Select Machine avoided: Private equity buys the firm, takes control, becomes focused solely on returning the shareholders' investment, cuts costs and personnel or takes the company lock, stock, and barrel overseas—whatever it takes to maximize return, without regard for the employees, the community, or any of the other real stakeholders.

Employee ownership and democratic governance are not for everyone, however. As the stories I've told illustrate, the conversion to employee ownership of any kind is complicated and difficult. It's hard to do. There are people who should never attempt to make their businesses employee owned; they are the people who don't believe in it. For them it will never work.

I have come to the conclusion that the foundation, the fuel, and the inspiration for the modest successes we have had at South Mountain Company is the profound ethic of employee ownership and all that spills from it and gathers around it. The employee-owned workplace is, in my view, the spawning ground for a restorative future.

The Workstead Act of 2010

William Greider, in *The Soul of Capitalism*, calls the Homestead Act of 1862, which awarded free land, if the recipients worked it and stayed on it, to more than half a million American families, a "a public works project of grandly egalitarian intent" that "was probably the nation's greatest single stroke of economic development channeled directly through people. . . ." He goes on to say: "In present times, some advocates suggest a parallel between employee ownership and homesteading. Instead of land . . . government, it is argued, should provide access to capital to finance the broadened distribution of equity ownership. . . ."[33]

In the next State of the Union address, I hope the president will propose the Workstead Act of 2010. About four million Americans are born each year. If, at birth, $10,000 were invested for each baby, it would become approximately $40,000 at age twenty. If, in addition, we offered $40,000 to each person turning twenty each year (until those being born come of age), the total annual cost would be less than the recent Bush tax cuts for the wealthy. This sum would be available to each young citizen to invest in the business of his or her choice after becoming an employee. How good would it be for American business—for capitalism—if every new employee was an investor?

If we were to begin thinking of employee ownership the way we do homeownership—as a right to be enjoyed by all Americans—it might have a cascading problem-solving effect. I understand there are a host of worthy competing interests for funds. But this would be a fundamental investment in the future of our children, our economy, and our country. How good would it be for business if our children were the new source of venture capital? If they were, what would they invest in? Do you think, as I do, that they would want to own businesses they believe in, businesses designed to make a better world? If many did, this would be a change of epic proportions.

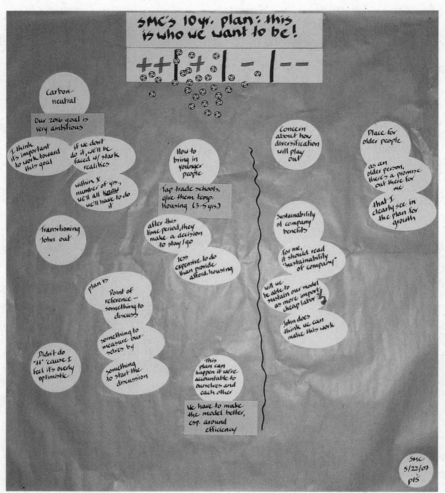

ROBERT LEAVER

▪ 3 ▪

Cultivating Workplace Democracy

Nearly all men can stand adversity, but if you want
to test a man's character, give him power.
—ABRAHAM LINCOLN

When we decided to restructure South Mountain in 1987, I mistakenly thought we were doing something more symbolic than substantive. Nothing could have been further from the truth. I could not possibly have imagined how meaningful and valuable it would be. It required a major psychological leap as well as a legal one. I suspect that it has been as rewarding for others as it has been for me, and there's no question in my mind—although I can have no definitive proof—that it has been a critical factor in the long-term success of the company.

I have been asked why our investigations led us to a worker-owned cooperative instead of, for example, simply creating partnership positions for Steve and Pete. A conventional partnership approach might have done the trick, for the moment, but we were seeking a long-term solution. We were also intrigued by the challenge of finding out to what degree sharing ownership and control could democratize and humanize the workplace. For us, like Bill Carris at Carris Reels, it was an experiment in change.

Is it possible for a group of people, especially one that is forever expanding, to assume the full mantle of ownership? Can everyone truly engage? Can people with different occupations, orientations, and backgrounds have similar relations and depth of commitment to the thing they have agreed to share custody of?

In our case it hasn't happened quickly or without difficulty, but it has happened steadily. Degrees of involvement vary, and the dynamics are constantly changing and evolving. It's no easy undertaking, and there are no guarantees of success. When success comes, it isn't likely to manifest in the ways we imagine. We are making fundamental changes in a complex human system.

Business management has become far more sophisticated in recent decades. The once common response to employee ideas—"You're paid to work, not think"—has largely been abandoned. But the generation of free-agent thinkers that has emerged is a generation of people thinking for themselves, and for their own advancement, without much concern for the common good.

In our case, it is essential that our owners learn that when they are acting as owners, they are wholly responsible for putting the overall good of the company above their own interests. The system encourages this.

In thinking about this dynamic, I am reminded of the way the Roman army handled daily rations. Rations were in the form of large loaves of bread, each sufficient to feed two soldiers. This presented a problem, since when the soldiers had little to do, they tended to fight among themselves, particularly over who got the bigger half of the loaf. The Romans developed a nifty solution. They passed a regulation that one soldier had to divide the loaf and the other chose which half to take. Employee ownership is a complex version of this kind of self-enforcing system. Each owner's actions on behalf of the others, and the company, are actions on his or her own behalf at the same time.

Such a shift requires that we learn new relationships while we keep the company afloat. As we bring more people to the table, we create

potency and capacity that did not previously exist. Gradually participants come to understand that the only power is the power of conviction and expertise: To create change we have only to convince one
another. It doesn't matter what you're trying to do—if you want to
replace the flatbed truck with a pair of oxen, all you have to do is to
convince the others that it makes sense. If we continue to use the
truck, it's because we agree to, not because it has been predetermined
or decided by one person that it's better than a team of oxen.

Everyone accepts the importance of balancing participation and efficiency. We know that since there is no map to guide us, we need to
be comfortable with trial and error and nimble enough to alter the
process as needed. We pave the road as we travel.

Sharing the Profits

The financial opportunity is the appetizer, setting the table for the
other courses. Personal equity is accumulated through profit sharing
and is recorded in each owner's individual internal capital account.
These are paper accounts (not cash accounts) backed up by the company's net worth. They begin with the membership fee that each owner
pays, and they grow after each profitable year. South Mountain has
two forms of profit sharing: All employees—owners and nonowners
alike—share 35 percent of the profits each year as cash bonuses, based
on hours worked during the calendar year (this partially mitigates the
hierarchical wage scale; we have distributed roughly $800,000 this way
over the past five years).

The remaining net income is divided between the owners' equity
accounts (50 percent, based on hours worked), and retained earnings
(the other 50 percent). The equity accounts measure the financial
stake of each employee-owner. Currently there is a total of roughly
$1.4 million in the owners' combined individual equity accounts. All
owners take that with them, in addition to their accrued pension (there

is currently approximately $1,700,000 in our pension fund), when they retire or leave the company. To be certain that the company will have the money to pay departing owners their equity share when the time comes, we have an investment fund dedicated to this purpose, and we've committed to always maintaining no less than 50 percent of the accrued equity in it. The cash in this fund is invested in socially responsible securities and bonds, and currently totals approximately $900,000. These funds could conceivably be used for other purposes (dealing with a financial emergency or a work slowdown, for example), but it requires the unanimous consent of the owners to do so.

Who Decides What and How

The employee-owners are the board of directors of the company. Only employees may serve on the board. Ownership is inextricably tied to employment; upon termination of employment or retirement, an owner's share must be sold back to the corporation, although retiring owners may elect to remain owners until their equity is paid off in full. Although we get plenty of advice from accountants, attorneys, bankers, and consultants—the best we can find—and we have the utmost respect for them and listen carefully to their counsel, they do not make policy decisions about the company; only employee-owners do.

The owners do not manage the company; they set policy, and management carries it out. The board has responsibility for issues that affect the future of the company, such as accepting new owners; significant compensation and benefits policies; profit sharing; general direction in terms of future projects and work; major purchases, investments, and expansions; company growth; new ventures; involvement in community projects; and major donations of time and money. The owners also provide general financial oversight, review and approval of annual budgets, and review and approval of year-end reports and future strategic plans. It is reasonably well defined what constitutes a decision needing board approval. But still, after twenty-plus years, there are times when it is not clear. We are continually testing these boundaries and refining our process. Informal adjustments and new understandings are crafted over time.

The board, with seventeen members, mostly discusses and reacts to proposals brought by management.

A typical board decision goes like this. Recently we began a new solar and wind division that is now a year old. The suggestion was made to the board that, for a variety of reasons, this may be a good venture for us to examine. The board directed management to explore the idea. Management worked with several people within the company to develop a concept and prepare a business plan. The board accepted the business plan. Management went forward with the execution of the plan.

All board decisions are made by consensus, but there is a supermajority (75 percent) backup voting mechanism for those rare instances when we are unable to reach consensus (see appendix 3, "Meeting Facilitation and Consensus Decision Making"). Each owner has one vote. In eighteen years we have only had to vote three times. The first time we voted, many years ago, was over a trivial matter that provoked strong disagreement. We couldn't reach consensus, and finally someone said, "We're spending far more time on this than it's worth—let's take a vote." Without resolving our disagreement we voted and moved on. Easy enough. In fact, I doubt anyone can remember what the issue was.

The second and third votes were about substantive questions; the dialogues were rife with conflicting views and debate. One was about our big, risky move to throw in our lot with a then-forming cohousing group, purchase fifty acres of land in West Tisbury, and develop both the cohousing neighborhood and a new business facility for ourselves. There were many implications and unknowns. The other was whether a particular employee, who had been with the company for the required five years, had the appropriate commitment to be accepted as an owner. On each occasion we had several long meetings before determining that we could not reach consensus. The ensuing votes were not close, however, and there was no discernible rancor in the aftermath because the airing had been so complete. We have found the backup voting provision to be essential to the effective use of consensus decision making. My guess is that today, were we to ask, all the owners, even those who disagreed at the time, would agree that on both occasions we made the right decisions.

We have been blessed with a congenial, respectful, thoughtful group of owners; there are few difficult struggles. As the ownership pool expands, there is more diversity, which leads to more disagreements but richer discussions and more thorough investigations. Monthly board meetings are informal, intimate, and humorous, but they are carefully facilitated; everyone has a voice, but the discussions don't wander or stray too far off topic. The average length of the board meeting is two hours. As a friend of mine says, "Anything longer than two hours is a workshop, not a meeting." Because the proposals have generally been through a broadly participative process before they get to the board, there is already a partial consensus that the proposals make sense. We have far more disagreements within our management committee, personnel committee, and other committees, because this is where new ideas and proposals first take root and get processed.

If pressed to identify a flaw in the way this all works, I would say that we may be just a bit too congenial, although I hate to rock that boat. Sometimes I think we need to increase our inclination to dig into our underlying differences and conflicts and surface them. On occasion, or so it seems to me, we reach resolution without deeply examining our differences because it isn't comfortable to do so. Accommodation is easier. It's a kind of "work avoidance," as leadership teacher and theorist Ron Heifetz terms it.[1]

The group of owners has the ultimate authority, but it delegates much of the trust and authority to management. Before the winter of 2003, I acted as CEO and general manager, responsible directly to the board of directors, and worked individually with others: designers, foremen, shop foreman, interiors, financial manager, and so forth. They were branches, and I was the hub. The only committee, other than the board, that had significant authority was our five-person personnel committee.

I took a sabbatical for the winter of 2003; we created a seven-person management committee to run the company in my absence. I took a second sabbatical for the winter of 2004; before my departure we changed the management committee to three people. When I returned, I joined the management committee, and we added a fifth, a rotating member of the board who serves for six to nine months. The management committee meets weekly and is responsible for managing the company; I remain CEO and chair the board. Deirdre Bohan chairs the management committee, and she is in charge in my absence.

Although we manage by committee, the buck stops with me when something needs a quick decision. Or with Deirdre in my absence. More often than not, the quick decisions that need to be made are about matters too minor to warrant broad participation—it's unnecessary, expensive, and inefficient to be overparticipatory. But sometimes, in the face of our participatory democracy, action must be taken. As David Lloyd George once said, "Don't be afraid to take a big step when one is indicated. You can't cross a chasm in two small steps."

Much of the company's management is currently done by Deirdre and I as co-managers, in close consultation with the other three members of the management committee. The five of us meet weekly. Peg MacKenzie, who chairs the personnel committee, has a similar relationship with me regarding personnel and human resources issues, and the two of us have a similar relationship with the committee.

We continue to distribute management in a highly collaborative way. More and more is done by committee. In addition to management and personnel, there are regular meetings of the following committees: design, production, shop, waste, charitable contributions, education, and more. The designers manage their own jobs, with design committee oversight. The foremen manage theirs, with production committee oversight. The renewable energy division manages their work, with oversight from management.

To successfully work in this way requires strong leadership every bit as much as good management.

Leadership is about holding the big picture and creating an environment within which people can grow. Management is about executing tasks to get things done. Both are essential, but it is impossible to have good management without strong leadership. Leadership is also the ability to motivate and enable others to do what they would not do otherwise. The Chinese mystic Lao-tzu said, "When the best leader's work is done the people say, 'We did it ourselves!'" Always present is the struggle to balance good leadership with effective management.

With so much collaboration and so many meetings, the meetings must be effective, concise, and productive. We monitor their cost to assure we are getting good value. Because we understand that facilitation is essential to good meetings, even of small committees, we provide internal training and encourage the development of competent facilitation practice. We have found that knowledge of facilitation technique produces better meeting participants as well as better meeting leaders. When people learn what it takes to run a good meeting, they gain greater understanding of how to collaborate successfully.

Our governance system is a democracy with clear divisions of responsibilities and authorities. Even with multiple owners and voices, and many committees, we are rarely bogged down in process. Part of the reason for this is the acceptance of hierarchy based solely on expertise, not power. Most hierarchies serve two purposes: efficiency and maintenance of power. "Once the power aspect is gone," says Terry Mollner, founder of the Trusteeship Institute, "people love hierarchy because of its efficiency, and they don't find it to be a barrier to healthy relationships with each other."[2] I think that's true in our case. Our decentralization efforts are not intended to reduce hierarchy; rather, they encourage more participation without decreased reliance on expertise. A cooperative corporation is more like a social sector organization than a business. No one has absolute power, so getting the right decisions made depends more on leadership than power.

And, of course, expertise. We don't want the crew to sit around on the job and draw straws for who cases the windows and who builds the stairway. We want a capable supervisor who knows the people he or she is working with and assigns responsibilities appropriately. In the end decisions must be made by those who have the ability to make them best. The decisions that get made on that basis reduce the number that must be made by consensus via the board of directors or the various committees.

Checking in helps, too. Management by walking around is my style: nosy, helpful, social, collaborative, opinionated, and demanding. The key to the success of this approach seems to be the suppression, or the calming, of that urge—sometimes—through the understanding that there is already a collaboration happening and that both the collaboration and I can get along fine without joining forces. That recognition changes the engagement from a pattern to a choice. Is this a good time to leave what I'm doing? Is this a good time to join their collaboration? For me? For them? It's hard to always know.

And it's always important to remember that the people who are here are here for a reason. As in any successful organization, we try to find the right people, inspire them, and trust them to do a great job. It can be difficult and frightening to let go, but the rewards are always greater than the risks. When we empower others, we build capacity that did not previously exist. For me the hardest part to learn has been that such empowerment must carry with it the understanding that they will do things their way, not my way, and to learn that this is okay, because there is always a collection of successful ways to do any one thing, not just one way. And the greatest reward is seeing that sometimes, when people do things their way, it turns out to be a better way, which is good for me, good for them, and, most important, good for the company. Sometimes it doesn't, and that's disappointing. But it's not the end of the world.

Recently we needed a new dust collection system for our woodworking shop. The shop foreman and the woodworkers worked with a dust collection system designer. The management committee had minimal involvement, recommended the large expenditure to the board, and it was approved. The shop crew worked diligently to install the system and did a superb job. When it was all done, however, it turned out that that the expert whom they had hired had only one thing on his mind: the most effective way to suck dust and clean the air. That was the limit of his expertise, and we now had an expensive new system that did the job but produced far too much noise (it actually rendered our conference room unusable) and was terribly energy-consumptive. This was a tremendous disappointment, and we realized, after some months, that there was no easy fix; we would just have to bite the bullet and start over.

The same team went to work, tirelessly, and assembled the necessary information to cover all bases. It's always demoralizing to have to start over, especially after having worked so hard and after feeling like you've let the others down. But a new system was designed and installed, and it works beautifully on all counts. The company took a big financial hit, but everyone was deeply satisfied with the results. It was not an efficient way to get the job done, but the learning that came from the experience is likely to save us countless missteps in the future. The right team had our full trust, but neither they nor we had asked all the right questions. Whatever it is that we may be doing, it's essential to have all the best information we can get.

A Communication Failure

Not only must we ask the right questions, but we must be careful to communicate all the important information to all participants. We reached an agreement to do a two-phase project—guest house and main house—on a small in-fill lot in Oak Bluffs. There was a small, ratty existing building at the back of the lot that had been lived in many years before. It was in rough shape, but approximately the right size for the guest house. We always try to renovate rather than tear down and start from scratch. More important, the building was located approximately ten feet closer to the road than would currently be allowable. On this very small lot that would be significant.

If we considered only the condition of the building we would have torn it down, but the location tipped the scales. We told our clients it would cost significantly more to renovate than to build new, but that it would be very advantageous in terms of the whole property. They agreed to renovate. The design was completed, permits were acquired, and construction began. It was a rough job. Everything had to be taken apart and put back together. It was incredibly time consuming and messy, and the crew was dispirited. They thought, *What is going on in the office? Have they finally lost their minds completely? This is a fool's mission—we should have just torn it down and done it right rather than struggling to patch together this hunk of junk.*

But they did a beautiful job and crafted a great little house. It was only later, at a company meeting, that several of them vented. They felt like we had made a bad decision that made their job harder and spent our clients' money wastefully. Only then did it come out that the driving force for the decision was the favorable location that we could not have used had we built new.

Aha! They got it. But we also realized that we had failed to communicate an essential piece of information to the crew. Without that information, they'd felt adrift. It is not enough to make decisions collaboratively. Everyone affected by the decision needs to know how and why it was made.

What Ownership Means to the Owners

In 1989 Peter Rodegast became our fourth owner. Before Peter was hired in 1983 he had studied architecture. He had experience in both building and design, and liked to do both. Over time his presence in the design studio became indispensable and he found fewer and fewer opportunities for carpentry, but to this day, when asked at annual evaluations if he'd like anything about his job to change, one of his refrains is "Well, I wouldn't mind pounding some nails at the job site." Mike Drezner, a teacher-turned-carpenter who was a bit older than the rest of us, was next in line, becoming an employee-owner in 1990. Gradually the ownership was growing as planned, but all was not peaches and cream.

Within two years of the restructuring Steve—one of the original inspirations for it—left the company. He was an effective owner, but he was involved in many causes. Each was more worthy than the next, but at the time he wasn't able to balance them (and new parenthood for good measure) with his responsibilities within the company. The distractions caused a crisis on the job. Due to his longevity and take-charge approach, he was one of our foremen, but his projects were suffering and the people on his crew began to complain. We anguished together and decided, with his concurrence, that he'd be better off trying something else. His departure was disheartening and difficult, but amicable and successful. We owe Steve tremendous gratitude for his important contributions to the early days of South Mountain. After he left, he and a partner founded a landscaping company, a design/build company much like our own. That company, Indigo Farm, has become a kind of sister company, doing most of our site planning, landscape design, and landscape construction for the past several decades. Eventually they, too, converted to cooperative ownership. They continue to thrive, and we continue to collaborate, although Steve is now engaged in other work (most recently helping to rebuild a temple in Mongolia!).

Our sixth owner was Vicki Romanauskas, our office manager, who signed on in 1991. In 1995 she became the second owner to leave. She left under very different circumstances; her departure was simply a time to celebrate her decade of employment, the contributions she had made, and her upcoming marriage, which was pulling her away from the Vineyard. During her four and a half years of ownership she had accumulated sufficient equity to depart with a significant nest egg.

In the thirteen years since, only one owner has left the company: Kane Bennett, a young carpenter who, in his five years plus with the company, became our youngest foreman. He was smart, capable, likable, and a skilled leader, but left to go to engineering school. In that same time we have gained thirteen new owners for a current total of seventeen. We project that there will be twenty-six owners in 2012 and thirty in 2017. Incorporating new members has worked well; all take the responsibility seriously and quickly become contributors. When we hire someone new, we assume that they will become an owner in five years—we are hiring a future owner. This makes us think differently about whom we hire and why. We're not thinking first and foremost about skill set and capability to do the job we need to fill, but about whether this person appears to be someone with whom we want to share ownership. This is an absolutely essential aspect of our business. The selection of new employees is as important as the structure. The five years is, in effect, a trial period, our opportunity to make sure we have the right person on board, and their opportunity to find out whether they want to stay on.

During that time our personnel committee clarifies, before each individual reaches eligibility, whether the employee wishes to accept the responsibility and whether the current owners wish to accept this person as a partner. An employee who makes it through five years without extenuating circumstances is likely to become an owner. Partly due to our cooperative structure, we have developed an elaborate evaluation system.

Each year, each employee (all employees, owners and nonowners alike) fills out a written self-evaluation questionnaire. We encourage employees to take as much paid time as they need to do this; we communicate the idea that "this is one of the most important tasks you will do this year." When all are submitted, the five members of the personnel committee devote a full Saturday to reading the self-evaluations together, making notes for personal evaluation meetings, considering goals for improvement, and deciding on pay raises.

Then each employee has a thirty-minute meeting with me or with me and one other member of the personnel committee (they choose whether to have another person and whom). This is a chance to talk about anything and everything. When evaluations are complete, individual goals and suggestions are distributed. Finally, a summary of new ideas and suggestions that came up for the company is distributed to all employees through our company newsletter.

One of the dangers of long-term commitment to employees is complacency. Some people tend to slide into a groove and lose their drive. Another problem is that some people have ceilings and limitations, and as the company grows and changes they are unable or unwilling to change with it. We are only now, after so many years, taking steps to improve our evaluation process so that it is rigorous enough to deal with these challenges.

After going through our evaluation process for three or four years, it's generally quite clear whether a person is qualified for ownership and whether they desire it. In most cases, during this five-year vesting period, we will part company with a person for whom South Mountain employment just isn't working, or they will depart on their own.

Even those who assume they will become owners don't always join after five years. Some may wait a year or two or three, usually because they are unable to handle the membership fee, or because they are at a stage in their life when they are uncertain about their future.

But ownership is not a requirement. Neither is it a right. It is a privilege to be enjoyed by those for whom it is appropriate and desirable. Some have remained here, working full-time, as long as ten years without becoming owners, but this is rare. Ownership just isn't for them, or so they think; some of us argue differently and encourage them to join. Since employee ownership is an integral part of the company culture, those who remain nonowners for a long time are, in subtle ways, isolated from important internal dynamics of the company, along with lacking the opportunity to make decisions that chart the company's course and build valuable equity. They miss out on a lot.

Prospective owners are expected to satisfy three principal criteria: an understanding and intent that employment at South Mountain will be their primary work for the foreseeable future; a demonstrated ability, derived from the evaluation process, to work effectively and cooperatively; and a commitment to understanding and honoring the company's core values of quality work, ethical business conduct, environmental responsibility, and concern for others. In short, we expect that a new owner will be a good representative of the company.

Ownership has different meanings for each of us. Here is a sampling of the opinions of a few South Mountain partners about the significance and spirit of employee ownership:

> Peter Rodegast: It's interesting to see how co-workers of all sorts evolve into business partners; it's different from just working with a few close friends. You end up with a diverse board and a variety of opinions.

> Mike Drezner: My notions of what ownership means have slowly changed as time has passed. Initially, I thought of it as analogous to [being] a shareholder: to have a voice in policy and business decisions but distance from personal matters within the company. I have come to learn that you do not decide the extent or nature of your involvement in company concerns. In essence, you become a parent to all South Mountain issues and your responsibility for the well-being of the company demands commitment. That understanding dictates a subtle change of perspective. You need to take what you know as an employee and use it only as a resource. The trick is to respond to South Mountain issues with honesty and objectivity and not to allow

responses to be influenced by comradeship, personal financial gain, or the desire to avoid thorny interpersonal problems.

Peggy MacKenzie: Since becoming an owner I have a deeper interest in just about everything that happens here. If I don't understand or agree with something I catch wind of, I ask questions so I get it, and I voice my opinion. Ownership is what each individual brings to it. I see it as a commitment as well as an opportunity. And frankly, it's a good investment, but somehow that's beside the point.

Derrill Bazzy: Even before ownership I felt I was part of the decision-making process, because South Mountain has always been the kind of company where all employees have a voice. Everyone can choose to be involved to whatever degree they like. What's different about ownership is the financial aspect. Ownership offers me the opportunity to make a good investment, and to make it in a company I believe in, have a say in, and plan to remain a part of.

Phil Forest: Employee ownership is a two-way street and has great significance to me and the company as a whole. Ownership is important because I have greater opportunity, responsibility, commitment, and benefits than if I were just an employee. I have the opportunity and responsibility to help guide our company's future, as best I can. Being an owner means commitment that this is my long-term primary work, and that I honor the goals and values we agree on and share. Being an owner means I benefit by having greater influence in shaping my career, receiving equity profit sharing and having a sense of empowerment, security, and belonging.

A feeling of belonging. Diverse views. Empowerment. More opportunity. Deeper connections. The system seems to encourage these. Our legal and financial covenants complete the framework within which the employee-owners share the wealth the company creates and control its destiny. This is not about a sense of ownership or a sense of control. Corey Rosen of the National Center for Employee Ownership once said that giving employees a "sense" of ownership is like giving them a "sense" of dinner.[3] This is the whole meal.

The "whole meal" sometimes creates greater capacity. Dunbar Oehmig was the owner of Walnut Street Builders in Burlington, Vermont, five young craftsmen who were all good friends and had worked together for years. Eventually Dunbar tired of being the sole responsible person in a company of peers, while the other four began to feel dissatisfied to be "just working for Dunbar."

The timing was good. Dunbar decided to work with his colleagues to restructure as an employee-owned cooperative. He says, "As soon as we started down the seven-month road to reorganizing, there was a ground shift in attitude, effort, and vision. Clearly the new model was opening the way for the others to contribute on a whole new level." They restructured in August 2003 as Red House Building Inc. At the time they were used to working on one or two jobs at a time, all five of them generally working together, but soon after the restructuring, circumstances and schedule changes piled up several jobs at once. Then they were offered an exciting project that they did not have the capacity to take on but that they couldn't bear to turn down. They took it on, geared up, and hired six new employees. Suddenly the company had more than doubled and they had four projects going at once. People had to take on dramatically new and different tasks and levels of commitment. Said Dunbar at the time, "Without the new arrangement we never could have handled this. No way. I never would have taken it on alone. We're doing okay with it, too. It's tough, but we're feeling our way and getting the job done."

New capacities. New ability. The whole meal.

Sometimes the whole meal fosters new solutions.

After twenty years in business, Graham Contracting, a successful design/build company specializing in high-quality residential and commercial renovations in the metropolitan Boston area, restructured to employee ownership. They ran into a big challenge, too—the opposite kind from Red House. Soon after the restructuring they suffered a major loss of revenue. The owners decided to forgo pay raises for the year. Founder Greg Graham and his wife Christy Boulding had always considered annual raises to be a given, almost a right. He was amazed at the reaction of his partners. A year earlier he never would have even thought to suggest it.

The whole meal comes in many forms—there's no right answer for every company.

Equal Exchange is a remarkable cooperative coffee company located in Boston. Founded in 1986, it is the oldest and largest Fair Trade company in the United States. They have a hundred employees, roughly 80 percent of whom are owners, and they offer coffee, tea, and chocolate products from more than thirty farmer cooperatives in eighteen countries. Their company and our company have many shared values, and yet we operate very differently. They have outside board members; we have none. Their CEO is not on the board; ours leads the board. They use majority decision making; we use consensus. At Equal Exchange membership is available after one year and a payment of $3,000. At South Mountain it takes five years and a payment of $12,500. All different, but the same structure.

The whole meal doesn't always turn out to be as tasty as we wish it were.

My good friend Merle Adams founded Big Timberworks, a wonderful company based near Bozeman, Montana, that designs and builds some of the most beautiful and inventive homes I've ever seen. A few years ago they adopted an ownership system not dissimilar to ours. I asked, "Looking back, Merle, four years later, what do you have to say?"

He replied, "It's been a rocky road, full of potholes. Wild animals have leapt in front of us, our tires have blown out, and we've slid into more than one ditch. Mostly there have been six guys in a car that'll hold only four, and some have stayed in and some have jumped out."

I was a bit taken aback by his dramatic assessment. "Whoa there, Merle, that doesn't sound so good. Say more. Knowing what you know now, maybe you'd go a different route if you had it to do over again, huh?"

He became more serious. "No. My life is better. The company is better. I'd do it differently. It all happened too fast. I should have extended the opportunity to just a few rather than many. It should have been more gradual. But the shakeout that's happened is full of lessons. The 20 percent who weren't suited to ownership responsibilities caused disproportionate disruption. So we understand now that we need to hire and offer ownership opportunities more selectively." The transition to employee ownership is never easy.

Says William Greider in the foreword to *The Real World of Employee Ownership*:

> Given the historic social weight of the status quo, no one should be surprised to learn that making a genuine conversion to worker-owned enterprises and self-management is very difficult to do. No one should be dismayed to see that sometimes the efforts fall well short of realizing the ideal. These are human systems being altered and everyone involved, in a sense, has to learn new work relationships—managers and workers alike—while also making sure the enterprise remains profitable and survives.[4]

The Jury's Still Out

I do not believe that restructuring to employee ownership will turn a business around. A healthy business and significant mutual trust are prerequisites. We must build businesses that are ready to take such a dramatic step. If we restructure a dysfunctional business, we can be sure we will have a dysfunctional worker-owned business when we are done. Employee ownership is not a curative; rather it is a complete new regimen to ensure long-term health.

I hope I'm not overfreighting the ownership aspect. I understand that employee ownership is not the only way to encourage more responsible and more democratic business practices. But dynamic fundamental differences occur when both control and profits accrue to the people who do the work. The apportionment of money in our current economic system is particularly vexing. How did it come to be that shareholders are the ones who accumulate most of the wealth? Business philosopher Charles Handy, in *The Elephant and the Flea*, tackles this head-on:

> I am still at a loss to understand why shareholders are given such priority in the Anglo-American version of capitalism. It is not as if they actually "own" the company in any real sense. They haven't in most cases even provided it with money. The first shareholders of each business did indeed give the company money in return for its shares, but thereafter those shares changed in hands through the various stock exchanges without any more money going to the company. The shareholders aren't financing the business, just betting on it.[5]

One thing seems certain to me. If businesses were owned by the people who did the work, if the people were no longer subjects, the rewards that resulted would be distributed far more equitably than they are today. That could only be a good thing.

Maybe employee ownership is like the current cultural battle over gay marriage: Each turns an institution, and a cherished tenet of society, on its head. Marriage has been changing for some time. The acceptance of multiracial marriages was a sea change. No-fault divorce was another—it took the "until death do us part" aspect out of the vows. Gay marriage is the next tumultuous step. Employee ownership is progressing through similar stages.

In *Democracy at Risk* author Jeff Gates writes about what a really democratic society would be: "Democracy is not a destination; it's our manner of traveling. It's not so much something we do as the way we are. And the way we are in relation to others. Therein lies its sweetness."[6]

It's an apt description of the sweetness of employee ownership that I sense at South Mountain Company. It's the way we have come to be. Employee ownership has become a part of our identity, as individuals and as a company. The searching-for-democracy journey we've taken has stimulated us to articulate and understand our common purpose as we try to find fairness, transparency, and shared responsibility. It has brought a sense of completeness to the company.

Together we've become, at once, better problem solvers and better dreamers. There's a lot to be said for ownership and the responsibility it encourages. So far, after two decades, employee ownership is working at South Mountain. The structure has withstood the test of time to date. It has been easily adjusted as change has been needed.

But what happens as ownership continues to grow? Will we one day find ourselves with thirty or fifty people making policy decisions instead of sixteen? Will our current system work at a different scale?

It should be readily adaptable. It has gone from three to seventeen without much difficulty. Adjustments have been made. When the board was small, it was deeply involved in far more decisions than it is now. I was the sole manager and I used the board for sounding ideas. As the board grew we created the management committee, and much of the processing now happens there. We always assumed, as we watched the board grow, that at some point we would create an executive committee, or management committee. My sabbatical drove us to do so, but it was time anyway. I believe our current system could accommodate a far larger board of owners; if we find that it doesn't, we will have to cross that bridge at that time, as we always have.

But as the slices of the equity pie become slimmer due to increasing numbers of owner-employees, will the urge to grow become irresistible? Will there be enough career opportunity within the company to keep employees satisfied? Will we find ways, as we build our cathedral, to withstand the pressures and keep our core values intact? Will the cornerstones settle beneath the load? These are major questions. Our foundations may be stressed by the pressures we face, but the outcomes will be determined by a democratic process that is seasoned, flexible, and adaptable.

Our employee-owned cooperative business is governed much like the town of West Tisbury, where I live. Like many New England municipalities, we have a town meeting form of government. One person, one voice, one vote. Just like South Mountain Company.

There are two fundamental differences. The first is that it's much harder—and not an absolute right—to join the South Mountain ownership than it is to become a voter in West Tisbury. The second is that in West Tisbury the majority rules. At SMC we make our decisions by consensus with a backup supermajority.

Does the town meeting run the town of West Tisbury? No, the voters set the policies and approve expenditures, like the SMC board of owners. The three selectmen, in concert with their staff, conduct the business of the town, like at SMC, where the management committee and various others attend to the day-to-day operations.

Does West Tisbury run smoothly and does the town meeting always make good decisions? Not in my opinion. And SMC? Precisely the same. Democracy is messy.

And what about rabble-rousers and troublemakers? What if the great young carpenter becomes a thorn-in-the-side, disruptive South Mountain owner? Well, it really doesn't matter. At town meeting we have to listen to the curmudgeons, cranks, and paranoids, but only to the degree that the elected town moderator deems appropriate. The curmudgeons, cranks, and paranoids have their say, and they have their vote, which is as it should be, but they are not permitted to control the process. So it would go at South Mountain if we mistakenly chose a disruptive owner. If it were bad enough, we would fire the individual. Owners can be fired, too.

TYLER STUDDS

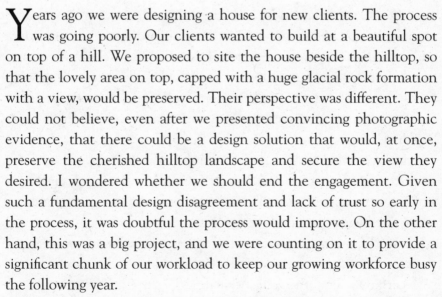

▪ 4 ▪

Challenging the Gospel of Growth

He who knows he has enough is rich.
—Lao-tzu

Years ago we were designing a house for new clients. The process was going poorly. Our clients wanted to build at a beautiful spot on top of a hill. We proposed to site the house beside the hilltop, so that the lovely area on top, capped with a huge glacial rock formation with a view, would be preserved. Their perspective was different. They could not believe, even after we presented convincing photographic evidence, that there could be a design solution that would, at once, preserve the cherished hilltop landscape and secure the view they desired. I wondered whether we should end the engagement. Given such a fundamental design disagreement and lack of trust so early in the process, it was doubtful the process would improve. On the other hand, this was a big project, and we were counting on it to provide a significant chunk of our workload to keep our growing workforce busy the following year.

I brought my partners to the site. We sat on the big rock and considered the problem. They shared my view that our design solution combined responsible use of a beautiful site and sensitivity to our clients' needs. We understood that if we withdrew from the project at such a late date, we might not be able to replace the work quickly enough and might run short sometime the next year.

We mused a bit. The silence was broken by my oldest partner, who speaks bluntly.

"Let's shitcan it," he said.

The next day I met with our clients and said, "This just isn't working the way we anticipated. Before we dig the hole deeper, let's call it quits." They were surprised, but after some discussion we agreed that it would be better to part company.

I was worried about our decision. I left the meeting wondering if this was a foolish conceit that we were taking too far. As it turned out, we were lucky, and another opportunity quickly filled the gap. We learned to trust our intuition when it told us not to risk the quality of our work in favor of security and growth.

Until that time we had responded only to demand. When work was offered, we accepted it, and when the volume of work required expanded capacity, we grew. This was standard operating procedure and we had no reason to question it. It was thrilling to have the opportunity. But this incident helped us contemplate the effects of growth, and we began to wonder whether this passive approach needed rethinking. We began to examine growth rigorously and evaluate the benefits and drawbacks.

It may seem odd for a company with thirty-some employees to have a self-conscious concern about growth. On the other hand, maybe it's why we've remained so small. While the potential to expand has been steady, we have scrutinized it carefully.

I do not know, from experience, what it would be like if our company were several times—or many times—larger than it is, so it's hard to talk with certainty about the value of smallness. I suspect that we could not retain many of the qualities we value if we were significantly larger. But it is a cherished business doctrine that without growth, a company will perish. Many ecologists and a few intrepid economists question whether the planet can sustain a global economy that enjoys perpetual growth, but the importance of individual enterprise growth is rarely challenged. Business literature contains surprisingly little that questions the advantages of growth, or that considers optimization of size. In fact, conventional wisdom implies that small businesses are those that just haven't had greater success yet.

Not that we don't favor some kinds of expansion—we do. But we do not embrace unrestrained growth for its own sake (Abbey's "ideology of the cancer cell"). We grow to achieve specific goals, but we are aware that when we choose to increase in size, we may disrupt and endanger treasured qualities. Such concerns do not imply that we must limit development. Economist Herman Daly explains this distinction: *To grow* means to increase in size by the assimilation or accretion of materials, while *to develop* means to expand or realize the potentialities of; to bring to a fuller, greater, or better state. Our planet, he explains, develops over time without growing, while our economy, a subsystem of the finite and nongrowing Earth, must eventually adapt to a similar pattern.[1]

If we apply Daly's insight to our companies and look at the implications of growth and the possibilities for development without expansion, we might conclude that remaining small, manageable, and familial has concrete value.

One proponent for limiting business growth is Jamie Walters, the author of a book called *Big Vision, Small Business*. She compares the concept to precious jewels: "It's more a matter of polishing a gem and perfecting its facets, if you will, than of acquiring an ever-expanding number of gems regardless of quality or despite the fact that they might be permanently depleting the mine."[2]

Others echo her concern. Yvon Chouinard, the founder of the iconic, pathbreaking environmentally and socially progressive outdoor clothing company Patagonia, says in his book *Let My People Go Surfing,*

> We don't want to be a big company. We want to be the
> best company, and it's easier to try to be the best small

company than the best big company. We have to practice self-control. Growth in one part of the company may
have to be sacrificed to allow growth in another. It's also
important that we have a clear idea of what the limits
are to this "experiment" and live within those limits,
knowing that the sooner we expand outside them, the
sooner the type of company we want will die.

Slow growth or no growth means the profits have to
come from our being more efficient every year. Unlike
the government, we cannot rely on an expanding economy to "burn the fat away." It's easier for a company to
make a profit when it's growing at 10 percent or 20
percent a year.[3]

Interesting view. It's easier to profit when growing.

But there's also a lot to lose. There is intense debate within the
movement for socially responsible business about a parallel growth-
related issue: how to keep control of socially responsible businesses as
they grow, and how to keep their original values intact. Scale is a critical issue. Many companies that start off with a mission and find early
success feel that they must go public to finance expansion. Once they
do, they are vulnerable to buyouts by larger companies and subject to
corporate law that requires a publicly held company to prioritize profits for shareholders. The takeover of Ben & Jerry's by Unilever is the
best-known example, but there are countless others. Many small natural and organic food companies, like Stonyfield Farm, Odwalla, and
Cascadian Farm—which have been emblematic of independent, live-
your-beliefs-no-matter-the-consequences commerce—are now owned
by the likes of Coca-Cola, Groupe Danone, and General Mills. Their
freedom to embed their values in their company and their brand may
be compromised. Wall Street now supervises.

Faced with such issues, some companies have taken a different
approach. Seventh Generation, the Vermont purveyor of environ-

mentally friendly household products, went public in 1993 but saw where that path was leading. Six years later the company began to buy back its stock, returned to private ownership, and now charts its own destiny. Patagonia has always been privately and very closely held, so when they decided to make a costly shift to organic cotton to satisfy their mission, they were free to take the plunge.

As Chouinard says,

> Being a publicly held corporation or even a partnership would put shackles on how we operate, restrict what we do with our profits, and put us on a growth/suicide track. Our intent is to remain a closely held private company, so we can continue to focus on our bottom line, doing good.[4]

Would employee ownership have the potential to apply similar shackles? Yes, it's always possible. But it's equally possible—terrible thought that it is—that Chouinard will perish on the Amazon River testing new products. What would happen then? Would the values remain intact? It's a serious question. Chouinard is very much alive, thankfully, and, judging from the skill with which he has steered Patagonia for decades, might have strong succession plans in place that I know nothing about. The heart of the matter is public versus private. Bo Burlingham, the author of *Small Giants*, says about this,

> We tend not to spend much time looking at privately owned companies, especially small ones whose stock is closely held. To an extraordinary degree, our view of business—indeed, our whole concept of what business is—has been shaped by publicly owned companies, which actually make up a small percentage of the entire business population.
>
> We've come to accept as business axioms various

ideas that, in fact, apply only to public companies. Consider, for example, the conventional wisdom that business must grow or die. That's no doubt true for most public companies. Steady increases in sales, profits, market share, and EBITDA (earnings before interest, taxes, depreciation, and amortization) are demanded and expected by a public company's investors, and decreases—or stagnation—send them running to the exits. But there are thousands of private companies that don't grow much, if at all; and they don't die either. On the contrary, they're often quite healthy.[5]

He tells the story of Anchor Brewing, the San Francisco microbrewery that started the whole trend with its Anchor Steam beer. The demand kept growing and growing until it began to outstrip Anchor's production facilities. Founder Fritz Maytag wanted to satisfy the demands of his customers but didn't want to expand. He assumed he just had to—it's the natural order of things, right? Needing outside capital, he began working on a public offering, but he was bothered by the whole process. He and his top employees started asking questions about how the business would change. Big questions, like "What are our goals in life?" and "Why are we in business anyway?" They realized that they loved it just the way it was, and they decided there's nothing wrong with staying small. It occurred to them that they were only doing the IPO out of desperation, but that they had been asking the wrong questions, and they decided, nervously, not to expand. They would just have to ration their product.

There are no outside investors and no nonemployee board members at South Mountain. Each owner is an employee. We decide what kind of business ours will be. The decisions are partly economic and partly philosophical, and the people making them have well-aligned interests. Our considerations have led us to believe that if our business practice is not governed by an unquestioned growth imperative, we will have greater flexibility and freedom and the character of the business will better match our aspirations.

I am not suggesting that every workplace should be modest in scale. An unquestioning attachment to smallness seems as careless as an equivalent affinity for unconsidered expansion. In our case we believe that excessive growth may narrow our horizons and limit good things like invention, personal fulfillment, and the overall quality of our workplace and our products. Most people I talk to want these good things in their work but find it hard to resist the tug of other, more persistent, forces. Too often we tend to think growth is the only path to greater profits and influence rather than improved proficiency. I am profoundly grateful to have partners who are committed to helping one another rationalize and plan for growth only when we believe the benefits outweigh the detriments.

Why Grow?

Staying small is about realizing when we have enough: enough profits to retain and share, enough compensation for all, enough health care, enough time to give our work the attention it deserves, enough communication, enough to manage, enough headaches, enough screwups. In *The Hungry Spirit,* Charles Handy says:

> In most of life we can recognize "enough." We know when we have had enough to eat, when the heating or air conditioning is enough, when we have had enough sleep or done enough preparation. More than enough is then unnecessary, and can even be counterproductive. . . . Those who do not know what enough is . . . do not explore new worlds, they do not learn, they grow only in one dimension.[6]

Sometimes frantic growth, I think, becomes a purpose in itself, or the perversion of other purpose. For example, our purpose might be to make the finest bagel or supply the best mortgage. But why do we need to produce all of either? Why not make just enough? The wish to make the best of a product and the wish to make all of a product may each preclude the possibility of the other. It may be impossible to satisfy all the demand for your excellent product without compromising essential elements of product quality. A different approach would be to learn how to do it, share the learning with others, and thereby encourage the establishment of small bakeries and banks embedded in their locale, well positioned to make the best bagels and mortgages for the people they serve.

That's what happened with Fritz Maytag and Anchor Brewing. Says Burlingham,

> He never regretted the decision. By the early 1990's the revolution Anchor Brewing had ignited was sweeping the country, and scores of other microbreweries were springing up to meet the demand. Although Maytag sometimes chafed at competitors' tactics, overall he viewed the increased competition with relief. Rather than resist them, he helped fledgling rivals develop their brewing skills. Their presence in the market left him free to build a company that he enjoyed and was proud of, that would give him the sense of accomplishment and fulfillment he sought, and that would allow him to lead the kind of life he wanted.[7]

Anchor's farsighted modesty led to opportunity for many others and a healthy industry.

Some say that to argue about growth in commerce is spurious. Of course you have to grow, they say: "Nature demands growth just as business does." Wall Street demands growth; business does not. Neither does nature. Nature seeks optimized growth and imposes limits. In the book *Upsizing,* author Gunter Pauli points out that if an oak tree grows to 150 feet, it is strong enough to resist wind, wear, and tear. But it doesn't grow to fifteen hundred feet, even when nature provides sufficient nutrients. Instead, it provides room for ten other trees. If it grew to fifteen hundred feet, it would become too fragile and lose its resilience and stability.[8]

Nature has many inherent limits that identify optimum size for different organisms, and we may be better off to do the same in our organizations and businesses. Often, however, there are legitimate reasons that necessitate growth in order to assure survival. Chroma Technology Corp., an employee-owned Vermont manufacturer and supplier of highly specialized optical filters for microscopes, must respond to the industry it serves. As the microscope manufacturers grow, they demand more filters. If Chroma can't supply them, they will lose their accounts. Their position in the supply chain requires growth.

The Weaver Street Market, located in suburban Washington, DC, had no intention of expanding, but a large development that combined residential, commercial, and retail uses was completed nearby and its residents wanted a market. They tried to get a major chain to open a store in their area, but none was interested. So the neighborhood asked Weaver Street to open a second market, and six hundred subscribers agreed to help finance the start-up. The residents of the community put their money where their mouth was. How could Weaver Street refuse to offer the service?

More often, however, it seems that the pursuit of happiness has become, for many, synonymous with the accumulation of wealth and power. We've been led to believe that we're supposed to grow, that we're supposed to win the competition for the survival of the fittest.

But our inquiry need not be about growth versus no growth; it better serves us to think about the quality of growth. Some things we want to grow and some we do not. We want to increase our responsiveness, our satisfaction, our effectiveness, our reputation, our legacy, our sense of accomplishment, our relevance, our capacity to improve the quality of our products, and our contributions to good lives for our employees and our community. We do not want to increase our waste, our pollution, our unfulfilled commitments, our stress levels, or our callbacks.

Charles Handy thinks broadly about expansion. He believes that growth doesn't need to mean more of the same but "leaner or deeper," supporting improvement rather than expansion. Bigness, he maintains, can lead to reduced focus, excessive complexity, and less effective control. He goes on to say:

> Once big enough [businesses] can grow better, not bigger. It is a formula which Germany's mittelstander (small family firms) have tried and tested to great advantage, content to corner and dominate one small niche market, through constant improvement and innovation. Rich enough, and big enough, they concentrate on the pursuit of excellence, for its own sake as much as anything.[9]

Handy's assessment is consistent with Daly's distinction between development and growth. Opportunities for development without growth are abundant.

South Mountain and Growth

The growth question came to a head for us in 1994, during a tumultuous period for the company. We had taken on several large projects that had caused us to double our revenues and add employees. Four new owners came on board. There were dissatisfactions and unusual stresses. People were feeling that "things are different than they used to be," and there were negative reactions toward new formalities and management systems. There appeared to be a general sense that we had grown too much, too fast.

At a company meeting we hung a sheet of paper on the wall with a heavy horizontal line and an arrow at each end. The right end said, DOWNSIZE GRADUALLY TO 1992 LEVEL. The left end said, CONTINUE SLOW GROWTH AS PRUDENT IN FUTURE. A vertical line marked the middle, which said, MAINTAIN PRESENT LEVEL; GROW INTO IT. Each person was given a sticky dot to place somewhere along that continuum. After all were done, we stood back to examine the results, and we found that about half the dots were collected just to the right of the vertical line, a significant number were scattered at locations to the left, and several were right on the MAINTAIN line. This was interesting. It was different from what I thought I had been hearing. Not one person actually called for us to downsize.

The graphic expression of the group's desire was right in front of us, and the discussion that followed clarified what it meant. The general group will was that we should back off on the accelerator a little, adjust ourselves to the recent growth and change, and err toward caution. Those who leaned toward more growth had specific reasons: With size, they reasoned, we had more ability to do community work and the potential for greater profit sharing. It's always essential to do the work to test the will of the group and to resist the temptation to rely on hearsay and conjecture.

Since then, we have held a similar meeting every few years. The kind of growth we carefully regulate is specific. If we can increase revenue, profits, and or community service without increasing the number of employees or the difficulty of working conditions for current employees, we consider it positive growth or, I should say, development. But adding employees always means greater management burden. When we hire an employee, we are extending a commitment to that individual. We are not expecting to let him or her go sometime in the future. In thirty years we have never had to lay off anyone due to lack of work. I don't necessarily think we can keep this record intact, but we'd like to. Fluctuations in workloads and new opportunities can be handled in a variety of ways, but not by adding employees unless we are willing to accept permanent (as best we can tell) growth. Adding workload without increasing staff, on the other hand, leads to added stress—longer hours, more to juggle, less attentiveness, and possibly diminished quality. Nobody feels good about that. Achieving a delicate balance among number of employees, workload, and workplace harmony is a constant and unremitting challenge.

Each time we determine that it makes sense to grow, it's with the understanding that people who come to work at South Mountain tend to stay. Before hiring, we must ask, "Are we hiring this person because he or she solves an immediate problem or need, or are we hiring because this is the kind of person with whom we'd eventually wish to share ownership?"

Between 1994 and 2003 we mostly agreed that slow growth was appropriate. In 2003, however, when the company met, a new consensus emerged. We agreed that, for the moment, we had reached an optimum size and it was time to apply the brakes.

Is this a conservative position to take? Perhaps. But you can't casually say "Let's shitcan it" if one hundred or more families are dependent on the company for a paycheck. You can turn down inappropriate projects when there are only thirty families involved and you have a reserve fund that can help navigate the rough waters of a slowdown. Strong financial position and small size preserve options.

But isn't this position radical as well as conservative? I think so. To forgo opportunities for growth means the employees of this company have chosen to value the quality of their work life over the size of the potential compensation that might come with more growth. They have chosen the team of oxen over the flatbed truck, because in this case the oxen are the appropriate means of getting the job done.

At the same time we try to remain flexible and open to the excitement of new opportunity. We have found that we can increase capacity without growth by developing new kinds of connections. Over the years we have cultivated a group of relationships with small architecture firms and craft-based general contractors. If we wish to accept work that will exceed our capacity temporarily, we ask these companies to join us. We make it attractive for them to join our office staff or job-site crews. For them it's an opportunity to work with a larger company without losing their independence. They like the camaraderie and new learning opportunities. We are able to expand and contract without disruption or permanent commitments, and we benefit from exposure to the ideas and methods they bring. These are not temporary employees; they are independent practitioners to whom we subcontract identifiable and well-defined pieces of work.

Our decisions about growth do not spring from a firm analytical basis or an identifiable straight-line logic. We are engaged in the exhilarating work of figuring out what we want to be, what we are able to maintain, and how we can get the most—every day—from the time we spend at work. This requires people who are unencumbered by rigid doctrine and empowered by the responsibility for their own workplace satisfaction. It has become a more appealing task to try to profit within the confines of small size than to profit by growing. It feels more humane, more manageable, and more challenging than pursuing maximum profits.

The 2003 sense that we had reached optimum size didn't last long. As will become clear later, new driving forces came into view in the years 2005–2007 that would cause us to change our view.

Making Opportunity

When we talk about emphasizing quality over quantity, there is a parallel between the houses we make and the business we have become. While the size of the American family shrank by one-third over the past four decades, the size of the average new house in this country grew by 50 percent. Energy costs, climate change, and new sensibilities are changing that.

The astonishing and unforeseen success of architect Sarah Susanka's *The Not So Big House* and her several follow-up volumes emphasizing quality over size is testimony to this trend. The dynamic craft of creating high-quality compact houses (or anything else, for that matter) is deeply connected to the idea of making businesses that also prize quality more than size. Susanka says, "It's time for a different kind of house. . . . A house for the future that embraces a few well-worn concepts from the past. A house that expresses our values and our personalities. It's time for the Not So Big House."[10]

In our work we embrace the same standards she proposes: small scale, high quality, protective land use, environmental care. Why wouldn't we want our business to have the same attributes? There's a place for the not-so-big business as well. This is not to say that there's no place for good big businesses or good big houses, but only that sometimes they are unnecessarily so, and often the goodness declines with the bigness.

With small scale come particular challenges in providing opportunities for career development. We need to do some of those things that large companies often do well, like offering training, providing varieties of work experience and room to move within the company, and contributing generously to community projects. We can do these things only modestly.[11] When we manage to provide diversity of experience and opportunity for movement, the talents and interests of our employees determine these directions.

Thirteen years ago, when our bookkeeper moved away, we hired Deirdre Bohan to replace her. Within a year she had developed good systems and reduced what had been a forty-hour job to a twenty- to twenty-five-hour job. She came to me and said, "I don't have enough to do." I asked her what she wanted to do. "That's up to you," she said.

"No," I said. "I mean what do you really want to do?"

She told me she had a long-standing interest in practicing interior design; it was one of the reasons she wanted to work at SMC. We had been wishing to add an interiors component to our work and had always done it informally and unsystematically, but we had never before had the impetus or resources to pursue it seriously. We decided to devote the time Deirdre had created—twenty hours a week—to her education. She put together a well-rounded program that used the resources of several design schools. She pursued it vigorously and now runs a highly professional interiors department (along with chairing our management committee). We do the complete interior on most projects we undertake, enhancing our impact on the final product while creating a new profit center.

We sometimes assign unconventional duties based on particular capabilities. Michael Drezner, a carpenter and owner, manages the investment of our pension fund and reserve fund. He is a longtime student of finance and the stock market, and over the years he has developed his skills by managing these two funds in collaboration with a socially responsible investment adviser named Christina Platt, who has worked with us for decades now. The two accounts contain more than $2.5 million at this point, so this is no small burden to bear.

While these two examples demonstrate the possibilities, they also highlight the danger of staying small and hiring from within. What if the efficient bookkeeper is a mediocre interior designer? What if the steady carpenter invests money unwisely? So far our experience has been positive whenever we've made such moves. Recently we have made education a priority, so that we can create more opportunities for employee enrichment. If we continue to hire for ownership potential rather than specific skills, we are likely to have a versatile workforce in years to come.

There are still times when I wish we were a larger company with the ability to offer a broader range of possibilities to our people. Yet we still manage to challenge the limitations that come with our small size.

Rule of 150[12]

Growth can be an extreme sport. When a company is growing quickly there's a thrill a minute. It's the same type of sensation many people seek by rock climbing or hang gliding. Some of us are willing to forgo such thrills in our work in exchange for familiarity and stability. Some try to get the best of both, and these people have made important discoveries.

When organizations become large, there is often the concurrent inclination to make small units within the larger structure to maintain qualities like conviviality, effective communication, and flexibility. Malcolm Gladwell's *The Tipping Point* explores how little changes can have big effects and turn ideas, products, messages, and behaviors into major trends. In the book Gladwell writes about the theories of anthropologist Robin Dunbar, who, in the interest of learning about optimum size, has studied how groups of varying numbers work. A striking collection of examples supports his conclusion that there is a Rule of 150, which says that 150 is the maximum number of people who can share a social relationship with one another. Therefore, organizations work best if they remain within that rough limit.

The number reveals itself in a variety of interesting settings. Dunbar looked at twenty-one different hunter-gatherer societies around the world and found that the average number of people in each village was right around 150. The pattern holds true for military organizations, whose planners have a rule of thumb for the size of a functional fighting unit: 150 to 200 soldiers. Reduced hierarchy, fewer rules, and fewer formalities are required for the group to function as a team if it remains at that size. Group behavior operates on the basis of personal loyalties and relationships in a way that is impossible with larger groups.

The Hutterites, a religious group that has lived in self-sufficient agricultural colonies in Europe for centuries and in North America since the early 1900s, also adhere to this concept. When a colony begins to approach 150 members, their policy is for that group to split and a new one to branch off. A leader of a Hutterite colony told Gladwell,

> Keeping things under 150 just seems to be the best and
> most efficient way to manage a group of people. When

things get larger than that, people become strangers to one another . . . you don't have enough work in common, and . . . that close-knit fellowship starts to get lost. . . . You get two or three groups within the larger group.[13]

The W. L. Gore Company stands out as the most celebrated proponent of this approach in business. Gore, a privately held company that is responsible for Gore-Tex and a spectacular variety of high-tech products, is widely considered to be one of the most consistently innovative, best-managed, best-to-work-for companies in the United States. It is a $2 billion enterprise with eight thousand employees in some fifty locations worldwide. Each location, whether its primary function is administrative, research, manufacturing, or sales, has no more than—you guessed it—150 people. The company's management has been able to retain the feeling of a small company by adhering to the Rule of 150 and by spreading ownership and responsibility throughout the company. The employees of each plant are called "associates." They work together with little hierarchy and widespread involvement in decision making. The company is owned by the Gore family and the associates. The associate stock ownership plan (ASOP) provides equity ownership and financial security for retirement for employees. All associates have an opportunity to participate in it. The stock is privately held; it is not traded on public markets. The ASOP, not the Gore family, is the majority owner of the company. This is an unusual company in many ways, and it has neatly balanced an absolute limitation on unit growth with an open-ended approach to overall company size.

Other businesses have also found the Rule of 150 to be useful. Chatsworth Products Inc., a medium-size, highly successful California manufacturer, is 100 percent owned by its employees. It is also broken into smaller units. In *The Soul of Capitalism*, Greider tells of Chatsworth's successes and quotes CEO Joe Cabral:

Most business managers think I'm crazy. I've been told, "Joe, you can't do these operating units as small as you envision them." Our philosophy is, we don't want any unit beyond a certain size—our magic number is around 150 people—because you need an environment of family. Everyone working together knows each other, they care about each other, and they're willing to help each other out. When you get above a certain size you end up with walls and workers become just faces rather than people or, god forbid, numbers.[14]

The Rule of 150 is powerful indeed.

Franchising Democracy and Local Wisdom

I have suggested here that it is often unwise and counterproductive for small businesses to grow. There may be other ways the argument falls short, but here is one for certain: If we develop a service, product, or business model that improves people's lives, we would want to make it available to as many people as possible, right? Dave Smathers and his partners at TeamWorks in Los Altos, California, have developed the beginnings of a network of social businesses aligned with the vision of Nobel Peace Prize winner Muhammad Yunus and the Grameen Bank. They transform low-wage service work such as housecleaning into cooperative ventures that allow workers to earn more, receive benefits, become owners, participate in a supportive culture, and accumulate long-term personal assets. Says Dave, "In our case, given our mission of creating better opportunities for workers . . . we do want to get big!!!"[15]

But if we grow our businesses to do so, they may become distanced from place and people and lose qualities we wish to maintain. I wonder whether we might be able to keep our cornerstone business principles intact, while expanding influence and effectiveness, by using the practice of franchising in unconventional ways.

Franchising is familiar to all of us. It's a popular and successful form of business. More than 35 percent of all US retail sales are made by franchises, and the practice continues to grow. It became prominent in the 1950s, but well before that it had already dominated key sectors of the economy, like automobiles, gasoline, farm machinery, and sewing machines. By the end of the 1960s it was used to sell nearly every kind of goods and services. Franchising combines large and small businesses into a single administrative conglomerate. It's a way to grow businesses quickly by creating many independent enterprises that must, however, conform to rigorous standards of operation designed and enforced by the parent company. The term originates from an Old French word meaning "to make or set free," but, ironically, most franchises have little freedom.

A franchise is a business that is authorized to sell another company's goods or services in a specific area in exchange for an agreed-upon start-up fee and regular royalty payments. A company that has been successful with a product or service can use this method to extend its business geographically. There are two kinds of franchises: those that distribute products and those that distribute business formats. Ford is a product franchise; McDonald's is a business format franchise. The product concessions came first, but as company owners learned that the franchise itself could be marketed as a distinct product, the business format led to a wave of new franchisers—hair salons, sewer cleaners, insurance firms, tax preparers, pest-control companies, copy shops, pizza shops, photo processors, Laundromats, and tai chi instruction.

Franchising offers a low-risk avenue to business ownership. In one sense it has had a democratizing effect, since someone with little to invest can go into business and have access to some of the benefits of highly capitalized business operations. It is also a way for small business to adapt to competitive conditions. At the same time, franchising contributes to the rapid homogenization of the nation's (and now the world's) business landscape. Consuming has become an experience that is repeatable no matter where you are—the same signs, same advertising, same products, and same experience. We have demonstrated a predisposition toward branded goods of uniform and proven quality over unique and unfamiliar products, but the character of consumerism may be changing. There is evidence that people are now beginning to want differentiation and customization and are searching for authenticity and choices. In her book *The Substance of Style*, social commentator Virginia Postrel says,

> The increase in aesthetic pluralism spurs competition to offer increasing variety. . . . The holy grail of product designers [has become] mass customization. Industrial design guru Hartmut Esslinger . . . imagines modularly designed products that could be recombined "to offer 100,000 individual versions," expressing as many personal styles. "Mass production offered millions of one thing to everybody," writes another design expert, upping the estimate. "Mass customization offers millions of different models to one guy."[16]

If Postrel has correctly identified a trend, franchisers may have to create antidotes to the monotony of sameness. But for now, the conventional franchising wisdom has a number of key tenets: consistency among outlets, identical customer experiences at all locations, and systemwide decisions made by the central office. Don't become a franchisee if you are an entrepreneurial type who likes to make your own decisions.

As a franchisee, you may even be told when to take out the garbage and what to do with it. Dave Thomas, the late founder and CEO of Wendy's, whom we saw in television ads standing at the grill, said, "Training our people is the most important thing we do. And the training never ends. We even teach them how to clean the tables. Believe it or not, there's a right way and a wrong way."[17]

Is that so?

Great Harvest

The antithesis of the Wendy's way can be found in the philosophy of an exceptionally intelligent company called the Great Harvest Bread Company. This small bread maker, headquartered in tiny Dillon, Montana, has developed a unique method of franchising and communication that is as different from that of Wendy's as fresh-baked whole wheat bread is from burgers and fries. In its approach to franchising there are elements of Postrel's ideas of mass customization. There are 206 Great Harvest bakeries in thirty-nine states selling some of the best bread you will ever taste. Each is a franchise. The owners of Great Harvest believe in their product, but they also believe in freedom, innovation, and the integrity of the community of owners who are their franchisees. All the bakeries are locally owned and operated and are unconstrained except by several basic principles contained in a simple franchising agreement that derives from a foundation of respect and trust. The only required provisions are to ensure the quality of the product: You must buy your wheat from approved sources and you must grind it fresh every day. That's it, and further, there is a provision in the contract that says, "Anything not expressly prohibited by the language of this agreement is allowed."[18] Have you ever heard of a contract like that?

I've oversimplified slightly, but it is entirely true that Great Harvest is franchising both a distinguished product and a progressive business ethic in a fundamentally unique way. I first encountered the company in the book *Bread and Butter*, the story of Great Harvest told by Tom McMakin, who started working there in 1993 as the company's newsletter editor and ended up managing the business for its founders and original owners, Pete and Laura Wakeman. I once made a point of visiting a few Great Harvest bakeries when my daughter and I were looking at colleges in the West. Each was different, each was a pleasant place to visit, and the bread was uniformly superb. At one point, between cities, I asked Sophie whether she was hungry.

"Starved," she said.

"Wanna stop and eat?" I asked.

"No, that's all right. I'll just butter us up another slice." Great Harvest. We lived on it for days.

I wanted to know more. I spoke to the current CEO, Mike Ferretti. He and a small group of investors bought the company when health issues caused the Wakemans to sell. Mike is careful and restrained when he speaks about Great Harvest, but his modesty does not mask his pride. He thinks of McDonald's, Starbucks, and other similar chains as being in one category and Great Harvest in another. The differences are striking. He, like McMakin, thinks of Great Harvest bakeries as "freedom franchises." The company encourages independence and initiative. Other franchisers have regimented corporate regulations and rigorous advertising rules. Franchisees must toe a well-defined line. Company field agents are cops whose job is to patrol and enforce.

At Great Harvest quality begins with the selection of franchisees. Mike says, "We take the selection process to an extreme." They feel an ethical obligation to do so, for both the company's sake and the sake of the franchisee. To open a new Great Harvest bakery is a major investment and life change, and the central office wants to be as certain as possible that success will follow. There is a series of interviews and visits back and forth. The interviews "are two-sided; we have to be right for each other." The new association is treated as the beginning of a partnership, just as hiring new employees at South Mountain is the process of identifying future owners. Once the selection is made and the location is approved by the parent company, there is extensive training and support, which continues during the first year after the new bakery opens.

An unusual aspect of Great Harvest's model is the implementation of quality standards for both customer service and products. These standards have been developed in consultation with the outlets and are implemented and monitored by "a council of bakery owners," not by the front office. "They're the ones who can best evaluate what's most important. It's a jury of peers," says Mike. So after bakeries do the required—source the right wheat and grind it fresh daily—they are expected to produce superior bread coupled with excellent service, but each decides how to achieve it. There are no standards for recipes, store design, or product selection. The philosophy is "Do it your way, but do it well." The central office establishes "handrail" philosophical guidelines, not strict rules. There is plenty of information and assistance available if you want it.

Another critical part of the Great Harvest system is a self-regulating conversation among owners that has been going on for many years. All are connected to a company-run computer network over which ideas, problems, and issues are shared and discussed. This system has become the primary means of communication within the company. Everyone hears and knows as much as they wish to. The front office has never removed a single comment, although, Mike says, "Sometimes we've sure wanted to." With this approach, the field agents have a different role than policing. As McMakin describes it, "What our field representatives do on their visits . . . is different. Their aim is not to assess how well an owner is complying with the corporate manual, but to act as bees, buzzing from bloom to bloom, cross-pollinating as they go, making sure knowledge passes from bakery to bakery."[19]

The franchisers' job is to create opportunities for owners to exchange ideas. In addition to the online discussion, they organize conventions, regional meetings, and owner-led trainings; facilitate group buying and marketing cooperatives; and pay for owners to visit one another's stores. The result of all this, says McMakin, is that

> [what] makes Great Harvest hum is that owners of bread
> stores have the best of both worlds—they are in close
> association with others who are doing exactly what
> they are doing, and this proximity sparks in them all
> sorts of interesting ideas. But they also are completely
> autonomous, free to implement in their stores the

ideas that excite them. Being organized as a freedom franchise allows all of us in Great Harvest to combine quick learning with the power of rapid adaptation.[20]

Great Harvest is significantly different from most franchisers in other ways, too. The royalties that the bakeries pay decrease every five years. As a "reformed CPA," as he puts it, Mike Ferretti recognizes that this is unusual. But it's practical and logical, too. It is only partly a reward for length of service. Long-term franchises need less support, which reduces the front-office workload.

Great Harvest has unusual aspirations about growth. Its long-term goal is to open, on average, one to two new bakeries a month in perpetuity. No more, no less. That's how the owners feel the company can be most effective. This means, of course, that as each year goes by the company's growth rate is actually declining. By operating in this steady manner, the owners do not need to swell their office staff (there are currently twenty-eight central-office employees with 206 bakeries operating) and face the prospect of having to grapple with market fluctuations by downsizing. The company remains intimate, personal, and nimble. Instead of committing to the growth of their business, the owners of Great Harvest have committed to the establishment of many small businesses, each of them unique, as part of a broader learning organization.

I asked Mike whether he knew of other companies like Great Harvest. His answer: "I don't want to be glib about this, but I'd say there are probably many, but none, I'm betting, with more than fifty franchises." Many companies, he continued, will do anything they can to attract early franchisees, but once they get into the twenty- to fifty-outlet range and there is established demand for their franchises, the goal of the companies shifts to the exercise of greater and greater control and faster and faster growth. He knows of no other company of its size that operates like Great Harvest. A central aspect of the company's long-term business plan is to remain private, so, like Gore, Patagonia, and

Seventh Generation, the obligations that public corporations have to maximize returns to stockholders and satisfy Wall Street will not affect them.

It is valuable to compare the Great Harvest experience with that of the Body Shop, an icon of socially responsible business known for its activism. Advocacy positions covered their trucks and store windows in the early days. Body Shop founder Anita Roddick also had a commitment to independence, irreverence, and individuality for her franchisees. She and her husband were strong on social mission, but when it came to business, they adopted the conventional paradigms of big growth and going public. Once beholden to Wall Street, they ran into problems of a sort that Great Harvest has never encountered, at least not yet.

The idea of franchising South Mountain has been tumbling around in my head ever since architect Gordon Tully came up to me after a talk many years ago and said, "You should franchise what you do."

Reading *Bread and Butter* caused me to think more seriously about the idea. I had never before imagined or encountered a conceptual framework for spreading a business practice that made sense to me, but this one did. We don't make a product—like bread—that can be readily franchised, and our business is so decidedly place-based that it does not seem to lend itself to franchising. I'm beginning to wonder, however, whether that's just the point: Could the thirty years of information and experience we have accumulated—about making a small, locally committed, democratically organized design/build business that's profitable and long-lived—somehow be distributed as a "knowledge franchise"? Since the publication of the first edition of this book many have encouraged us to pursue this idea. To explore the terrain we are beginning to create a new profit center from consulting and educational activities. Will this lead to a new franchising model? Someday maybe. We'll see. I can't quite envision it yet.

Small Time

Nor can I envision our company with 150 or more people. I can almost imagine it with forty or fifty, as we expect it to have in ten years, or maybe sixty. Even now I don't always remember the names of all the kids of my workmates. Since many people are scattered at different job sites, I may not see someone for weeks. Occasionally it takes months or years to have follow-up conversations to the mutually probing exchanges we had around the time of a person's hiring. I wish I knew everyone better. I wish I made more time to catch up on people's lives, and shared more of mine. I wish there were more chances to explore the intricacies—the hips and valleys, the copes and scribes, the successes and failures—of the projects they're doing.

The pursuit of concentrated power and wealth may be like chasing a porcupine—if you're not careful, you just might catch it. I've come to believe that we need to think more broadly about the meaning of growth, and that the concept of "enough" has a place in our internal debates. As our ownership pool grows, we may have to expand our ability to create individual equity as the larger numbers dilute the distributions. If one of our goals is to extend our influence through growth, we may have to find inventive new forms of it, like implementing new forms of franchising. Careful examination and control of growth has become South Mountain's third cornerstone, a prominent link in our chain of values. It's a tug on the sleeve that has our full attention; the gospel of unrestrained growth is not the right doctrine for us.

There's a story about a fisherman who was sitting on the beach with his wife one afternoon enjoying the surf and the sun. He had enjoyed a big catch that morning, so he came in for the day. A wealthy businessman heard about his success and approached him.

"Why didn't you keep fishing and bring in twice as much?" he asked.

"Why?" said the fisherman.

"Because you could make more money. Maybe buy another boat and hire some employees."

"Why?" the fisherman asked again.

"You could keep growing, increase profits, and buy more boats. If you worked long and hard at it after some years you'd grow rich."

"Why would I want that?"

"Because then you and your wife could retire and relax on the beach," said the businessman.

"But that's what I'm doing now."

It's a good story, but I still don't know that we have it right yet. Is it about challenging the gospel of growth, or about clarifying our mission as we navigate through the challenges of growth? It's a combination of the two.

BRIAN VANDEN BRINK

· 5 ·

Balancing Multiple Bottom Lines

Sometimes I lie awake at night and ask, "Where have I gone wrong?"
Then a voice says to me, "This is going to take more than one night."
—Charlie Brown

Not long ago I was deeply moved by a decision of the South Mountain owners. One of my partners, who had recently adopted a child, presented a proposal for an adoption benefit. It was well researched, and he made a good case. Birth parents have all their expenses covered by our medical insurance, while adoptive parents have none. He proposed that our maternity and paternity leave should be formally extended to adoptive parents, that they should receive a $2,500 to $5,000 cash benefit to offset part of their expenses, and that the new benefit should begin with the next adoption. Discussion led to the conclusion that if we're trying to create parity between birth parents and adoptive parents, the $5,000 figure was too low. We settled on a larger number. After a final inquiry to affirm consensus, one of the owners asked, "How many think this should be retroactive?" Nearly everyone's hand went up. Again we probed for consensus and found it. This meant a large unexpected payment would go to the partner who had suggested the benefit. A tear rolled down his cheek, and he sat in silence, unable to speak.

When everyone feels there is enough for them, the impulse to share the abundance has a chance—just a chance, I'm saying—of prevailing. It becomes clear at moments like these that the financial bottom line is only a tool in service of the multiple bottom lines by which our company measures its ultimate success.

Describing the Wine

We all know it at some level, but when we get down to business it is all too easy to forget: Using money as the sole measure of prosperity fails to recognize that people have lives, families, and communities. Many people value the quality of their work environment as much as, or more than, the size of their paycheck. In addition to making a reasonably good living, we need to be satisfied by our work. We need to meet the expectations of our clients and business associates, to contribute to the stability and vitality of our community, to care for the environment, and to maintain a workplace that is safe, healthy, and rewarding. We need the pleasure of good service, the joy of humor, the treasure of strong relationships, the fulfillment of collaboration, and the security of stability and longevity. Our enterprise must create sufficient profit to be able to serve all these worthy ends, but profit is simply the engine that drives a bottom line composed of many parts.

Our third cornerstone principle is balancing multiple bottom lines while consigning profit to its appropriate role.

In recent years many businesses and nonprofits and even some governmental agencies have begun to account for multiple bottom lines. Usually they have added environmental and social accounting to the traditional economic tracking to make a triple bottom line. The term *triple bottom line* (TBL) was popularized in 1998 by John Elkington in the book *Cannibals with Forks: The Triple Bottom Line of 21st Century Business*.[1] In the years since, the term has caught on. Some of the larger accounting firms are now "offering services to help firms that want to measure, report, or audit their two additional 'bottom lines,'" according to Wayne Norman and Chris MacDonald, in an article in *Business Ethics Quarterly*.[2] Norman and MacDonald are critical of the way the term has been used, however, since there is no methodology for measuring and comparing social and environmental bottom lines to the accepted accounting standards that define financial reporting. Their research led them to the conclusion that the term *triple bottom line*, as used today, is vague and misleading and promises more than it can deliver. "In short," they say, "because of its inherent emptiness and vagueness, the triple bottom line paradigm makes it as easy as possible for a cynical firm to appear to be committed to social responsibility and ecological sustainability."

South Mountain claims no triple bottom line. We are absolutely committed to social equity and ecology as well as profits, but we do not measure and account for our social and environmental impacts, or our relative successes and failures in these nonfinancial pursuits. Rather, I am using the term *multiple bottom lines* broadly and metaphorically. It is an indicator of the variety of parallel concerns, values, and issues that drive us. Each of these is as important as the economic bottom line, but none can exist without healthy financials, which are the only ones we carefully measure. As somebody once observed, "It is easier to count the bottles than to describe the wine."

But not always. It is, in fact, a long-term goal at South Mountain to do more counting and deeper analysis. We have begun the process of evaluating our carbon footprint, but we have a long way to go. The best corporate responsibility report I've seen is that of Seventh Generation, the Vermont purveyor of environmentally safe household and personal-care products. They do one every two years. It is thorough, accessible, and, most of all, relentlessly revealing about both their successes and their shortcomings. What a superb model! We're not there yet.

Describing the wine is not enough. We can't become who we wish to be just by saying it, and it has taken years of toil and turmoil to find the track that leads us toward being the kind of company we'd like to be.

This aspect of building a company is like tending a garden, and each of the bottom lines is a row that needs to be prepared, planted, cultivated, weeded, and harvested. Because we're the owners, this is like a kitchen garden. It's not for making goods for sale but for seasoning the food by creating balance and quality in our lives and work.

When people pay their South Mountain member's fee and sign the ownership documents, they become legal owners. But they are owners only in a sense. It's like walking out of the attorney's office just after closing on a new piece of property. You may own it, but it's not truly yours until you've experienced a sunset, a full moon, a downpour, a swarm of mosquitoes, a gusty day in the fall, an ice storm. It's not yours until you've come to know the trees and shrubs. It's not yours until you've tended the garden. The property is not yours, in fact, until you have confronted at least one skunk on the path to the front door.[3] That's how it is with our business. Work experiences and shared decisions accumulate within each individual, gradually making the company his or hers. The skunk on the walkway heightens our senses as we tiptoe down the path to ownership. Tending this garden, and taking responsibility for stewardship of a diverse set of commitments, makes multiple bottom lines meaningful and real.

Growing Pains

A February 1993 company meeting, with all employees present, may have been a pivot point in our understanding of multiple bottom lines. It was a day when grumbling about wages and other dissatisfactions coalesced into productive dialogue. In those days our company meetings were sporadic affairs. To me they sometimes felt like being at a dance with no music—we kind of wandered around without purpose. This meeting felt particularly disharmonious. It was suddenly galvanized when Mike posed a series of questions to everyone.

"What's important to you?" he asked. "Do you need greater compensation? Or are other parts of what the company does more important to you? Obviously everyone can use more money. That's not the question. The issue is one of priorities and balance. What are your priorities?"

These were the right questions at the right time. Heads rose, eyes lost their glaze, yawns disappeared, and people spoke from the heart. The voices of discontent we had been hearing, it turned out, did not represent the general will and feeling. Among the statements that found widespread support were:

- We would be less happy at work if South Mountain were less concerned with social progress. Affordable housing, sliding-scale work, care for the environment, contributions to social causes—all of these were apparently critical to peoples' satisfaction with their work.
- We should have a formal annual evaluation system and an equitable, accessible wage schedule. Company members supported transparency and a thorough discussion of compensation fairness.
- Job security is essential. Profits were seen by most not primarily as an avenue to their own personal financial independence, but as a vehicle for ensuring the longevity of the enterprise and their role in it.
- We should continue to build our reputation as a socially engaged company. It was pointed out that the company's good reputation was partly a result of our community work; therefore, social activism directly affected job security and profitability.
- We need a diversity of work opportunities. People expect to be here for the long haul, and we wanted to help the company create new kinds of work for us to do as we become too old to spend our days running around on rooftops.[4]

The many points of agreement that emerged from discontent at this watershed meeting allowed the board to move forward with a better understanding of multiple needs, and it inspired more company meetings, more engagement, and a new respect—among nonowners—for what it meant to be an owner. I wrote a memo to all employees after the meeting that said, in part (I've paraphrased some of this for clarity and brevity):

> Thanks to all of you for your forthrightness, sincerity, heartfelt concerns, and ideas. . . . I believe we've reached a turning point. For a while we've been successfully engaging employees in steering the course of the business when they become owners. We've been less successful at bringing the rest of you into this process. There's a simple reason why it is valuable to do so—it's an opportunity for each of you to assist in making things more like you wish them to be. We'll never build a perfect house, nor will we ever be a perfect business. We'll never even agree about what a perfect business would be (or a perfect house, for that matter). But the expression of your needs, desires, and ideas for improvement will make us a stronger and more responsive company and will make personal satisfaction for each of us more likely.
>
> The meeting pointed out many areas that need work. The necessary changes will happen slowly, over a period of years. I'm sure at times it will seem like we're moving backward instead of forward, but you don't discover new lands without losing sight of the shore for a while. I look forward to the journey. Thanks for your company.

At another meeting three months later, we concentrated on compensation and evaluation issues and agreed that competitive evaluations should not be the criteria for pay scales. We also agreed that it was time to put our heads together to define and articulate our mission, our

core values, and our purpose. This was a moment of new consciousness. Before that, the questions we had tackled together were mostly
about how to do what we do better than before. Now we were asking
ourselves, "Who are we and why?" This was key to our emerging understanding of multiple bottom lines.

The next company meeting, in February (when the Vineyard is
always bleakest), evoked an outpouring of protest and complaints.
The venting was prompted by the observations of an employee who
had begun work with us when he and his wife had taken a one-year
sabbatical from their regular life in Connecticut. He was a valuable
addition, as he'd been a contractor himself for twenty-five years and
had a wealth of experience to share. They had had such a good time on
the Vineyard that they went home at the end of the year, finished their
nearly restored house, sold it, and moved back here, and he'd come
back to work at South Mountain.

Now he said, "Things are different than they were when I was here
two years ago." And it's true that they were. He had returned to a larger
and busier company, a company that was experiencing new stresses
and tensions.

As the meeting evolved, it became clear that the stress experienced
by members of the company was coming not only from work issues
but also from their lives outside of work. There were new babies, new
houses, and additions to old houses. The new employee to whom it felt
"different" was a good example. Two years before he and his family were
experiencing an idyllic sabbatical in a new and welcoming place. Now
they'd uprooted their lives and they were busy buying land, dealing with
banks, drawing plans, adjusting to new jobs—nearly everything in their
lives had changed. It wasn't only the company that was different.

We learned a lot from that meeting. We found, for example, that
our new job schedules were causing trouble. We had never had such
detailed schedules before, and everyone seemed to be worried about
them. We became aware, too, that people were worried about budgets,
which had become more accessible in accordance with the group's

wishes. The only thing that had changed was the exposure; making the schedules and budgets available made them available to worry about. What was happening—with overload, schedules, budgets, and wages—was that information was beginning to bounce around and reverberate. It had safely rumbled around in my head for years. Then it had gradually spread to the group of owners. Now, as they learned to balance the complexities, the owners were beginning to spread information throughout the company. New knowledge is sometimes tough to swallow. An appetite for information had developed, and despite the new stresses the information caused, or perhaps because of them, the capacity to absorb it began to increase. These tensions reflected our development into what former Royal Dutch/Shell Director of Strategic Planning Arie de Geus calls "a learning organization."[5] In our case, we were learning to balance multiple bottom lines.

Other emblematic board discussions helped us define our bottom lines. At one point, in 1996, I suggested the use of the phrase *ecological building* in the tagline on our stationery. There was strong negative reaction. A litany of examples was tossed out to point out how distinctly *un*ecological our buildings and our work are. We build houses that are sometimes larger than they need to be and use excessive resources. We do a less-than-exemplary job of reusing and recycling construction waste. Everything we do has aspects of negative environmental impact. I responded that our environmental bottom line had received the same degree of emphasis as our social bottom line. There is a strong internal commitment to incremental progress in our use of energy, our approach to waste, and our support for and development of environmentally sensitive and low-impact land-use strategies.

Of course we're not doing a perfect job, but aren't we trying to do the best we can, and doing a better job of it than almost anyone else we know, and therefore don't we have the unassailable right to define ourselves that way?

This tack didn't work; I got nowhere. As I argued my point, I slowly came to realize that the critics were right. It took me a while to get it, but I came to understand their view that it was presumptuous to label ourselves as ecological builders. We should do the stuff, let the work speak for itself, quietly highlight the ecological aspects of our work when the opportunities present themselves, and leave it at that. I admired the passion and precision with which this call for restraint was articulated. It was an important identity issue. As a group, we eschewed greenwashing, preferring silence to inflated or questionable claims, even if we might be the only ones questioning the claims. (Now, a little more than a decade later, we do use such terms. Questioning the label strengthened our resolve to do better. We are on much firmer footing. We are doing a much better job. But we are still careful and restrained about the claims we make.)

I tell this series of stories and events to convey the rhythm of the conversation—which I now am able to identify as being about multiple bottom lines—that has become essential to our company. The dialogue has been the vehicle that carries us to a deepening of our shared values and mutual commitments. We have not made these up; we have discovered them. To track back along the trail that led to them, before I wrote this chapter I spent two long days reading through six large loose-leaf binders of our meeting minutes and attached memos dating from 1985—when we first began to meet formally—to the present. The review was by turns tedious, embarrassing, funny, uplifting, instructive, and gratifying. It's a rich vein, and it was remarkable to mine it all at once. Since then, we have had all these minutes professionally indexed to make them more usable as they accumulate over time. Twice a year the indexing is updated. This is an immensely important record of our journey; it is the thread of our multiple bottom lines.

Mining Collaboration, Curbing Competition

About ten years ago I read *No Contest: The Case Against Competition*, a book by educator and social theorist Alfie Kohn. It was a memorable experience of affirmation for me; Kohn articulated clearly so much that I felt deeply.

Kohn has been described as the country's leading critic of competition, although he is said to be quick to point out that there is not much competition for the title. In his thoughtful and well-researched critique of our winner–loser society, he shatters myths regularly. Using a combination of his words and mine, I will try to convey to you, in a few pages, what he takes a few hundred to reveal far more completely and competently. I want to do this because Kohn's thesis explains another crucial part of the South Mountain bottom line, and that of other collaborative organizations, businesses, families, and classrooms around the world. Kohn's insights run against the grain of US culture and question much that we take for granted. They contain valuable information for those interested in a more compassionate economy built around healthier workplaces and communities.

Kohn describes how human nature is characterized more by the urge to cooperate than by the will to compete. He argues that competition systematically damages relationships and crushes self-esteem. Most competitors lose most of the time because by definition not everyone can win. The race to win turns most of us into losers, and as Lily Tomlin once said, "The trouble with the rat race is that even if you win you're still a rat." Kohn puts no stock in the theory that competition builds character. He maintains that competition actually holds us back from doing our best, in school and at work.

If all this is true, or even partly true, why do we hold competition in such high regard? Why has it become, as one author says, "almost our state religion"[6]? Because, says Kohn, when we think about cooperation we tend to associate the concept with fuzzy-minded idealism or, at best, to see it as workable only in a very small number of situations. This association may come from confusing cooperation with altruism.

Cooperation is a shrewd and highly successful strategy, a pragmatic way to get things done effectively, but we have been trained to compete and, more important, to believe in competition. The message that competition is appropriate, desirable, required, and unavoidable is drummed into us from nursery school to graduate school. The results of this teaching, which permeate every lesson, are used to prove competition's inevitability. If you make it so, of course, it will be so.

Kohn recognizes isolated progress toward a collaborative ethic in our classrooms—some teachers are coming to honor cooperation as the primary method for human interaction—but he thinks most teachers don't understand the concept of cooperation. They use it to refer to obedience; to cooperate, for them, is to follow instructions. This misunderstanding means our education often lacks critical learning about cooperative behavior.

I am continually amazed that we are not taught in school how to lead meetings or to be effective meeting participants. Very few people are trained in meeting facilitation. Due to this unfortunate oversight commerce, government, and community life all suffer from our lack of meeting facilitation and collaborative decision-making skills.

Kohn's findings indicate that success and competition are conceptually distinct and unrelated. He goes so far as to say, "Superior performance not only does not require competition; it usually seems to require its absence."[7] He relates the findings of several research projects to support the conclusion, including one exhaustive overview:

> David and Roger Johnson and their colleagues published a[n] . . . ambitious meta-analysis (that is, reviews of others' findings) in 1981. In what is surely the most conclusive survey of its kind, they reviewed 122 studies from 1924 to 1980 . . . including every North American study they could find that considered achievement or performance data in competitive, cooperative, and/ or individualistic structures. The remarkable results: 65 studies found that cooperation promotes higher achievement than competition, 8 found the reverse, and 36 found no statistically significant difference. . . .

> The superiority of cooperation held for all subject areas
> and all age groups.[8]

Kohn also points to other experiments that consider how we are taught to compete and how our perceptions are shaped once we become competitors. Experimenters have found that whereas cooperative individuals realistically perceive that some people are cooperative like themselves while others are competitive, competitive individuals believe that everyone is like them, that it's human nature to compete.

Even natural selection, Kohn argues, is a cooperative process. Contrary to the prevailing ethos of Darwin's survival of the fittest, nature is a proponent of collaboration rather than competition. Natural selection does not require competition; on the contrary, it discourages it, and survival generally demands that individuals of the same species, as well as those from different species, work with rather than against one another. Close examination demonstrates that animals cooperate with one another except in extreme conditions.

Kohn refers to the work of Russian dissident Peter Kropotkin, who was apparently the first to show that the animal kingdom is cooperative. In his 1902 book *Mutual Aid,* Kropotkin demonstrated that those periods in which there is heightened competition among species members are always harmful to the species. The tendency of nature to cooperate, Kropotkin said, although not always realized, is the constant message that comes to us from every landscape—*mutual aid* is the watch phrase.

Most of *No Contest* is devoted to a systematic unraveling of what Kohn calls the "four central myths" of competition: (1) Competition is unavoidable; (2) competition motivates us to do our best—we would cease being productive if we did not compete; (3) contests provide the best, if not the only, way to have a good time; and (4) competition builds character and is good for self-confidence.[9]

When confronted with the question of eliminating competition in favor of cooperation, people tend to say that we can't possibly keep our world vital, exciting, and productive without competition, which is everywhere in our society—in business, politics, sports, and academics. Competition has helped us to scale great heights, we're told.

The effectiveness of competition as a mode for reaching specific, highly targeted goals—such as maximum profitability—cannot be argued. My experience has taught me, however, that we do better across a multiplicity of goals, producing greater, more lasting satisfaction, when we work in cooperative modes, balancing the needs of multiple stakeholders.

Another examination of the impact of a single-minded pursuit of competition is contained in the work of Dr. W. Edward Deming, widely acknowledged to be responsible for the Japanese post–World War II industrial revolution, an American who only later became known as the "guru of quality" for US industry as well. In the 1950s, as the Japanese economy was rebuilt following the devastating effects of the war, Japanese goods were the butt of worldwide jokes. *Made in Japan* was a euphemism for "cheap and shoddy." Today decades of success by Sony, Toyota, Honda, and the rest have obliterated this memory.

At the request of the Japanese government, Dr. Deming worked to shift the world's perception of the quality of Japanese goods. He succeeded at this, in a very short time, largely by teaching the Japanese, through his total quality management system, to organize their workers in teams, to learn from the people on the factory floor, to drive out fear and banish exhortation, to do away with competitive bidding and arbitrary numerical targets, and to promote pride in craftsmanship. Japanese products were soon emulated throughout the world, and American companies were soon adopting the teachings of Deming.

For Deming, the practice of having employees compete with one another is "unfair and destructive." Not long before his death in 1993, he read Alfie Kohn's book and said, "We have been in prison from wrong teaching. By perceiving that cooperation is the answer, not competition, Alfie Kohn opens a new world of living. I am deeply indebted to him."[10]

Kohn is not asking us to do away with incentives or tests but to stop using them to determine a "winner." He is not asking us to do away with games, but to remove the emphasis on winning. Our favorite team does not have to win every game, or win at all, to stay close to our hearts. Red Sox Nation endured its team's failures for eighty-six years. That doesn't mean we don't love to see them win; it's just that a good job in a losing effort is equally worthy of celebration.

I hope the spirit of Kohn's theory—that people in an equitable and cooperative setting will attain a goal with more efficiency and creativity than people in a competitive setting—is being cultivated at South Mountain. It's a spirit that cannot be imposed; it can only be offered. I hope it takes hold more and more. I hope we can accept our urge to compete, but continue to remain vital with a minimum of rivalry and contention, and I hope we will always dignify and honor our collaborative successes. They are the key to the road ahead.

In *What Matters Most* author Jeffrey Hollender (the CEO of Seventh Generation) quotes Bob Massie, the former executive director of Coalition for Environmentally Responsible Economies (CERES), a group of forward-looking companies that have committed to consistent environmental improvement. Massie, says Hollender, thinks the most important cultural shift occurring now is a spiritual one that moves us from competition to cooperation. Massie notes,

> Take a walk through any airport . . . and look at the business books. They're all about teamwork and cooperation and making the firm more like a family. Look at the way the stakeholder concept is taking hold, all over the world, which is truly a triumph of cooperation over competition.[11]

Let us hope that this triumph continues to expand. There's a long way to go, and the need is great. But there are wonderful examples. In the Emilia-Romagna region of northern Italy, where thousands of small businesses are the heart of an energetic manufacturing economy, businesses are finding that they can cooperate for a general, rather than an individual, benefit. Small businesses in the same line of work, which would normally be competitors, have begun to pool resources for greater buying power, for control over particular industrial processes, and for shared distribution. Everyone benefits, and small companies gain some of the advantages that are usually available only to large companies. These collaborative methods have helped the district become one of the world's most dynamic and prosperous economic regions. In his book *Making Democracy Work*, Robert Putnam says of the region, "A rich network of private economic associations and political organizations . . . ha[s] constructed an environment in which markets prosper by promising cooperative behavior and by providing small firms with the infrastructural needs that they could not afford alone."[12] This region, home to four million people, has virtually full employment and a per capita income 5 percent higher than the national average. At the core of this strikingly successful economy are thousands of employee-owned cooperatives, which have a strong collaborative relationship with the regional government.

This might be the kind of economy Kohn would design if he were an economist.

Handshake Business

Collaboration and cooperation can also relieve us of a colossal waste of time and money: assigning blame. Even in today's litigious world, we can substitute handshakes and mutual understanding for the elaborate contractual protections that are necessary in a business environment defined by competition.

A client of ours once came to see his house as construction was ending. A large and important window didn't feel quite right. It was exactly as shown on the drawings, but in real life the size of the panes didn't feel right in relation to the other windows. It was subtle, but it was so. I said, "Maybe you should live with it for a while and see if you get used to it."

His unforgettable reply: "I can get used to it. I can get used to almost anything. I can get used to a hatchet in my forehead, but why would I want to?" Right. We don't want people to get used to what's wrong with our buildings. Was it our fault the window was wrong? Was it theirs for accepting the drawings as presented? It doesn't matter; it's our job to get it right. There is nothing gained by assigning blame. We replaced the window. It's far better to understand ourselves as collaborators with the owner; we are each engaged in the project of making the best building we can.

As difficult as it may be for some to believe, an attitude of shared purpose can allow the handshake to be the principal mechanism for doing business. It wasn't so long ago that most commerce was transacted as a set of informal understandings shared among company, customers, and community, and I believe that a spirit of cooperation and commitment to multiple bottom lines can restore much of this lost understanding.

South Mountain has a three-page contract that, with only minor adjustments, has served us well for twenty-five years for projects up to $4 million. When new clients question the simplicity of this document, we explain that its purpose is just this: to remind us, if we ever forget, about what we agreed to and what we're shaking hands about. They and we share the same small community, similar aspirations for the work we are undertaking together, and a sense of trust in each other. That's why we have agreed to work together. We're not going to wind up in a court of law; if we do, we all lose. And in thirty years, we never have.

The contract is, quite simply, a supplement to our memories.

Rather than concern ourselves with whether our language covers every eventuality, we just ask ourselves a few questions: What, exactly, do we wish to remember? Have we said that here? Is it a good reflection of our relationship and our mutual understanding? If so, it's a good contract. We choose those with whom we do business according to our ability to achieve this degree of mutual trust, and they choose us, presumably, for the same reason.

People who do business in other locations have said to me, "That's all well and good if you can afford to choose your clients or customers. Working in a prosperous place like the Vineyard makes that possible." But this belies the fact that on the Vineyard, as in any other bustling economy, there is no lack of competition. The island contains a wealth of design and building talent; it's a miniature Silicon Valley of building expertise. The island's history of boatbuilding has attracted scores of craftsmen, and many have shifted to house building. When development and construction are booming and opportunities are great, professionals and tradespeople from Cape Cod, Boston, and New York swoop in. Someone's always offering a bargain, just like in Sioux City or Tallahassee or anyplace else. Wherever you work, if you believe in what you do and are committed to principles of quality and cooperation, you can't afford not to choose the work you are willing to do and the clients you are comfortable serving. We have found that when we elect to work with people we don't trust (or those who don't trust us), we are likely to lose both money and sleep. That has nothing to do with the Vineyard.

Years ago we designed and built a house for a couple. He is a writer and she is a judge. I remember the moment, sitting across the table from them, when it came time to address the construction contract for their house. We discussed the meaning of its contents. When we were through talking, I slid the contract across the table to them.

She took it first, flipped immediately to the signature page, signed, pushed it to her husband, and said, "Sign it, dear."

He turned to her, incredulous, and said, "Aren't you even going to read it?" She said, "Of course I will. Later. And if there's anything that needs to be changed, we'll call John and change it. Go ahead and sign it." And he did.

Coffee Break

Our commitment to multiple bottom lines is expressed not only through wrestling directly with issues of accountability and corporate culture, but also in a host of informal ways that define the overall feeling of the workplace. When we talk about serious business, we can't overlook coffee break.

Our office coffee break is a time for the designers, the business staff, and those who work in the shop (and anyone else who happens to be around on any given day) to sit and talk. Each of the job sites also has a coffee break that happens in much the same way. But these days the office coffee break is the one I'm mostly at, so it's the one I know best. Our coffee break belongs to Jim Vercruysse; it's his creation, in a way. Jim is one of our owners and has been running our woodworking shop for nearly fifteen years. We always had coffee break (I think) and we didn't always have Jim (I know), but some people seem to become symbolic of things they didn't actually invent. That's the way it is with Jim and coffee break. He makes sure it happens (even though it happens when he's not around). He loves food and he loves to cook, so he is the inspiration (although not necessarily the provider) for the good food that sometimes shows up at break.

Lunch at South Mountain is similar to coffee break, another time of gathering. In fact, one of our newer employees, Betsy Smith, said to me at her first evaluation meeting, "I was a little worried to hear that most people eat lunch here. I need my space. When I worked at Honeywell—not that I didn't like my job, but I just had to get out of there. And I never went to coffee breaks at Honeywell; that's where the old guys would sit around and complain about how good it used to be. But here you hate to miss it. It's so much fun and it's where stuff happens. I love it."

Betsy's work is not glamorous—she answers the phone, she files, she organizes, she does the mail. But it's tremendously varied and important. She buys flowers for clients and presents for new babies, she assembles slide shows, she helps people find what they're looking for, she helps people find other people, she makes all kinds of arrangements, she handles our insurance accounts—she's a critical hub. Invariably she has multiple active projects going. She has told me that this is her dream job. Her job description, and everyone's, for that matter, should also include "implementer and evaluator of multiple bottom lines." Betsy said that one of her goals, when she was looking for a job, had been to find one where she was actually proud of the product. Now she contributes to the making of beautiful houses and the doing of good things in the community—that's what she really does, while she's doing all those other particular tasks. She will soon be an owner.

At coffee break and at lunch the conversation can go in any direction. Political talk. Sports talk. Talk about movies, people, trips, art, music, and Vineyard events. Or, talk about South Mountain business, South Mountain people, and hot local issues. Some of the most important communication in the company happens at these times. Mostly it's a time to converse in an unstructured setting, for breaking and emerging news to be communicated, and for trying out new ideas before they're fully cooked.

It's a time for figuring out what's next. I think of it as our expression of pleasure with the workplace we have created and who we are. Coffee break as an institution may seem trivial when set next to the complex and abstract concept of multiple bottom lines. But it nurtures something nontrivial in our process and business culture. It is an informal declaration of the mutuality and shared decision making at our core. It is a place where multiple bottom lines can mingle, relax, breathe, and find their own happy medium.

Multiple bottom lines lead to the notion that work should be a place where people can "work to their heart's content," as Sony founder Masaru Ibuka wrote in his original purpose statement for his new company. Work is a place where people should be content. It should be a place where people are proud of what they make, like Betsy, and proud of how they conduct themselves. That's what we're aiming for.

Nearly thirty years after our seat-of-the-pants beginnings, we are still small enough to stay closely connected to our roots, to do business on a handshake, to all gather in one small room, to know one another as people and not only as co-workers, to recognize one another as collaborators in pursuit of multiple goals. Living the language of our mission, goals, and purposes, and learning to collaborate together, has shaped a dedicated, skillful, compassionate body of decision makers. Nobody's getting rich, but we are living comfortably doing the work we enjoy in the location of our choice. All of us are able to make good livelihoods because no one of us is getting rich. Perhaps we have unconsciously internalized the wisdom of Chinese philosopher Lao-tzu, who said, in the third century BCE, "He who knows he has enough is rich." We are rich in multiple bottom lines.

Fellow Workers

In early December 2002 one of our employees was arrested, for the second time in less than a year, for driving while intoxicated. He had been with us many years before, had left to go to sea for a while (he is a skilled and experienced mariner), and had returned. He's a meticulous carpenter and has always been well liked by his fellow workers. He had only recently gotten his license back from the first incident. Now it was clear that he was in real trouble.

Several of his friends on his crew, along with another close friend in the company and one of our owners who'd had alcohol problems himself decades ago, decided to meet with him. Peggy MacKenzie, the chair of our personnel committee, pulled the meeting together. It was held in our conference room at the office.

He told me later that he walked into that room in a state of dread. He felt doomed, knowing they were going to tell him what a screwup he was and that they didn't much want him around unless he could get it together, which he obviously couldn't. But something different happened in that room. He said he walked out of the room, about an hour later, feeling loved. That probably wasn't easy for him to say to me, but it flowed out as naturally as could be. He walked in with dread and he walked out loved. He checked into a detox facility within a few days, with assistance from those same friends. A year later, to the day, the same five people took him out to dinner to celebrate his first year of sobriety.

I was lucky enough to spend a day skiing with him the following winter, and he told me about the dinner. As he talked, I realized that he had become a different person. I had never known him this way before. Gratitude and emotion filled his articulate account of the changes in his life. I thought, *Look what happened here—this is astonishing. Now, that's the way to run a company.* But the thing is, we're not running it that way. Our company didn't make that change happen; his fellow crew members did, combined with his own strength of character, of course. It sprang from the personal values they all bring with them to work, not from any kind of management decision. Maybe a work environment that is more than a job encourages that kind of response. Maybe a company culture that encourages sympathy and cooperation helps inspire the kind of camaraderie that leads to such kindness. As Jim Collins says in his seminal study of enduring visionary companies, *Built to Last,* "You do not 'create' or 'set' core ideology. You discover core ideology. It is not derived by looking to the external environment; you get at it by looking inside. It has to be authentic. You can't fake an ideology."[13]

You can't fake it. It's there or it's not. You discover what it is. Those cornerstones in the pile—they really have to be there, you really have to find them, and you really have to place them in the wall.

RANDI BAIRD

▪ 6 ▪

Celebrating the
Spirit of Craft

I want to live in a society where people are
intoxicated by the joy of making things.
—WILLIAM COPERTHWAITE

Clients for whom we were building on an eighty-acre property requested a single house large enough to accommodate their children and a growing cadre of grandchildren. The site we chose had beautiful old gnarly oaks that nobody wanted to lose. We proposed a scheme for two buildings rather than one. They would be connected by a roofed breezeway that stepped down and curved from one building to the other in a graceful descending arc, navigating the landscape in a way that allowed us to preserve the most important trees. At the same time, the two-building approach broke down the building mass into a scale more appropriate to the wind-sculpted low-slung site. Our clients accepted the proposal, we completed the design, and construction began.

When it came time to link the buildings, it became clear that our breezeway design wasn't right. Built as conceived, it would have upset the balance and harmony that our site designers had so carefully achieved. The design team met on-site to explore alternatives. We suggested many solutions to one another, but none resonated.

Then one of our designers, Derrill Bazzy, said, "It's clear what the right design is: no roof at all, just a path winding beneath the tree canopy." "Of course," we responded. "That's it!" The clients, however, had specifically accepted our design with the condition that there would be a protected walkway between the two houses. Would they go for this new idea? It was my job to approach them.

I remembered being impressed, years ago, when a friend and I were visiting the Japanese woodworker George Nakashima at his studio in Bucks County, Pennsylvania. Nakashima took us for a tour of his shops, four small buildings separated by white gravel paths and Japanese gardens. It poured rain in sheets that day. At each building the door-ways were set behind sheltering porch roofs, and on each porch was a bin of umbrellas. As we walked from building to building, we'd grab an umbrella, carry it with us, and deposit it outside the next. A clever system. When I met with our clients I told them the story. "So that's our design solution: You carry your roof with you, if needed, and at other times you'll walk under the trees and the stars." They immediately agreed, suggesting only that the umbrella stands be prominently located and beautiful to look at.

Design is looking for needles in haystacks. All too often, we stop before we have searched diligently for the ultimate solution. To be able to consistently bring an unrelenting approach, we need to overcome fear, the designer's toughest adversary. It's fear that keeps us, as our former landscape designer Sanford Evans says, "from suspending judgment long enough to arrive at a good solution." Frightened that we won't find a solution, we gravitate toward the easy or the early concept and bail out too soon. We can never completely conquer the fear, perhaps, but experience helps us recognize it and move forward despite it. Embracing the uncertainty, we can stay with our apprehension long enough to find just the right needle in the haystack.

If we were not practicing the processes of designing and building as a single craft, we might not have solved the problem posed by that breezeway. The design for the walkway roof looked good on paper, but as we stood on the site and absorbed the space, we all had the same visceral reaction. The structure we had proposed was simply a violation. You had to be there, with posts ready to rise, to know it. If not for the building crew, who were ready to dig in until they looked carefully at what they were about to do and alerted us to the problem, we might not have known until it was too late. And if they had been working in a company that had a "you're paid to work, not think" philosophy, they never would have bothered to make the call; they just would have dug the holes and built the breezeway.

This chapter is about the craft of designing and building. Celebrating the spirit of craft has become our fifth cornerstone.

Making Things

Our primary work at South Mountain is making things—like houses, breezeways, and pathways—that are visible, tangible, and functional. Along with houses, we make many things that are parts of houses: additions, interiors, cabinets, furniture, lighting fixtures, landscapes, and even, sometimes, collections of houses—small neighborhoods. We try to make things—neighborhoods and houses and parts of houses—that will have lasting value for generations. It's surprising how few people in this country actually make things like this anymore, and how few make things at all.

Some people make things that are visible, tangible, and functional, but not durable, like butter, aspirin, and haircuts. Most people make things that are not things at all, like insurance, mortgages, financial transactions, diagnoses, therapies, and sales. According to the US census of 2000, less than 10 percent of employed people work in production occupations. There are as many people in media, sports, and entertainment as in manufacturing. More people deliver and move things around than work in the construction trades. In this country, we just don't make much anymore.[1]

Manufacturing continues to flee the United States in pursuit of cheap labor. The Bureau of Labor Statistics' year 2006 chart of the thirty fastest-growing US occupations is made up almost entirely of jobs in which people do things for other people. Communications analysts, personal and home health aides, and software engineers are the top three growth occupations. Nurses, retail salespersons, medical assistants, security guards, janitors and cleaners, child-care workers, accountants and auditors, truck drivers, maintenance and repair workers, teacher assistants, and a host of other similar occupations fill out the list. Down near the bottom we find carpenters, the only people on the list who actually make anything. Manufacturing workers? Nowhere to be found.

I'm glad, of course, that we have all these people to help, teach, advise, cure, and account for us, as well as fix our teeth and do our taxes. But do you find it unsettling, as I do, that tens of thousands of our very brightest people are working in hedge funds and investment banks and private equity firms and producing nothing—absolutely nothing—except money? I do, and so does my young friend Jake Mazar, who is graduating from Boston College this year. He wants to do something, with meaning, but he feels like he's all alone, that most of his fellow graduating seniors just want to climb a ladder, a moneymaking ladder. I think that maybe that ladder is leaning against the wrong building, and that many of us suffer from not making things. Like Betsy in our office, who wants to be proud of the products made by her company, the quality of many people's lives—both workers' and consumers'—is improved by authentic products made by authentic craftspeople.

Although not everything we do is about making things—we, too, give service, advice, and assistance—the making of things is central to our enterprise. To ensure the quality of our products, we have developed a process of integrated design, a way of assembling expertise and creating dialogue through which good solutions can be found and good value created. Everyone involved is important, including the clients, building designer, site designer, interior designer, carpenters, foremen, craftspeople, subcontractors, suppliers, bankers, building inspectors, town boards, and neighbors. All influence the design. An extended, intricate web of relationships creates each project. To conduct this process effectively, we need to oversee all aspects. Over time we have developed the skills to do it. On nearly all of our projects it is our responsibility to do development and planning, design, building, furniture and woodwork, the interior, and aftercare.

The Master Builder Approach

The integration of design and construction in the making of a building is known as the master builder approach. (A 1794 reference to this term in the *Oxford English Dictionary* says, "When a building is to be erected, the Model may be the contrivance of only one head.") Having the master builder as both designer and constructor was the predominant method of building in the Western world before the industrial revolution, but it is not how most buildings are made today. From the beginning my colleagues and I had an intuitive sense that the design/build approach was the right way for us. As we learned to build, we also learned to design. At that time in our lives, there was no separation between work and play. All activity had both in it. I didn't know what a vacation was. Vacation from what? Trips always had a purpose, but that didn't make them more work than play. It was just as much fun picking up a load of wood at the sawmill as it was stopping at the swimming hole along the way. Both were part of a process. Similarly, there was no separation between designing and building.

The master builder approach assigns responsibility for all aspects and trades to one entity, unlike today's conventional method, which fragments responsibility into a process that some have called the "relay-race" approach. The conventional method, a product of our overspecialized professional culture, begins with a client who describes a set of requirements. An architect makes a program of spaces and designs the building. The architect hands the design to engineers—who may not understand the design intent—to check for structural integrity, superimpose mechanical systems, and design the foundation. The completed drawings go out for bids to contractors who have been remote from the design process and may have even less understanding of the rationale. They may not agree that the building should be built as designed. Subcontractors, further disconnected and having their own predilections, bid on parts of the work. A landscape architect is employed to design site functions and equipment. Plantings and landscape construction are assigned to another contractor. The interior is passed to others.

The rigidity built into the process by complex contractual arrangements and segregated responsibilities makes it difficult to make changes. When changes do get made they tend to create unintended consequences, because the channels of communication and degrees of oversight are not always clear and effective. None of the various participants may have a large enough view to know that when a wall is moved to line it up with the structure below, which may not be where it is supposed to be, it may affect the lighting, the mechanical systems, the window placement, and the furniture layout. When the building is completed, nobody understands the whole well enough to show the occupants how to use it, care for it, and operate and maintain the building's systems. As the baton is continually passed, those who could fix problems when they arise (as they always do) are no longer there. When there are problems, each practitioner blames another or feels no particular responsibility. Squabbling and lawsuits are commonplace.

It's only in the past century that building has come to be practiced in this way. Some are trying to make relay-race building work better through greater collaboration, but in many cases the method remains contentious and problematic. As pressure builds to make buildings more and more ecological, practitioners are finding that they must collaborate deeply with all participants in order to be successful, and integrated design and building processes are becoming more common.

A master builder who guides and oversees the planning, design, and construction and has direct accountability to the owner can lead an effective process. In our case this is not a single person but a whole company. South Mountain is the master builder, or, more accurately, the whole South Mountain team is a "master collaborator." As master builder, we hold the conviction that design and construction go hand in hand. We combine the theoretical aspects of design intent with the knowledge of what it takes to perform a successful construction job. This is a direct process—just South Mountain and the client, fully responsible to each other. Although many other important contributors are involved and become part of the team, this central relationship provides clarity and integrity to the complex process of making settings and buildings. As master builder, we are the protectors of the process and the product. We are responsible for the land, the neighborhood, the town, and the clients' interests. We are accountable for the needs and feelings of the many people who do the work.

The master builder system is predicated on the understanding that sites and buildings are layered; they develop over time and need care, adjustment, and continuous knowledge. The work is never done. The relay-race approach postulates that an architect will develop a miraculous concept, others will turn this wonderful vision into reality, and when it's done, it's over, and it sits on display like a sculpture for its lifetime, which is sometimes surprisingly short.

Bilbao

On the way to Mondragon, Spain, my friend Lee and I flew into Bilbao. We planned to visit Frank Gehry's famous Guggenheim Museum. We landed at Bilbao's surprisingly beautiful and well-conceived airport. This is an airport you actually want to spend time in. We did. Everywhere we turned we found thoughtful craft, lovingly attentive detail, extraordinary daylighting, and playful drama. We were delighted with this modern complex designed by Spanish architect and engineer Santiago Calatrava. Suddenly we looked at each other, as if struck simultaneously with the notion that if this was the airport, then it must be true—Bilbao is a true architectural mecca.

When we were able to tear ourselves away, we picked up our car and drove downtown, parking in a long, sloping lot beside a railroad track, in the shadow of the striking, soaring Guggenheim. We walked the asphalt, hiked up a long, poorly made stone stairway, and stood on the stark plaza at the museum's entrance, the pavement broken only by one lone stunted tree. The signature titanium siding was sloppily installed and rusting in spots. We were shocked by our immediate impression of mediocrity. Inside was no different. The spaces were dramatic, but we couldn't quite figure out where the art was. High-quality materials were poorly joined and inappropriately assembled. Mystified, we wondered what had gone on here. How could such a monument be so disrespectfully made? Was it built by the lowest bidder? Were the workers who were charged with construction disdainful of the project or opposed to what they were being asked to do? Was this truly the realization of Gehry's grand vision? Or had the design been passed through so many hands that we were looking at a diluted, half-baked version of the original intent?

As we left, the bell rang on a cathedral a few blocks away. The sound was deep and resonant, issuing forth from a building created by a master builder hundreds of years ago. The cathedral had endured, and would continue to. In contrast, the Guggenheim appeared to be the temporary winner of a relay race, beating its chest in hollow victory, disconnected from the surrounding neighborhood and the city, a sentinel rather than a participant. Is this building like a hit song that spends six weeks atop the charts, becomes dated, and fades into obscurity?

Perhaps there is a lesson here, however, about celebrating risky failures. I think of the Guggenheim as a massive failure, but we need these failures. Without them, there would be little innovation. Sometimes craft is overly conservative. There are always new approaches to invent, and we do not want to be hamstrung by precedent. Breakthroughs keep coming in materials, energy, building systems, and aesthetic forms and insights. We hope to create a healthy balance between innovation and precedent. If students in architecture schools were encouraged to take as much responsibility for serving neighborhoods and communities as for mastering studio critiques and their own ambitions, we might see better balance. The more stakeholders we gather, the more intelligence we focus, the more we will get buildings and communities that are not merely, as architect Bruce Coldham says, "settlements between the various designers and consultants, all defending their own turfs."

Essentials of Craft

Taking responsibility for all the elements of making buildings and landscapes—development and planning, design, building, furniture and woodwork, the interior, and aftercare—gives us a chance to craft good buildings and landscapes. Integration of practice promises that all the parts may work together appropriately. If they do, they will serve their purposes well and presumably will be kept, and enjoyed, for centuries. This is our hope for the places we make. At the core is craft, the critical unifying aspect of our work.

Craftspeople have strong feelings about their products and their practices. Sometimes there are elaborate discussions in our shop about a single piece of wood—recognizing how the grain runs, how it grew, and where the strength is; considering the orientation that will work best for the function intended; speculating about how to tease out all its beauty and how it will finish. Conversation ranges seamlessly from the overall qualities of the product to the most subtle and detailed elements of the process. We have more disagreements about wood and joinery than about money.

Craftspeople take their time. You can't rush quality; it develops at its own pace. You can't rush the skills of craft, either. They have to be absorbed over time. I used to be a woodworker, but I didn't grow up with woodworking. I took it up with passion, but it came to me slowly and incompletely. My son Pinto, however, has been around it his whole life, and I've noticed that he has it through and through, in ways I never could. He practices it like a skater who has been on the ice since the age of three. His knowledge has the depth of a farmer working land that has been in his family for generations.

When we work as craftspeople, the pleasure of work can soar above the tedium that—at least some of the time—characterizes all work. When we make something well designed and executed, it is a telling of the truth. A thing well made reveals how we think and what we admire. Craftsmanship translates well to different scales—everything we make, from a knob to a neighborhood, can be imbued with craft. And it translates to different arenas as well; letters, contracts, drawings, phone calls, schedules, budgets, and relationships can all be as well crafted as a stool or a stairway, and for somebody, at least, each of these is worth embodying with craft. Work is a chance to develop worthy expressions of craft in all its parts. The spirit of craft leads us, like the Balinese say, "to do everything as well as we can."

The imperatives of craft create an internal set of standards devised by the maker (child development experts say that this sense of being in control is one of the most important characteristics of play). The craftsperson or team of craftspeople makes the whole thing, from start to finish.

The purpose of craft is generally not dramatic innovation but evolution and improvement, so standards are based on practice that refines the craftsmanship over time. It's not practice for something else or performance against an arbitrary or competitive standard. When we make a piece of furniture, there's a complete outcome, but it's practice because it's part of a continuum that is never complete. We are forever polishing our skills.

The superior work that results from creating a workplace that engenders the spirit of craft is what makes it possible for us to fulfill the wishes of those for whom our work is done. They are expecting something authentic to be made especially for them. But they are not our most difficult taskmasters. The difficult ones to please are the makers themselves. We, the makers, are never satisfied. Every design has flaws that we don't see until it's built. Each building could be detailed more coherently, each chair could fit the body just a tad better, and every color could be one shade closer to artful perfection. We grumble, we assess, and we curse our carelessness and foolishness. We are gratified when a tight fit leads to an elegant result. That is the craftsperson's lot.

I'm still heartbroken (that sounds extreme, but I can't think of a better word—it's more than sad, I know, so maybe it's slightly heartbroken) when I look at something we've done and see a room or a roofline or a detail that should have been better. I wish we'd come closer to the target. Often we put our heads together, in such situations, and think hard about how we could have, and whether it's too late. Sometimes it's not. Even when the solution takes serious reworking, we repair the cause of our slightly broken hearts when we can.

Panic happens, too, although less often than heartbreak, and it's usually unwarranted. There's almost always a way out from under our mistakes. For me such panic is partly a carryover from our early days on the Vineyard, before we understood the powerful abilities of wind-driven rain. We made buildings that regularly leaked whenever there was a storm. Leaks are loathsome. Nothing except fire harms a building more than water or diminishes, to a greater degree, the sense of shelter that buildings provide.

In those days, when I would wake up in the middle of the night and hear the wind howling and the rains pounding, I knew the morning would bring phone calls and trouble. Over time we solved those problems through practice, observation, reworking, and repairing, but for many years the onset of stormy weather would provoke in me that sudden moment of alarm.

Hard to Find

It's not easy to find or train good craftspeople. The work is hard, great discipline is required, and the financial rewards are not as great as in many other sectors. The culture directs us elsewhere. Craft is no simple path.

There's an ad that airs on the Weather Channel. Two snowboarders are standing on the side of a snowy road with their gear, trying to thumb a ride up to the mountain. "Yeah, dude, I think I'm gonna major in ceramics," says one. "It's so Zen. Just you and the wheel. I can see myself in ten years sitting in a little cabin, living off the grid, throwing pots in some beautiful setting."

Just then a Range Rover stops and picks them up. They get in, settle into the plush seats, and gaze around, awestruck by the lush interior. They look at each other with raised eyebrows. The other kid says to the first one, "Well, you could minor in ceramics."

But would it be so hard to find people with the patience, tenacity, and inspiration to devote themselves to craft if those same people owned the work and owned their workplace? Perhaps not.

Martha's Vineyard is one of the most difficult and expensive places to live that I know, and yet we have been able to find the people we need, some already living here and some moving here to work in our company. I don't want to minimize the difficulty of this—and we are finding that we must devote more and more effort and resources to employee housing to be able to find smart young people—but if they are being offered the kind of work they are looking for in the kind of atmosphere they want, with the possibility of ownership if they stay, it makes it that much easier. As business owners we have to look hard at what we are offering our employees.

The Design/Build Process

The master builder approach has been our way of working from the start. The process has endured, but what we do with it has changed. At the beginning, thirty-plus years ago, our geometries were simple, predetermined by our limited abilities. As our range has increased, we've learned how much more there is to know than we can know, and we continue to be excited by assimilating new knowledge and ideas that lead to the development of our own eclectic design language.

As we learn, our ambitions grow, too. There are qualities that we feel our buildings must have in order to be worth making. These are inspired partly by the Vineyard's natural environment, architectural heritage, and community and partly by our clients and our own aspirations. Well-crafted projects, in our view, embody a collection of qualities: They are artful, calm, comforting, light and airy, durable, flexible and easy to change, energy-efficient, healthy to live in, made from low-impact materials, surprising, uplifting, and, of course, satisfying to the needs and desires of our clients. All of this applies to both buildings and landscapes. Most of all we wish to make buildings that are loved.

We keep these qualities front and center as we establish criteria and priorities, gather information, and synthesize solutions. When our ideas jibe with those of our clients and we all understand our roles, the result is an extraordinary shared adventure. A critical piece of the design journey is something we have discovered that may be self-evident to others: There is no better design tool than the act of experiencing a real building with a client. We are fortunate that we do all our work in a small geographic area. We've built and kept strong relationships with our clients and made a point of cultivating access. Once we've completed early questionnaires, design programs, and a rough budget, we begin to spend large chunks of time with new clients in and around past projects. Here is where we find connections with them, gauge reactions, and start to weave the fabric of the new building. This is what computer-generated walkthroughs are used for. They're good tools, but I find that reality is even better. The conversations we have when we explore a space together with our new clients have more life and vitality, and more precision, than if we were only looking at drawings or models.

Memories return: *"The house I lived in that I loved best had windows just like this; I had forgotten all about that pattern."*

Tastes change and develop: *"We saw these log posts in photos and thought they looked like Lincoln Logs, but seeing them up close they feel natural, expressive, and appealing."*

Requirements change: *"This is twenty-five hundred square feet? There's no way we need more than this; the thirty-five hundred we were imagining would feel like a mansion."*

We work in those houses together. We talk, we reminisce, we measure, we model. Frank expression is common:

"This room reminds me too much of my grandmother's house in Queens."

"If only the window tops and the ceiling were six inches higher."

"Can't stand granite—reminds me too much of Martha Stewart."

"Ugly fixture over the dining room table."

Honest reactions and heartfelt expressions give us the information we need. A pattern evolves that's full of individual meaning and will lead to something entirely new and different: their home, a place that's uniquely theirs and different from all others. While engaged in this exercise, we remind clients that when their project is complete, we'll want to use their house for the same process with future clients. No one has ever denied us this; people feel that it is only right that they extend to others the opportunity that was extended to them. We are grateful, because it's one of the best tools we have.

Our job, as designers, is to ask, listen, and suggest solutions. The clients' job is to articulate needs, preferences, and desires. Together we test schemes and hypotheses to see whether they work for both parties. Conversations range widely, because design combines style, personal expression, technology, cognition, aesthetics, functionality, and the satisfaction of human needs.

Each of us is a designer. Each of us makes countless design decisions every day—what to wear, how to do our hair, which ear to pierce and where to put the tattoo, how to arrange the dishes in the dishwasher, where to hang the picture on the wall, how to load the trunk of the car. Each design decision affects us. The ultimate result of a good design process is a well-mixed blend, a combined expression of clients and designers. To be good at being a client requires being good at communicating how you feel in a house or a landscape. To be good at being a designer requires good listening and asking skills and having the good luck to see our way to good solutions. When the process works well, it's hard to look back and say what parts and which ideas came from whom. At the heart of the design process is trust—trust that a good solution will emerge from the collaboration, if given sufficient time and space.

The relationship between the client and the designer/builder requires honesty, forthrightness, and the fulfillment of expectations. We must build trust from the beginning. If our clients are lavished with commitments fulfilled, they will come to expect it and trust that things will continue that way. They can loosen up and enjoy the ride. The pattern of honesty assures that they can be equally forthright with us. We become allies and learn to work well together. We tell them when we feel that they're doing a good job, or not, and expect the same of them. When we screw up, we tell them we screwed up. Everything is on the table. This especially applies to the communication of bad news. It may be human nature to avoid bad news, but good work requires bluntness as much as kindness. At a recent meeting with a client, one of our designers presented schematic plans. Our client studied them, asked a few questions, and said, "You're in the right church, Derrill, right pew, too. May have to move down a few seats." Good client.

It's equally important that the chemistry be right. Experience has taught us that the best clients are people who are good at what they do, secure with their competence. These people are looking for some-one who works the way they do. They won't pretend to be able to do our job; they know they can't, just like we couldn't do theirs. They are looking for expertise, integrity, reputation, and shared aesthetics. We are looking for people who appreciate our philosophy, our methods, and our work, and who want to learn, with us, what the result should be.

There are clients with whom we fit and those with whom we don't. Mostly, it's clear to us which are the ones we should work for, and we work hard to make those clients see what we can offer. Many times they know it as surely and as quickly as we do. But when they're not so certain about us, this is when we have to sell, which means to reveal to them who we really are so they will know what we already know— that this is a good match. It's always disappointing when people we think would be good clients for us—and for whom we think we would be the right designer/builder—choose someone else. Sometimes it's because someone else has told them they could do it faster, or cheaper. Sometimes that's true, but often it turns out not to be. We have to take that frustration in stride—nothing can be done about it. But more often, I have come to believe, they really have made the right choice, and they would not have been satisfied with us. We're not for everyone and everyone is not for us.

We deal forthrightly, and early on, with money; we talk about it from day one. It is an essential design constraint, and we must be able to discuss it as frankly and knowledgeably as site, space, aesthetics, energy, dormers, and window seats. Because we have responsibility for the building as well as the design and a full set of construction skills and broad experience, we can more competently advise clients about costs as we design. It doesn't matter how expansive or limited a client's financial capability is. Everyone wants good value, and everyone wants to know what they're paying for. We begin the design process with a program (how much space will be devoted to what), a concept (what is the scope of the project and what kind of project it will be), and a budget. The budget informs our thinking all the way. It's no use to complete a design that excites and satisfies if it will cost twice what the budget calls for.

Whether our client is one person, a couple, a family, a town, a committee, a tribe, or a nonprofit board, this process is key. Our design/build method makes room for many to be involved and accommodates surprises and unplanned course changes.

In the movie *Little Big Man*, the Native American grandfather, played by Chief Dan George, one day determines that it is a good day to die. He makes his arrangements, calls for his buffalo robes, goes out onto the prairie, lies down, and waits. Time passes; it begins to rain. His grandson mournfully comes to check on him and discovers that Grandfather is still alive! How can this be? George rises with great dignity, gathers his belongings, and says, "Sometimes the magic happens, sometimes it doesn't." The chief is clear that his responsibility is to make a space for the magic, then to be ready for and accepting of the outcome, whatever it may turn out to be. This is also the key to the design/build process. All of our processes and tools are aligned, collected, and deployed for one purpose: to make room for the magic, in whatever form it comes, from wherever it comes, and whatever its meaning.

Standing there between the two houses, gazing at the landscape, struggling to design a roof for the walkway, we were all, however inadvertently, trying to make room for the magic.

"Aha," we are sometimes fortunate enough to say. "Got it."

Practices

Design magic does not come by chance. It must be invited. Many years of design/build work have produced a set of technical practices that are woven into the aesthetic and functional aspects of our work; the results we seek are predicated upon them. In each of our projects we embed four essential technical practices: (1) fully integrated site and landscape work done on a design/build basis; (2) specific tools and methods that promote durability so our buildings and landscapes age well; (3) extensive use of salvage, reclaimed, and carefully sourced lumber; and (4) high-performance green building and on-site energy production. These practices have evolved over the years and apply equally to our most highly crafted, expensively detailed homes and our most affordable housing.

Integrated Design/Build Site and Landscape

We create buildings, landscapes, settings, environments. We must learn to know the land, to recognize how our sites relate to the human and nonhuman communities around them, and to weld our buildings comfortably to the landscape. We do not have the skill to do that alone. We used to try, but many years ago we realized that the quality of our landscape design and construction was not up to the quality of our buildings, so we teamed up with Indigo Farm, a landscape design and construction company. The people of Indigo help us achieve more satisfying results. Their participation often leads to unusual and complex approaches to siting, yet when they are finished, the sites feel like they have undergone little intervention. In the end, the houses feel calm and settled in naturalized landscapes of appropriate landforms and native plantings.

Sanford Evans, Indigo's founder, thinks like a sculptor. He says, "I'm responding to the quality of the space and illuminating it. It's about loving where you are."

The houses must express that love, too. We might back a house gently into a hillside or step it up the hill rather than placing it in front of or on top of the hill. Branching patterns of the trees on a site are sometimes echoed in window muntins. The color of the house's shingles and window trim will match the silver-gray bark of the oaks and the light green of the moss that clings to them. Trees that must be cleared from the site are used to frame the porch or to hold up ceilings. The house (and the other "improvements" we make) is a foreign object in an existing landscape, so we attempt to gently celebrate what is offered and relate to the stories residing in the land.

We work with landscape designers from the beginning to the end of every project, from the initial conceptual siting to the last flowering plant. One of our early projects with Indigo illustrates what the collaboration can achieve.

New clients bought a property directly adjacent to a site on which we had built a house for other clients. The two sites shared an access. But when we looked at the siting for the new house, it became clear that using the established access would bring cars to the wrong place on the property, subject the house to the glare of headlights, and diminish the scale and privacy of both properties. Sanford saw that if we created a new access up a steep hill farther down the main road, we would enhance the site in several ways. To do so, however, would be complicated and expensive, and we doubted that our clients would approve the plan. It was too far-fetched. Nevertheless, we were certain of its value. When we presented the plan, our clients fully understood and endorsed it. The radical departure dramatically improved both properties.

Some years ago Indigo restructured and became an employee-owned cooperative much like ours. Both companies have matured together. Sanford has now retired and been replaced by a young landscape designer named Mike Turnell. Although we sometimes add a landscape architecture firm, WCA Associates, to the mix, they only enrich the collaboration and bring a slightly different set of skills and perspectives.

Buildings That Age Well

Once I took my mother-in-law, a surgeon, to tour some of our houses. As we headed home she said, "You know, I've spent my life working my fingers to the bone to help and save people. But all the work I've done will soon be gone. What you do is lasting. It remains here forever."

I wish she were right. I didn't have the heart to tell her that most houses built in this country barely outlive their mortgages. Some of her patients will last longer.

The only thing we know for sure about buildings is that they change over time. Uses change, configurations are altered, finishes are updated. Parts wear out. Systems degrade and need replacement. New technology must be incorporated. We try to think of our buildings the way landscapers think about landscapes. No landscape is ever completed when it is first created. It develops and matures over time. What if we made our houses the same way? Let's plan many possible ways to expand and alter our houses. Let's create forms that easily accept additions. Let's frame in the door to the future addition, bay window, and extra skylight, and let's plan for the built-ins. Let's imagine future solar collection and leave plenty of unobstructed south-facing roof area. Let's expect that extra dormer in the roof. Let's build certain walls so that they can easily be removed to open up spaces as needs evolve, and let's use engineered floor systems that don't need bearing walls. If we do this work well, we will enable these houses to develop as a landscape does. In a decade or two or five, house and landscape will be very different from what they were when they were first occupied.

Stewart Brand, author of *How Buildings Learn*, the seminal book about what happens to buildings after they are built, demonstrates that the only buildings that last are buildings that are loved. These are the buildings that are maintained and carefully readapted over time as different occupant needs develop. If we make buildings that are beautiful and functional and easy to maintain, operate, and change, they stand a better chance of being loved. We have now maintained, altered, and renovated some of our buildings for a quarter of a century. We learn from them every day. We keep a small crew busy repairing and doing small alterations and additions to the buildings we have built. They serve as an important feedback loop, telling us what's working and what's not.

In a book called *The World Without Us*—which is, as the title implies, about what would happen if humans suddenly disappeared from the planet—author Alan Weisman says,

After 500 years, what is left depends on where in the world you lived. If the climate was temperate, a forest stands in place of a suburb. Amid the trees, half-concealed by a spreading understory, lie stainless steel dishwasher parts and cookware. The chromium alloys that give stainless steel its resilience will probably continue to do so for millennia.[2]

On the other hand, he says, all the other forces of nature (led, of course, by water) will assure that, without humans to maintain them, the buildings themselves will be gone within fifty to a hundred years.

As we learn new techniques to encourage durability, and as we have committed to the long-term maintenance of our buildings, we have developed several unique tools to encourage extended building life. All new cars have an owner's manual. Why don't houses? Houses cost ten times as much and have a significantly longer life. Finishing a house is a bit like letting a dog off a leash; now comes the test to see whether she's truly ready to behave. But we know she won't behave without guidance. For a house, that guidance equates to operating and maintenance instructions for its owners. When you buy a house, its documented history should be a part of its contents. We provide every house with a detailed owner's manual that includes a listing of all project participants; recommendations for ongoing service relationships; building chronology; complete as-built specifications; design and program information; regulatory documentation; sewage disposal, well, and water-quality information; a history of all the materials contained in the house; operating and maintenance instructions for the site and building; and equipment manuals and warranties.

In addition, we've developed a second important tool that we call a "roughing book." It's a series of photos of all walls and ceilings, keyed to a set of plans, taken after everything was installed in the walls but before they were closed in. This gives us perpetual X-ray vision into the walls and ceilings. Our subcontractors have come to rely on the roughing books. Once a client returned home on a Sunday night, heard water dripping into the cellar from the wall above, and called the plumber. He arrived, took a quick look, and asked for the roughing book. He found the photo he wanted, which showed the location of the pipe he had figured was leaking, saw where there was a joint in the pipe within the wall, made a neat incision in the drywall, went right to the leak, and resoldered it. No fuss, no mess, no search-and-destroy mission.

These documents truly begin to shine years later, when it's time to add a room, move a wall, or make a built-in. The longer a building endures, the more valuable these tools will become, as memories fade and more alterations and repairs become necessary. If I were a banker, I'd require an owner's manual and a roughing book for every building I financed. If I were an insurer, I'd do the same. If I were a Realtor, they would make my job easier. If I wrote the building code, I'd put this requirement in it. If I were a buyer, I'd be pleased to find them on a shelf in the pantry, like hidden treasure in an attic.

The message of the owner's manual and roughing book is this: *We expect this building to last a long time. We want to assure that it does. We expect it to change during its lifetime. We wish to make it easy to change.* To make it last and to make it easy to change, we have to make it easy to maintain and we have to communicate—to the people in the future who will work on it and live in it—what it is and how it was made.

It says something else, too. It says, *We're proud of the way this building is made. We wish to hide nothing.*

We also periodically survey past owners and take our medicine. What's wrong and what's right about your house? What would you do differently? What should no new house be without? What should no new house be cursed with? Our clients give us honest replies. Sometimes they tell us things we wish we didn't have to hear, but the information is critical to our future success. One couple, for whom we had built a passive-solar house that included a problematic dyed-concrete floor, answered our question about what houses shouldn't be cursed with by saying, "A floor that comes off on your socks." Soon that concrete was covered with tile.

Salvage, Reclaimed, and Carefully Sourced Lumber
We have always used materials that we believe to be worthy of our efforts. Wood is an essential ingredient of our craft, and for many years we used quantities of old-growth redwood, cedar, cypress, and Douglas fir. As we watched the quality of the material decline and the cost rise, we also became aware that we were using material that was disappearing at a rate that far exceeded its renewal. In response, we decided to source wood in new ways. We made the use of salvaged and reclaimed lumber a priority, and our practices changed dramatically as a result.

We soon discovered that there are wonderful and widespread salvage resources, but that using reclaimed wood is an intricate and subtle undertaking. Successful use requires a good supply network, substantial inventory (because you can't just go to the local lumberyard and buy it), specialized equipment, and careful coordination of design processes to encourage best use. A saying goes, "Never try to teach a pig to sing; you'll waste time and annoy the pig." We learned how important it is that the particular material be appropriate to the specific use. The material cannot be shoehorned into places where it doesn't belong.

When we first began to use salvage consistently, there was internal resistance within the company. Salvage required new skills, took a lot of work, made a lot of mess, and demanded extra care and dexterity. It seemed to cost a lot, too, because we had to inventory rather than order as needed, and because there appeared to be so much waste. Some of my partners worried about the buildup of a large inventory. But the practice gradually became institutionalized, the benefits became clear, and this endeavor soon became a special source of pride, a distinction felt by all of us. Today it's as hard for us to remember the pre-salvage days as it is to remember when *Made in Japan* meant cheap imitations.

In some ways the transition to salvage was a trip back to our roots. In the 1960s and early '70s we had salvaged from necessity. In 1972, for example, Chris and I, along with some close friends, bought a scruffy piece of rocky woodlands on Belden Hill in Guilford, Vermont.

We moved onto the land, set up camp, started clearing land and making gardens, and began to build, with roughly $500 in our collective pockets and all the time in the world. We needed it. With hand tools (we had no power), a chain saw, and a couple of raunchy old trucks (a Diamond T flatbed and a Jeep pickup without doors), we went to work collecting material. We disassembled several barns, scrounged old windows, collected piles of roofing slate, and lugged home anything that resembled lumber. To make foundation piers we found a pile of old railroad ties that had been replaced by new ones and tossed beside the tracks in Brattleboro. We asked the stationmaster if we could have them, and he said, "If you can haul 'em, you can have 'em." Easier said than done.

Late at night, when no trains would be coming, we drove the Diamond T onto the tracks. The ties were about a quarter mile from the access point. The going was rough, and we hadn't gone more than a few hundred feet before we were hopelessly stuck. By the time we got the truck out, it was nearly daylight. This wasn't working.

The railroad tracks in Brattleboro are located on a narrow shelf between Main Street (about seventy feet above) and the Connecticut River (about fifty feet below). Both drops are precipitous. We tried to pull the ties up to a parking lot on Main Street by hooking onto them with ropes and towing with the truck. The steep, rocky bank foiled this attempt, knocking around the unwieldy ties until they broke the rope or slipped the knots. Finally we went out on the tracks on foot and pushed the ties over the bluff and down to the river's edge. On the riverbank, we laboriously gathered them one by one and lashed them together into a big raft, and my friend Smokey Fuller poled them down the river, like a Mississippi flatboat man, to a boat launch downstream where the rest of us waited with the Diamond T. Smokey landed the raft successfully, and we finally had our foundation piers.

Four of us must have spent the better part of a week to get those thirty ties. They were worth only about $150, but that $150 was nearly a third of the budget for the whole house, and now we had what we needed for our foundation. That's the way it went.

These days our salvage wood comes from many sources, including wine and beer tanks, pickle and olive barrels, whiskey barrel racks, water towers, dismantled barns and warehouses, logging leftovers, driftwood, and river bottoms. The sources of supply provide interesting stories and compelling histories that give the wood a new kind of life. Our clients are taken with these stories; they become a part of the soul of the houses. For example, our staple wood is reclaimed cypress that is mined from river bottoms. This material, known as "sinker" cypress, is timber that sank to river bottoms in the South during the time, mostly around the turn of the past century, when the great old-growth cypress forests were logged. We buy from several small operations in southern Georgia and the Florida panhandle. One of them salvages logs from the bottom of the Choctawhatchee River, cruising more than a hundred miles of river hunting for sunken bounty. He pulls them from the river, mills them into rough boards, and ships them to a kiln and mill, where they are dried and dressed to our specifications. We've been buying multiple trailer-loads of this reclaimed cypress each year for more than a decade. I met Adlee just once. I traveled to his home, saw his mill, and rode up and down the river on his funky homemade pontoon vessel, which has a deck-mounted winch that pops the logs off the river bottom after scuba divers locate and attach cables to them.

Officials of the state of Georgia once impounded Adlee's equipment, claiming that the sinker logs belonged to them. They turned out to be wrong. In the old days, the many small landowners along the river who owned the cypress swamps would fell the trees during the dry season. In the rainy season, when the rivers were high, the loggers would float the timber downstream to sawmills. First they would brand their logs individually, so they could be identified and sorted at the mills. It was like a cattle drive. Because the logs were so plentiful, those that got caught in eddies or vegetation weren't bothered with, and thousands eventually sank. Adlee and his crew prospect for these logs.

When he first started, Adlee learned the history, and over the years he systematically approached people in the area, asking them to dig out the old brands from the barn or the attic. He purchased and collected them. On the day of his court date, he entered the courtroom pushing a wheelbarrow full of sections of logs with old brands stamped on them. Then he produced the corresponding branding tools and showed them to the judge. He said, "Your Honor, I truly believe these logs belong to me. They've got my brands on 'em." The judge agreed and directed the state government to leave Adlee alone.

We use the superb wood that Adlee and others reclaim for exterior and interior trim, woodwork, cabinetry, and furniture. It lasts forever on the outside, and its patina, warmth, and varied color are beloved by clients on the inside, as is the story of its origin.

Some of our best salvage teachers have been people we originally met through the North American Timber Framers' Guild, including Merle Adams, Jonathan Orpin, Jake Jacob, and Max Taubert, who specialize in sourcing and using this extraordinary resource in the resurgent timber-framing industry.

Before 1850 most American houses were made with braced timber frames. But once sawmills became commonplace, mass-produced nails became available, and construction subsystems were developed that used small-dimension wood, houses became faster and cheaper to build. The artful and durable timber-framing methods fell into disuse.

In the 1970s a few visionaries, led by Tedd Benson and Ed Levin in New Hampshire, began a revival of this craft. Structural and challenging, beautiful and graceful, full of spirit and strength, with a strong and authentic aesthetic, the scale and precision—at once—of this work make it unusually attractive. It's also congenial; preparing timbers involves a lot of hand work that people can do gathered in close quarters, either in a shop or in the field. As the Mohawk Indians took to high iron work on bridges and skyscrapers, the counterculturalists of the 1960s took to the craft of timber framing. It was not an aptitude. Some think that the Mohawks have a special way with heights; it has been proven not to be true. What both groups enjoyed was an *affinity*, and the skills were learned.

We have always used timber-framing methods in our work, but we've never classified ourselves as timber framers, because the timber work we do is a small part of the system of the whole building. For many of our employees, though, timber work is the epitome of craft—furniture making writ large.

We also try to use woods that come from our area or region. Even better than salvaged wood shipped from somewhere else is wood that is cleared directly from the site on which we're building. In our wind-swept and sandy coastal area this is tough, because mostly all we have is twisted, gnarly, undersize oak trees. Still, we've begun to put these trees to use as naturally shaped posts and beams, with surprisingly pleasant results. Driftwood, too, has become a source of high-character railings, porch frames, and furniture.

When salvage or local wood is unavailable, we try to use lumber from certified sustainably managed forest. Our exterior walls are covered with white cedar shingles from trees grown on the lands of Seven Islands Land Company, a family-owned business whose holdings include more than a million acres of Maine woodlands. They have spent substantial time and money to have an independent evaluator, Scientific Certification Systems, investigate their operation, certify their commitment, and make recommendations for how they can move their program even farther along the road to sustainability. The Maibec company in Quebec buys their cedar from Seven Islands. They make wood shingles. We buy their shingles.

Incrementally, our sources of supply become more refined and the percentage of well-sourced wood in our buildings increases. We use a hierarchy of criteria to make choices that ultimately get us what we want—fine material that suits both our craft and our environmental principles.

Green Building Techniques

Buildings have significant environmental impact. Resources are used for their construction, energy is used to obtain and process these resources and to operate the building, and habitat and natural landscapes are disrupted by their siting. A successful design/build process must be well informed about these impacts.

We use a wide variety of "green" strategies to help us minimize the environmental footprint of our buildings and landscapes. These strategies fall into three basic categories of environmental design and building solutions. The first is the bundle of standard South Mountain techniques that we incorporate as a matter of course, such as minimizing square footage and volume; renovating whenever possible instead of demolishing and rebuilding; finding uses for construction and demolition waste; siting buildings to minimize visual and habitat impact; providing for future solar use; protecting existing vegetation from construction damage; avoiding the use of pesticides, chemicals, and toxic materials; using native plant species in the landscape; placing glass and windows where they will bring in the most sunlight, daylight, and natural ventilation; maximizing water conservation; employing salvage and locally produced materials, those with a high recycled content, and those that are easily recyclable at the end of their service life; and, most important, achieving first-rate energy efficiency.

The second category includes strategies we offer at significantly greater cost to clients who wish to further reduce the environmental impact of their home: heat-recovery ventilation; passive-solar heat; solar hot water; state-of-the-art glass and superinsulation techniques; composting toilets; enhanced denitrifying waste disposal systems; and solar and/or wind-powered electricity. At this point we are employing these techniques on virtually every project we do, and we are attempting, in some situations, to make zero-energy homes, or net energy producers. For many years, we pushed our clients to go farther; now, in some cases, they are pushing us, challenging us to do even better. I never thought we would regularly be installing composting toilets in million-dollar houses, but it's happening now as awareness grows.

Finally, there are specific community-planning approaches that we try to incorporate into development projects: attaching houses or clustering them tightly; adjusting older buildings to new uses and today's standards; creating shared systems and functions whenever possible; designing pedestrian environments that isolate vehicles; limiting pavement and maximizing green space; preserving and creating prime agricultural land; and locating close to public transportation.

The goal is to design and build in a truly restorative way. It's an elusive long-term goal that we can't pretend to achieve, but we are always trying to move closer by doing better tomorrow, with this essential part of our practice, than we did today.

Our work with renewable energy has led to the creation of a thriving new division within South Mountain that provides energy conservation, solar, and wind to island homeowners, businesses, and institutions who are not our regular clients. This will be discussed in detail in chapter 10.

Our three categories of green building strategies originated with Marc Rosenbaum, the most intelligent, knowledgeable, and inventive systems engineer I know. We use his consulting services consistently. During our decades of collaboration with him, he has been a tremendous teacher, constantly encouraging us to reach farther and extend our ecological endeavors. Rosenbaum and all the dedicated practitioners and thinkers we have come to know through association with the Northeast Sustainable Energy Association—Terry Brennan, Bruce Coldham, Chuck Silver, Alex Wilson, Jamie Wolf, and a host of others—have been great teachers, and great friends.

Modest Goals

Perhaps the most important and elusive lesson of the practice of our craft is that even with all our lofty goals and expectations, it turns out that our most successful projects are characterized by a sense of modesty. We are not wildly innovative (only mildly so, I'd say); nor are we drawn to the highly dramatic. I'm glad of this. I think it's important to know who you are and what you do well, and to stay focused on this.

We recently hired a new architect. About six months after his arrival I took him and three other new employees for a half-day tour of some of our houses. Afterward I asked Ryan what he thought. Was there variety, or was there a sense of sameness?

He said, "It was like checking out the produce at an awesome food store. Many varieties, all mouthwatering." Our houses are as different as broccoli and sweet potatoes, but they are connected by a thread of intention and an evolving practice of craft.

In the late 1600s the finest musical instruments originated from three families in the small Italian village of Cremona. First were the Amatis, and it is said that outside their shop hung a sign: THE BEST VIOLINS IN ALL OF ITALY. Not to be outdone, their neighbors, the Guarneris, hung a bolder sign: THE BEST VIOLINS IN THE WORLD. At the end of the street was the workshop of Anton Stradivarius, and on its front door was a simple notice: THE BEST VIOLINS ON THE BLOCK. South Mountain is trying to make the best buildings on the block. Good buildings, well-loved buildings, not "important" buildings. Buildings that, first and foremost, serve the needs of the people who inhabit them by supporting and nurturing their health, satisfaction, productivity, and spirit. Buildings that spring from a strong sense of place and deep collaborations, that celebrate the spirit of craft, and that seamlessly arrange the elements of our creations.

Stewart Brand quotes the duchess of Devonshire, speaking about a particularly unassuming room in her spectacular manor house, Chatsworth, which she has restored meticulously:

> Being in this room on a winter night, alone or with
> one or two great friends, the sparkling coal fire with its

low brass-bound nursery fender, the familiar things all around, sitting on a chair which becomes a nest with letters and papers and baskets and telephone scattered on the floor, dogs comfortably settled by the fire, or near the draught of the door according to their thickness of coat, is my idea of an evening happily spent.[3]

Says Stewart about this passage, "The distribution of the dogs—and her perception of them—signals a room thoroughly grown into. Professional designers have borrowed all manner of Chatsworth fabric patterns and historical references and design inspiration, but they will never get the dog part right."[4]

At South Mountain, we are struggling to get the dog part right.

And while we do, how lucky we are to have the opportunity, over and over, to express the desires of our clients through the voices of our craft.

RANDI BAIRD

· 7 ·

Practicing Community Entrepreneurism

Man stands for long time with mouth open before roast duck flies in.
—CHINESE SAYING

In 1980 a fifty-nine-year-old woman named Madeline Blakeley called. Her husband had recently died. She was a librarian, they had no children, and they had always lived in rented apartments. Her dream was to own a piece of property. She had $7,000 in cash. A Realtor showed her a lot priced at exactly that, but all her friends advised against buying it.

I went with her to look at it. The steeply sloping lot was adjacent to the main road from Vineyard Haven to Edgartown. The road was loud; trucks roared by, downshifting as they rounded the corner. The property sloped due south to a beautiful little valley, a perfectly matched solar exposure and view. Except for the proximity to the road, it was a lovely site. There was nothing else available that was even remotely in her price range.

I suggested that she could build an earth-bermed, partially underground house. "The southern orientation aims away from the road just enough, and the berm would dull the noise as long as the house doesn't open to that side. We can design the traffic right out of the picture." She was excited. Even though she didn't think she could afford to build, the idea that the land could eventually be sensibly used was appealing. She bought the property.

At the time the Farmers Home Administration had a rural housing program offering very low-interest loans to moderate-income people. I explored it for Madeline and an old friend of ours, a young single mother named Cathy Weiss, and it looked feasible. We designed passive-solar houses suited to each site, submitted them to Farmers Home, and requested that they raise the mortgage limit from $40,000 to $48,000 due to the promise of carefully analyzed and documented energy savings. After extensive bureaucratic wrangling, the increase was approved.

The houses were built, and dreams came true. Madeline and her dog moved into a sunny earth-integrated house and lived there for many years; Cathy raised her daughter in her house and lives there still.

In the 1950s Madeline and her husband, John, had lived in Brockton, Massachusetts, where they were friendly with another couple, Edwin and Olga Heath. When Madeline and John moved to the Vineyard they fell out of contact. In the mid-1990s Madeline received a letter from Edwin. His wife, Olga, had died, too. They met (after thirty years of separation) and fell in love. Edwin loved her Vineyard house, but age and health dictated that they be in Florida, where he lived, so they moved there and got married. She sold her house. It was heartbreaking, but she liked the woman she sold to; they remained connected, and thereby she retained her connection to her house.

I lost track of Madeline after she moved to Florida, but when the first edition of this book was published, I tracked her down and sent her a copy with an affectionate inscription. She wrote back, a wonderful letter in longhand about what that house had meant to her. She talked about each of the people who had worked on the house—Pete, and Steve, and Marco, and Mitchell, and me (I think that was all of us at the time).

Edwin Heath died in 2004. In her eighties, and somewhat ill, Madeline had one dream left—to move back to the Vineyard for the final years of her life. But there was little hope of that—it was far too expensive. Undaunted, she put her name on the long list of people waiting for housing through Island Elderly Housing. Miraculously, her name was drawn a short time after. She accepted the apartment offered, sight unseen, and packed up.

Twenty-six years after I first met Madeline, she called me and said she was settled in on the island and wanted to come to see our new shop and office, and the cohousing neighborhood next door where we live. Her neighbor Joyce dropped her off. Once inside she stopped, looked around, and sighed deeply. "My God it's beautiful," she said, and continued toward the main office, with a look of wonder on her face as if she had just entered a botanical garden in full bloom—touching everything, gazing around, taking it all in.

She looked older, of course, and moved more slowly, too, with the help of a mahogany cane. But the eyes and voice had not changed a bit, and her character—sharply observant, powerfully candid, deeply emotional, wonderfully expressive, and remarkably vital—was the same as always.

She spoke to each person she encountered. Her presence was magnetic. She strolled through the offices like an old master, pointing out things of interest, but humbly, not grandly. She was awed by everything she saw and everyone she met.

After touring, we sat down in my office to rest, to talk, to have a glass of water. She said, "John, I don't know if I've ever told you this, but you and the others didn't just build me a house. It was so much more. I found myself in that house. I loved everything about it, and everything about being there, and every day I lived there I found myself again, in some other way, and found something else in the house to bring me pleasure."

Not long after, she called me and said "When I die, I am going to have some extra money—not a lot, but some significant sum, I think. I want to leave that money to South Mountain, to be used for a solar education project for the youth of the island." But a lawyer had advised her to give it now, while she was alive, so that she could see the fruits of her gift.

We began to brainstorm what to do with the $50,000 gift.

Ironically, another old client had come to us not long before, a woman who has always been very community-spirited, and said, "I have some extra stocks that I don't need, and I want to use them to hire you to install a wind turbine at the high school. I want those kids to see it every day and learn from it." She hoped the turbine would inspire kids at the high school to pursue careers in renewable energy.

Phil Forest and I took her message to the school board; they were as excited as we were. She paid 90 percent of the costs, and we contributed 10 percent. We applied for a grant from the Mass Technology Collaborative; it was approved, and all the proceeds ($30,000) are in an account that will assure the long-term maintenance and repair (and dismantling if ever necessary) of the machine. The ten-kilowatt ARE442 was installed on a hundred-foot tower, but soon after she came to us Nan, the donor, was devastated by an aggressive cancer and sadly—so sadly—passed away before the turbine was raised. A bronze plaque at the base of the turbine honors her memory.

Given that, we hoped to do something with Madeline's gift that would complement the turbine—a solar-electric installation. But we didn't just want to put $50,000 worth of photovoltaics on the roof; we wanted to do something more expressive and dramatic. Phil had an idea: to cover a portion of the high school parking lot with electricity-generating photovoltaic panels—a solar carport. If this comes to fruition it will generate electricity for the high school, provide shade for cars, and create a charging station as plug-in electric vehicles become more commonplace.

More important, perhaps, it will be a model of great things to come. Parking lots constitute a large area of available real estate that can be used for their primary purpose while also becoming solar power stations. If, for example, we were to cover all the parking lots at the high school, we could generate approximately one million.kilowatt-hours of electricity annually—almost 70 percent of the high school's total annual use! (And we could generate all the rest, and more, by adding more solar panels to the roof.) Madeline's $50,000 will be used as seed money, and the project will be called the Heath Solar Power Station. The installation will be dedicated to her beloved Edwin Charles Heath.

This whole story is an illustration of full-circle community entrepreneurism—the commitment of business to bringing new ideas, investment, and problem solving to a local community. This has become the sixth cornerstone of our work. We give to the community, the community gives back, we reciprocate in turn, and onward it goes.

Preserving Community

Stable housing is an essential component of the American dream. The Vineyard's desirability is responsible for a serious affordable housing crisis. It wasn't so long ago that young people could find caretaking gigs, shacks in the woods, welcoming campgrounds, cheap land, and a host of housing options. Locals could build homes on the family back lot and stay here to raise families. Today, however, staggering increases in real estate prices have made it impossible for many to afford homes. As housing prices soared, the community became endangered.

A decade ago we began to suffer significant outmigration by people who saw no hope of entering the housing market. Others, who were fortunate enough to have bought cheap land a quarter century ago and managed to cobble together a house and a livelihood, had excess equity. They could not possibly afford the house they owned if they had to buy it at today's prices. Suddenly they found themselves the owners of real estate worth $1 million. They could buy a major chunk of western North Carolina or northern Maine for that. The future on the island looked grim for their children. People were bailing out. We were losing the essential fiber of our community, and the new buyers of those homes rarely filled the same important civic roles vacated by those departing.

A community consists of a place and those who have a relationship with that place: the land and the people. Land conservation is a familiar concept, but now we have to think about people conservation as well. Affordable housing is less about houses or land or development and more about people who belong in a place being able to afford to stay in that place.

Neighbors and nannies, schoolteachers and social workers, truck drivers and technicians, artists and arborists, plumbers and plasterers, the town clown and the town drunk, whistleblowers and curmudgeons, peacemakers and troublemakers, politicians and taxpayers, grandmothers and grandfathers, sisters and brothers, those of different ages, abilities, incomes, colors, religious beliefs, sexual orientations—we need all these people. Each time any of them is forced to leave our community due to escalating real estate prices, the Vineyard becomes a lesser place. People conservation also relates to important jobs going unfilled, or being filled by those who are unqualified, or turning over quickly as people lose their housing patience and hope. It relates to a commuter workforce instead of one made up of familiar faces and old acquaintances. It's connected to stress, anger, child abuse, alcohol, and divorce. When we begin to lose continuity of generations, we lose an essential element of community character.

Tom Chase, the director of the Islands office of The Nature Conservancy, says:

> Every time we lose a Vineyard family of long-standing, we lose a grey cell from our cultural memory. Gradually we forget the traditions of land stewardship. Affordable housing is not only about people caring for people, but also people caring for the land. Enough Islanders have to be around so knowledge of the land accumulates and transcends generations. Without restoration of our natural habitats and generations of stewards, we might as well live anywhere.[1]

The story of affordable housing is a story about long-term community preservation. Ever since we built those two houses for Madeline and Cathy, South Mountain has been assembling small affordable housing projects; it is a staple of our work. We believe it is one of the most important community services we can offer—high-quality housing for the people who live here. Our high-end work subsidizes this work that has so much meaning for us.

The Island Mobilizes

In the year 2000 we began to step it up. Since then our company has banded together with many others to lead an intensive long-term local effort to solve our housing crisis. An islandwide public–private partnership has emerged. Community passion has ignited this effort, and local funding mechanisms are driving it. We think of the affordable housing issue as more than a social or political issue—it's also a design challenge. Our approach is broad and diverse. We support a mosaic of housing solutions that are small-scale, scattered-site, high-performance, mixed-income, and that, in all cases, respect the Vineyard's traditional community patterns. It is a primary objective to use existing housing stock whenever possible. We have equal commitment to stable rental housing and permanently protected homeownership opportunities.

Part of the effort was a comprehensive housing needs assessment funded by the Island Affordable Housing Fund. The assessment pointed out that this is a community issue that affects everyone, and it helped us to begin to engage everyone in the solution. The needs assessment was particularly helpful with potential donors. Although those who come to the Vineyard to enjoy our beauty create change, they also bring new wallets—and wealth that can be harnessed to preserve and enhance. Local money is key.

In 2005 we asked our consultant, John Ryan, to update the assessment. He proved that he doesn't fit the usual consultant's motto, which is, "If you're not part of the solution, there's good money in prolonging the problem." He said that market forces were accelerating housing difficulty, but although the median home price had grown ten times faster than wage increases, "The island's residents have made remarkable progress, creating 95 new affordable ownership opportunities, 83 year-round rentals, with another 165 units permitted, in litigation, or in construction. There's reason to hope and celebrate." Today that list of options is even longer.

Not only does our affordable housing work change our community, but it changes our company as well. It has caused a new interest in a particular kind of growth. It has caused people in our company to want to sharpen our ax so we can do more and better work. The more we profit, the more we can give back while we still meet our personal needs. It's good for our company to do this work. It's good for business. The community values us in new and different ways because of our association with these efforts.

Subsidies

In runaway real estate markets, affordable housing needs deep subsidies. What little can be done without subsidies produces shoddy housing that communities find unacceptable and occupants find to be distinctly unaffordable over time due to high maintenance and energy costs. Subsidies are essential to projects that respect both their residents and the community at large. Affordable housing should be similar, in many respects, to luxury housing, except more compact, somewhat less detailed, and, most important, differently financed.

Historically, in the modern era, whenever we have been successful at housing our country's poor—and even the middle class—it's been due to subsidies. The GI Bill after World War II was the greatest affordable housing subsidy ever. It helped the families of our returning soldiers and partially fueled the postwar economy. It's interesting to note that by far the largest current housing subsidy in America—to the tune of roughly $80 billion a year—is the mortgage interest deduction. Each of us who owns a home with a mortgage deducts our mortgage interest from our taxes. This huge housing subsidy benefits the middle class (properly, I think) and also the wealthy (improperly, I think). It has no benefit, however, for the millions of low-income people who really need it. Subsidies must be appropriately directed.

In our community a wide range of people, and not just poor people, need subsidies. People making 140 to 150 percent of the median area income for our county are shut out of the local real estate market. Cops, teachers, nurses, tradespeople, and even town managers need housing subsidies here. It won't be long, the way we're going, before doctors and lawyers needs subsidies, as they do in Aspen.

Addressing this situation requires tremendous commitment and creativity, but this community has demonstrated such qualities in the past, especially with land conservation. If someone had said in 1988 that by 2008 the Vineyard would have a dozen new public beach accesses and a growing network of public trails across the island, no one would have believed it was possible. Everything was headed in the opposite direction. The Martha's Vineyard Land Bank, voted into existence in the late 1980s, has accomplished this and more. Private land conservation groups have also been tremendously effective. As a community we have actively and generously funded land conservation of roadsides, vistas, beaches, farmland, and ecologically significant habitats. At present roughly 20 percent of the island's land area is under some form of permanent protection. Now we are seeing that people conservation is equally important. Our business has been one of the many entities that have banded together to lead this new effort.

Martha's Vineyard is a rarefied place, and it faces particular problems. But housing issues are virtually universal in all attractive places, all the places that people want to live. Desirability trumps affordability. There's a bumper sticker that says, HOUSES: EVERYONE GETS ONE

BEFORE ANYONE GETS A SECOND. I can't imagine what the Vineyard would be like—or what South Mountain Company would be like, for that matter—if our housing market were governed by that principle. But somewhere between the draconian egalitarianism of this bumper sticker and the sticker shock of a real estate market run amok is the balance that can keep the Vineyard community healthy.

Development

We were in a Chinese restaurant with Chris's mother. She cracked open her fortune cookie and found a blank piece of paper. She asked the waiter whether he'd ever seen anything like that. He nodded gravely and said, "Umm . . . your fortune—no news is good news." That's the way many people feel about developers: No news is good news. Real estate developers are widely disrespected and mistrusted, but *development* need not be an ugly word. Development is invention.

Our affordable housing efforts have led us to development work. At South Mountain our first development question is: Are we proposing to invent something that the community needs? If not, why bother? Let's design something else. When we examine community needs, we find the demand for affordable housing nested in a constellation of other needs:

- Open space preserved in perpetuity.
- Restoration of agricultural land.
- Places for low-impact businesses that will not contribute to strip development.
- Community systems for converting waste to nutrients, to protect our sole-source aquifer.
- Neighborhoods that encourage social interaction.

So . . . let's invent all that.

My belief that we can do so stems in part from my tour of Danish cohousing neighborhoods in 1990. The cohousing concept, which originated in Denmark in the late 1960s and 1970s and has since spread to other countries, takes many different forms, but there are five general principles that set it apart from traditional residential developments:

1. The development is limited in size to twelve to thirty-five homes (large enough to avoid being a fishbowl and small enough that residents can all know one another).
2. The automobile is relegated to the perimeter, leaving pedestrian space within.
3. Houses are tightly clustered or attached to promote social contact and leave open space undisturbed.
4. A "common house" is included where residents often share one or more meals a week, where guests can stay, and where a variety of activities take place. Not only a community hub, the common house provides space not needed on a daily basis, thereby allowing individual homes to be smaller.
5. The residents are the developers, making decisions as a group and, in the process, creating community bonds.[2]

Island Cohousing

One evening, years ago, during a talk about Vineyard housing, I floated the idea of a cohousing neighborhood on the Vineyard. Two couples approached me afterward and said, "This is just what we need here. Why aren't we doing it?"

I replied, "I've just been waiting for a few people like you. Let's go." Those two couples, Randi Baird and Philippe Jordi and Sylvie and Paul Farrington, became the energy and the glue behind the beginning of Island Cohousing, which grew into a broad partnership among our company, sympathetic bankers, flexible regulatory officials, and a group of dedicated people who shared a dream and wished to develop and live in this kind of neighborhood. South Mountain was hired to conduct a land search, facilitate the formation of the group, and develop, design, and build a deliberate neighborhood. Through trial and error, dialogue, and persistence, we invented, together, a development that combines the elements I've mentioned. Its commitment to affordability did not diminish its commitment to be as green, beautiful, and democratically inspired as we could make it.

Early on we decided to do a combined project that would include both the cohousing neighborhood and new facilities for South Mountain. The timing coincided with the company's need for more space and a larger property. We decided to pursue the synergy of co-locating our business with this innovative development. We were able to acquire a large piece of wooded land that satisfied all needs. South Mountain would share land and infrastructure costs to reduce Island Cohousing's costs, and Island Cohousing would be able to provide the business with the space it needed.

Taking full responsibility for this project was a stretch for South Mountain. It was a larger endeavor with greater complexities than any we had previously undertaken. The South Mountain complex, and the sixteen Island Cohousing houses and facilities, served two separate entities with fundamentally different needs. Both were tough clients. Both had stringent cost constraints in an area with high costs and very restrictive zoning. All told, the combined project violated then-current zoning in eleven different ways. The regulatory hurdles were tremendous, and the potential for delays and conflict was real. It was a risky, difficult project.

The regulatory process promised to be difficult. We had to apply for zoning relief (to overcome our noncompliance) under Chapter 40B, a Massachusetts statute known as the "anti-snob zoning law." The law was enacted in 1969 to allow developers of affordable housing that met specific criteria to bypass local zoning that obstructed affordable housing or had the effect of making such projects financially unfeasible. Chapter 40B provisions offer housing developers a powerful stick. It has been used well in some cases and abused in others. In our case, the town was fully supportive, and this "friendly" 40B would permit the project without forcing the town to make potentially undesirable and hard-to-enact zoning changes in order to accommodate it.

But it was bound to receive intense scrutiny. It included the location of a business in a residential area, something that had never been done before in a 40B project. As well as town approval, it needed approval from the Martha's Vineyard Commission (MVC), a regional planning agency with broad regulatory powers. The commission determines whether proposed development projects of significant size (which are known as "developments of regional impact") will be more beneficial than detrimental to the community. Developers often see the MVC as a difficult adversary. Because our purpose was fundamentally aligned with that of the commission—to shape a better community—we were able to work collaboratively to achieve an even better plan than the one we started with. When the commissioners finally voted approval, they issued a decision with fifteen conditions. All of these began with the words, "We accept the applicant's offer to . . ." We were pleased that our project was able to answer their questions.

Once we had steered through the regulatory maze, there remained a host of complex financial, design, construction, and social issues to work through. Aspirations were high. All members of the group wished for first-rate ecological land use and building quality. They wished for low prices. They wished for community diversity. They wished to accommodate those less fortunate. We had to learn together how difficult and expensive it is to achieve all this, how tricky the balances are, and how substantive are the sacrifices that must be made.

Nearly half the houses were subsidized in two ways:

- Light subsidies achieved by internal price structuring that shifted a higher percentage of the shared costs (development and design costs, infrastructure, and common facilities) to the larger houses.

- Deep subsidies from a combination of cash fund-raising from private donors and discounted mortgage
  rates.

The first method kept the price low for smaller houses; the second allowed four of the houses to be sold to qualified buyers earning less than 80 percent of median county income at a price they could afford. The subsidies required that we raise $300,000 in cash. Most of the money was raised from our past clients, who responded magnificently. Their contributions, and others, coupled with a foundation grant and a major contribution from the Martha's Vineyard Co-op Bank in the form of discounted interest rates, pushed us to our goal. These houses have permanent limited-equity affordability restrictions.

Along with the internal and external subsidies, there were four other significant cost-control mechanisms: production building methods and customization control, carving off and selling several building lots to offset land costs, reduced rates for South Mountain's design and construction services, and infrastructure sharing. The toughest was the first: working with a diverse group to maintain cost-effective design and production building. This was achieved by designing for flexibility in such a way that we avoided building sixteen custom homes. Customization has often been a virus that infects cohousing projects, because the members of the group making the overall design decisions each harbor different individual needs and desires. It's impossible at once to achieve low cost, high quality, diversity, and custom homes for all. If this is not well understood, it is likely that costs will spin out of control.

We had the good fortune to benefit from the experiences of others who had been through this process. We toured other cohousing projects and queried extensively. We listened carefully and took the advice of those who had covered similar ground. Ultimately, we limited customization while making room for individual needs and desires. We developed a single core plan that had a fixed number of expansion options. A one-page menu determined what each house would be, and a master chart tracked the options in all houses. The group's self-discipline enabled agreement on a tremendous number of choices, right down to the tile selections and interior paint colors.

The strong environmental aspirations for the project collided with the severe cost constraints. Choices were necessary. We told the group that the standard and not-so-standard green building approaches that South Mountain regularly uses (including finishing our houses—inside and out—with salvage and certified lumber, first-rate energy efficiency, and extensive use of recycled materials) would have only minor cost implications. Other possibilities would have major cost implications. We discussed generating our power with wind and photovoltaics, installing a district heating system fueled by wood that grows each year on our land, saving and protecting the native vegetation instead of mowing it down for construction convenience, converting our human waste into valuable nutrients by using composting toilets, and more. Some measures might be possible in the future; some would not.

The group decided to put its limited resources into two important and costly measures that could be done only now, and not later. The first was mapping, protecting, and saving hundreds of key trees and areas of native vegetation on the wooded site. To facilitate construction of dense housing, most sites are fully cleared before construction begins. After completion, trees and vegetation are planted. For many years after, the sites look raw and young. Protecting and working around existing vegetation is difficult and costly. We figured that this measure would add approximately $75,000 to the cost of the project. But what kind of landscape would that money have bought, spread over the four-acre disturbed area? Very little. Just a year after completion, once the plantings and lawns around the houses had grown in and the buildings had begun to weather, the neighborhood felt like it had been there for ages.

The second measure was to equip the neighborhood with composting toilets—a big expense, a lifestyle change, and a risk. Many in the group were strong supporters of this measure because it did two things at once: made waste into useful nutrients and protected the island's sole-source aquifer. But given the unusual nature of composting toilets, would people want these houses, would banks finance them, would appraisers value them, would the town allow them? These questions turned out to have positive answers, and this is one of the few new neighborhoods in the country that has no flush toilets.[3]

Architecturally, Island Cohousing is less about the houses and more about the spaces between them. In lieu of a street, a pedestrian common separates the buildings. Extensive shared facilities—the common house, a swimming and skating pond, a community garden, woods and trails, and a basketball court and playground—favor neighborliness and community interaction. But such design elements can only facilitate what in the end is a difficult balance. Neighborliness cannot be mandated. Pushed too far, the notion of community can become forced, phony, and contentious. The diversity in incomes, backgrounds, and values of cohousing residents can lead to controversy, stress, uneven levels of participation, and occasional bouts of what Paul Farrington calls the "dysfunc-shui"[4] of neighborhood. Working out differences is not without conflict. There are a few people who don't much care for one another, and this will probably always be the case.

But we have succeeded, to some degree, in creating a neighborhood that enjoys some built-in provisions that make it work differently from most. The neighborhood has a special sense of community. There are more connections among the residents, the connections are less random, and there is a splendid, convenient environment for kids, who can just walk outside or next door and find their playmates in an unusually safe setting.

It's instructive to watch our developing ability to work together, think together, and live together in a neighborhood. There are issues with kids, parking, pets, participation, consideration for others—all that one would expect. There is also a reserve of good feeling, which ebbs and flows, but which holds us together. Gradually, we have learned one of the essentials of consensus decision making: the art of gentle persuasion and compromise. We continue to deepen our appreciation of the cultural shift embodied in the concept and practice of cohousing and see in this shift much that is hopeful for the future of our neighborhood, our community, and our island. It's been a wonderful place to live—full of great moments, great failures, great frustrations, and great progress.

Ultimately, the creation of Island Cohousing served as a partial catalyst for surprising regulatory reform. The town planning board looked at this project, and at several other affordable housing projects with zoning difficulties, and said, "These are exactly the kinds of projects we mean to encourage. Yet they violate our zoning in so many ways." This discussion was one of the factors that evolved into a process of rewriting the zoning regulations. The voters approved the new zoning bylaws, and today we could propose Island Cohousing or the others without violating the regulations in any way. Small stones can make big ripples.

Jenney Way

Just after Island Cohousing was completed, I gave a talk about affordable housing at a local church. An older couple, Ralph and Olivia Jenney, approached me later and said they'd like to meet. We did. They had land in Edgartown, and they wanted to do some estate planning that included committing a part of their land to affordable housing. It turned out to be an extraordinary property.

The land is in downtown Edgartown, five acres hidden in the middle of a well-developed old neighborhood of small homes. It's an odd-shaped parcel, patched together over time with tentacles that reach out to several surrounding streets. When you travel down the narrow dirt driveway to the Jenney house, you enter an enclosure surrounded by dense vegetation. It feels like you're away on an old farmstead, rather than in the middle of town. Ralph and Olivia wished for half the land to remain in their family, with the rest devoted to an affordable housing development right in their own backyard. This is one of those rare examples of someone saying, "Yes, in my backyard." I was impressed.

Ralph and Olivia were willing to sell the land at a bargain price to the Island Affordable Housing Fund. We negotiated an agreement and began the preliminary design process. The opportunities were tremendous. The walk-to-everywhere potential of the in-town site became an immediate driving force. It was clear that at this location, if possible, the homes should be occupied by municipal employees, teachers, health workers, local working people, and longtime neighborhood renters ready for homeownership. Unlike the Island Cohousing project, we would strive here for full affordability—a range of subsidized homeownership opportunities and no market-rate houses. It would be a mixed-income neighborhood for all who were currently shut out of the Vineyard housing market, which included people making from 60 to 150 percent of median area income.

The land would ultimately be owned by the Island Housing Trust, a community land trust we had spun off from the Island Affordable Housing Fund in 2001. The fund raises money, the trust develops and owns property, and the two organizations are closely linked and share some board members.

Before beginning the formal permitting process, we organized several public meetings for area residents. We presented the preliminary plan, answered questions, and listened to suggestions. The reactions were mostly positive, although residents also pointed out existing problems in the neighborhood.

Public officials were all supportive of the project. At an informal meeting with the Edgartown Planning Board, the only substantive remark we heard was, "Can't you squeeze in a few more houses?" No, we responded, this is what the property can bear.

Wherever we went the project generated enthusiasm. The regulatory process involved application to the Edgartown Planning Board, which would hold a hearing and then turn the project over to the

Martha's Vineyard Commission. Once we had received approval from the MVC, the project would be returned to the planning board for local approval.

At the first planning board hearing, it was clear that we had misjudged the political landscape, expecting the process to be a cakewalk. This would be nothing of the sort. It turned out to be more like wading through a swamp with mosquitoes biting our faces and alligators nipping our heels. The room was full of people bearing a litany of complaints. Some were rational and reasonable; others were not. Some we could accommodate; others we could not. There was acrimony and there were accusations. Three or four strong-willed not-in-my-backyard opponents had aroused the entire neighborhood. We had no idea where the hostility had come from and were completely unprepared. We had not bothered to bring out supporters because we hadn't thought it would be necessary. The planning board was surprised, too.

Sometimes, as the proponents of projects we think are progressive and important, for which we have made sacrifices to bring to the community, we are attacked. When this happens, it is important—to avoid becoming discouraged and hurt—to remember that the attacks are not personal, even when they seem to be. We are always a part of a system in which we have taken up a particular role. It's the role that is being attacked. Understanding that it is the chair we're sitting in that is being attacked, rather than our own person, we can mostly remain calm and relaxed, we can listen carefully, and we can maintain respectful relationships with our attackers. We always have to remember that we have chosen to sit in that chair.

The MVC hearings were similarly contentious, but now we were prepared. After several lengthy hearings and a variety of delays, the MVC approved the project unanimously, with minor conditions.

We returned to the Edgartown Planning Board. I was worried about the Jenneys. This was taking much longer than any of us had figured, and some of the testimony was insulting to them. Would they grow weary and back out? No, their commitment remained firm. In the end the planning board, faced with a project they supported and an angry group of townspeople, did a superb job of devising conditions that in no way diminished the project but that defused and partially addressed some neighborhood concerns. They voted unanimously to support the project with the conditions they had imposed.

Nevertheless, a few malcontents—seasonal residents who didn't even live there full-time—decided to appeal the planning board decision. When they filed their appeal, the *Vineyard Gazette* wrote an editorial that chastised them, saying,

> The future of our Island community is most often decided in small steps—a board vote here, a commission approval there. Such decisions should be made after fair and open debate, and with plenty of listening. But appropriate progress is jeopardized if individuals refuse to recognize the legitimate outcome of a thoughtful process.[5]

We were able to settle, but it was a terribly costly and time-consuming delay. Now several years later, however, Jenney Way has become a wonderful little neighborhood tucked within another.

A grant from the Mass Technology Collaborative's Green Affordable Housing Program allowed the installation of solar-electric systems on four of the houses. All of them were designed and built to meet LEED (Leadership in Energy and Environmental Design) platinum standards, the first houses on the island to do so, and the first affordable housing in Massachusetts to do so. In the spring of 2008 ten lucky families, chosen by lottery, bought well-built, low-energy, low-maintenance homes for $160,000 to $330,000 (depending on income) at a time when the median house price on the Vineyard was pushing $700,000 and the very bottom of the market (small shacks needing lots of work) was about $400,000.

Our affordable housing work differs from our custom work in this way: Our custom clients come to us, asking us to fulfill their dreams, while our affordable housing projects are mostly self-generated—we identify needs and create projects, proactively, as community entrepreneurs. Over time, our focus has expanded from buildings and technology to community-planning efforts. On our small island we're finding that the need to create new hopeful stories is compelling, that the rewards for doing so are great, and that the potential to make progress with affordable housing, and preserving community, is within reach. Some of the programs themselves have made great stories.

House Moves

When land gets scarce and pricey, its value can far exceed the worth of the buildings located on it. People begin to tear down perfectly good houses to make room for new construction. With sufficient creativity, homes that owners no longer want can become an unusual resource.

Several years ago the Island Affordable Housing Fund began to get calls from people wishing to donate their houses if we could relocate them. Regrettably, we had to decline, because it's far too expensive to develop land, move a building, renovate, and update. Then it occurred to us: The funding mechanism is right there, embodied in the houses! Now when we field such offers, we say, "Here's the deal. You donate your house to the nonprofit fund. We'll get your house appraised to determine the value of your charitable donation and we'll remove your house if you will contribute in cash the gross tax benefit you will receive so that we have the money it takes to do the work."

The concept takes people aback at first, but after consultation with their tax professional, many agree, as long as they are in a position to take advantage of the tax breaks, which can be used over a period of five years. Recently one substantial property was assessed for $244,000 for the house only, not including the land below it. The total tax benefit to the owner who donated the house to us turned out to be 52 percent, and we received a check for $127,000. Another was a beautiful 1841 Victorian house that was in splendid condition but was too small for today's extended-family vacation life. The cash donation that accompanied the donated building came to $80,000. The owners pay only what they'll save; in addition they save the cost of demolishing and disposing of these buildings, which is not inconsequential, and they provide a service to the community. Everyone comes out ahead, except the IRS, but the process is entirely legal.

The town of Edgartown, the nonprofit Island Affordable Housing Fund, and South Mountain collaborated on a pilot project. Four homes were moved to four adjoining parcels owned by the town. The homes were equipped with perpetual limited-equity deed restrictions to guarantee that they'll be affordable forever, and they were offered via lottery at remarkably low prices to carefully qualified local residents. One of the recipients was a dignified, white-haired gentleman in his fifties who had worked in the school system for many years. He had lost his rental when his landlord had decided to sell. Purchasing a house had seemed far beyond his means, and he thought he would have to leave the island, where he had lived for nineteen years. It was a great moment when his name was drawn out of the hat, thereby selecting him to receive one of these houses. He was overwhelmed with joy and relief and broke down when we spoke with him immediately after his selection.

Not long after, I called him to ask him to testify in support of another project at a public hearing. He happily agreed. I told him I was planning to show a video that included our previous interview with him and asked whether he would find this embarrassing. He said he would, but he'd be there anyway: "You know, these days it's okay for a grown man to cry. I cried at the award, I'll cry again at the closing, and I'll cry the first time I walk through the door of my new home."

More and more houses are coming up for removal. A major problem is that it takes a long time to assemble a project, find land, develop it, and move the house. Owners aren't always willing to wait so long. We hope to convince the towns to set aside land for storage of houses.

Eventually we could have "used-house lots." When potential owners finally get their land together and are ready to build, they'll be able to inspect the houses, point, and say, "We'll take that one."

The physical process of moving houses down narrow country roads and through tightly packed villages is a remarkably complex undertaking. Power lines, road width, overhanging limbs, the size of the house, the shape of the house, other traffic on the road—all have to be juggled. Sometimes you have to break a house into parts, move it, and then put it back together. Sometimes you have to cut it apart horizontally because it's too tall to fit under obstacles between its old and new locations; other times you have to cut it apart vertically, because it's too wide to traverse the narrow roads. Sometimes you have to do both. Only when you're lucky do you get to move a house whole.

At one point during a recent move, our job foreman, Peter D'Angelo, stopped by my office to talk about the dangers and difficulties of the job. We talked awhile and then he left for the job site, where the house, which was already mounted on two trailers that had been moved out into a field, was to be split in half and rolled to its new location several miles away.

Late that morning I got a call from him. "You remember what I was saying about the dangers?"

"Uh-oh," I said quickly. "What happened?"

"Everyone's safe. But not the house. When we separated the two halves and moved the first half out, the second part toppled right off the trailer and crashed on its side."

After he'd reiterated that all were okay, I asked, "So what are you doing now?"

"I'm trying to decide whether it's salvageable—whether to bother moving the sound half, whether to set a match to the whole damn thing, or what."

I drove out to the site. The scene was surreal. Because the move required power, telephone, and cable television lines to be disconnected and lowered, the site was jammed with utility trucks, linemen, police escorts, and workers. They were standing around in small groups staring at this strange, two-story half-a-house lying on its side. Peter and Mike, the mover, had already figured out a scheme to right the house, repair the damage, and move it.

There was little talk about what had actually happened, and no talk about who was to blame. Everyone began to put things in order for the move, like cowboys pulling the herd back together in the quiet moments after the end of a stampede. The utility guys headed for their trucks, the cops moved out to the road and switched on their flashing lights, the tractor started up, and the other half began to roll.

Not long after I left, Peter told me, the local newspaper showed up. When pressed by the reporter to make a tragedy out of a mishap, as reporters are wont to do, Peter quipped, "The closest thing to a real tragedy this morning was that while we were otherwise engaged, the neighbor's dog stole our supply of fresh-baked Humphrey's doughnuts."

Community entrepreneurs are always learning, and with learning comes a certain vulnerability and exposure. Our mistakes are right out there in public view. Which adds a certain sweetness to our occasional successes.

Solving a Problem

Supporting our housing efforts requires significant funding. This has moved, over time, from small, private fund-raising efforts to an array of sources. The annual Island Affordable Housing Fund event in the early years was called Houses on the Move, in which architects, builders, craftspeople, and artists all created small houses—anything from jewelry to ceramics, doghouses, saunas, garden sheds, and writers' shacks—that were all trucked to our Grange Hall for display and auctioned off.

In 2002, the first year, Houses on the Move raised $180,000. South Mountain's employee-owners designed and built a seven-by-nine-foot writer's shack out of found materials, including roofing made of the discarded aluminum printing plates from the *Vineyard Gazette,* which you could read inside through the skip sheathing of the roof. It was fully furnished and equipped with a well-oiled Royal manual typewriter. It sold for $40,000.

A ceramist fashioned a wonderful little pickup truck, overflowing with one family's worldly goods, including the dog. Symbolizing the summer shuffle, it sold for $3,000.

From those beginnings, a diverse communitywide approach has developed. Successful community entrepreneurialism gives towns and regulatory agencies the confidence to take larger steps. It gives public-spirited developers and builders the sense that if they are creative and willing to step forward, their projects may find acceptance. Vineyard towns are now actively developing town-owned lands. Zoning incentives are strengthening. The public regional housing authority has been energized, and is the essential manager of rental properties and steward of ownership selection processes. A community land trust (the Island Housing Trust) has formed to develop housing and own land in perpetuity. This happened for two reasons: (1) As the Island Affordable Housing Fund became more and more active, it seemed prudent to fine-tune its mission, concentrate on funding, and spawn another organization to focus on development; and (2) the community land trust model is the best organizational approach to assuring that housing remains affordable over time.

Commerce and community are united in this effort. Pessimism and lack of will have been, in large measure, overcome. This is not to say that there is no longer any not-in-my-backyard sentiment. Sometimes such expression is vigorous. Mostly, though, there is a solid new consensus building around a core of community support. Progress on these efforts cannot come fast enough. The community loses people every year due to the lack of housing solutions. As important as each individual project is the larger unfolding of a new direction for the community.

Most interesting to me is that this is not a story of how a problem could be solved, but rather a collection of extraordinary and inter-related initiatives that, together, are moving inexorably toward the prize dangling at the end of the maze: community stability. If you asked anyone on the street in Edgartown or Vineyard Haven whether there is an affordable housing problem on Martha's Vineyard, they would unequivocally say yes. If you asked them if it has been solved, they would unequivocally say no—but most would add, "We've made some progress, though."

I would answer differently. I would propose that, except for one major missing piece that may be almost in place, it is solved. I do not say this casually, I do not say that there isn't huge work ahead, and I do not say that the solutions in place don't need improvement and refinement. Yet I'm convinced that we will look back sometime soon—perhaps in five years, perhaps in ten, perhaps in fifteen—and say, "Amazing. We had a problem—a big knotty complicated problem—and we truly solved it." How rare. How wonderful. Here's why.

Funding is a three-legged stool. Two are fully built. The first leg was mobilizing and inspiring the seasonal community to understand the critical nature of community preservation, and the reason to contrib-ute generously. And that one's done. The second was convincing the residents—the voters—to implement a tax to fund the Community Preservation Act. That one's done, too, as a 3 percent surtax on prop-erty taxes. The funds are used for affordable housing, land conserva-tion, and historic preservation. The final piece of the puzzle—the missing leg of the stool—is a housing bank, and it's well on its way. The housing bank is a 1 percent transfer fee on real estate sales greater than $750,000. It will generate several million dollars each year. It has already been approved by Vineyard voters and now it needs approval in the state legislature. The Senate passed it easily last year, but the House—after being lobbied hard by off-island Realtors (island Realtors are overwhelmingly in favor)—defeated it in a close vote. This fall we hope to achieve passage. When we do, everything changes. The $4 to

$5 million a year we will have to work with means we will no longer need to think about how to do it—we will only have to think about how well we're going to do it.

We do have a long way to go. We need approximately a thousand permanently protected housing opportunities, and we have created a few hundred. The rest will come.

The fundamental underpinning of all this is permanent affordability restrictions that limit equity so that affordable housing properties remain forever in the pool. Without them, all this work and money will eventually go out the window when houses and land return to the marketplace. I have always felt strongly about permanent restrictions, but for a long time I mostly thought of them as a necessary evil. Recent observations cause me to think differently.

The recipients of affordability-restricted properties know that it will never—most likely—make sense for them to move within this community. The house they may have purchased for $150,000 would increase in value (under the limited-equity provision) to approximately $180,000 after five years and to approximately $210,000 after ten years. To sell would do nothing for them in a wildly inflated real estate market like ours. So they invest in their houses in ways that they might otherwise not do. They improve them, they beautify them, they tend to their gardens and maintain their property for their children and grandchildren.

Some say these permanent restrictions create a second class of homeownership, because owners cannot profit from sale of their homes. But homeownership has not always been the investment path that it is today. Homeownership used to be, in the 1950s and 1960s and before, a means to stability, not profits. Perhaps we are opening a new avenue back to that kind of homeownership. Let's imagine, ten years from now, that there are a thousand restricted housing units on the Vineyard. Rather than being a second class of homeownership, it will be a widely accepted form (as it is already becoming) that brings community stability—a cadre of people who are truly committed to their property, in the same way that, for instance, small farmers have always been. This is more like European homeownership than the current American view of homeownership as investment. This is a corollary effect of affordable housing programs that softens another hard-edged problem: the commodification of real estate.

As we see housing solutions coming to fruition, and we recognize the good work of the team of committed people working to take them farther, we have begun to shift our efforts to energy. We are still working (more than ever, in fact) at designing and building affordable housing, but we are working less on the funding and policy aspects.

Community Energy

One of the greatest drains on a local economy is the cost of energy. In our community, nearly every dollar spent on electricity, gasoline, fuel oil, and propane leaks off the island and into the ledgers of large energy corporations. This does not have to be. Through energy conservation and the use of locally produced renewable energy, we can spend energy dollars locally, where they will have a multiplier effect within the community. At the same time, we can do our small part to protect against climate change.

In the 1970s and early '80s, before we took on the challenge of affordable housing, many of our early community entrepreneurial efforts were devoted to renewable energy. Working with the Energy Resource Group, a nonprofit our company helped to found and fund, we built community solar greenhouses, conducted solar home tours, and developed energy audit and weatherization programs.

Recently we have returned to these endeavors. Our projects with former clients Nan Rheault and Madeline Blakeley were a beginning. As I write, we are collaborating with a private donor and the town of Chilmark in an effort to turn the drafty, energy-hogging Chilmark School into a comfortable zero-fossil-fuel facility.

We see plenty more of this in our future. We have also committed to dedicating a large percentage of our annual charitable contributions (we give 10 percent of our net profits) to community entrepreneurial efforts strengthening the local economy by encouraging local food, energy, and craft.

The controversial Cape Wind project, which will be located off our shore in Nantucket Sound, is an important part of our future, but it is only a start.[6] We need more Cape Winds—many more—but we can also make significant contributions to the energy mix with local, cooperatively owned wind, solar, biodiesel, and energy conservation efforts.

Community entrepreneurism is an essential part of the integration of our community and our company. The actions we take can make us a vital force for long-term restoration. They are at the heart of the give-and-take of commerce, community, and place.

BRIAN VANDEN BRINK

· 8 ·

Thinking Like Cathedral Builders

A society grows great when old men plant trees
whose shade they know they shall never sit in.
—GREEK PROVERB

During the last days of January 2000, South Mountain Company's twenty-five employees, along with several friends and planning experts, spent two days hunkered down together, thinking about the future of the Vineyard. Our goals were to sketch a future we would like to see and to decide what commitments we, as a company, were willing to make to help achieve it.

The prelude to this exercise was our sense that Martha's Vineyard is being overwhelmed by its own desirability and prosperity. Land values are rising and community life is changing. Most people are acutely aware of the changes, but our political leadership has not formulated an effective collective vision of the future. Instead, our posture remains defensive. We act as if we are under siege, weakly trying to fend off the inevitable.

We asked ourselves, "But is it inevitable? Can we imagine a future that would make it possible for our children and grandchildren to enjoy the Vineyard the way we have? Can we muster the strength and resolve to tackle the issues and forge a satisfying tomorrow that serves the interests of all? Perhaps . . ."

We invited a few people from outside the company to Future Sketch, as we called the meeting, to broaden our perspectives. We gathered early on a Friday morning. After introductions, author and historian David McCullough, one of our guests, opened the day. He spoke about the Chagres River, which was the major obstacle to the building of the Panama Canal, but which was eventually used in a simple but ingenious way to become a part of the overall engineering solution. He related this to the "river of money" pouring into the Vineyard, undoing a way of life. He expressed two ideas that became central to our discussions:

- "We must redirect the river of money [that causes such harm] to restoration of community."
- "Our future is a design issue—it should be the result of intent rather than circumstance."

With these two themes echoing, we started by sharing memories of the past. After contrasting the characteristics of the place we love with the nature of the pressures that were changing it, we began to consider the components of a positive future—one that might harness the forces of change to allow the Vineyard to continue to be a place we (and the generations to come) will love.

The Results

We assembled a collection of ideas to guide us, and inspire others, to chart a course that would make a difference. Some of the emergent concepts were more developed than others. Some were tied to initiatives already in place and in need only of encouragement or better funding. By the end of the session, we had identified eight crucial areas:

1. Achieving political unity.
2. Creating the Vineyard Institute.
3. Promoting adequate and appropriate housing.
4. Preserving and enhancing rural character.
5. Supporting the new traditional economy.
6. Making a transportation system that works.
7. Committing to environmental stewardship.
8. Maintaining cultural traditions.

In each of the eight areas, we characterized the problem, suggested solution concepts, and identified actions to be undertaken. Having worked through the eight issue areas and come to broad consensus conclusions, we shifted our focus. We asked ourselves, "Given the vision of the Vineyard that we see before us, what can we, as a company, do to further and support the future we've identified?" The discussion was lively. Ideas flowed easily. The result was a series of fourteen actions to pursue as a company, including developing internal regulatory processes to assure appropriate building scale and good land use in our work; devoting a larger portion of our profits and pro bono time to community efforts; making a greater commitment to affordable housing projects; intensifying our efforts to use renewable energy and materials and to eliminate waste; aligning our mission with the Future Sketch findings; and sharing our conclusions with others.

Throughout this discussion there was a discernible, cohesive force linking us, making us a powerful community of interest. We agreed that we had not crossed the line of "fouling our own nest," that we could still steer in the direction of a longer view and encourage effective solutions over time. We understood that our problems were the same as those facing all beautiful and desirable places. We recognized that already we had some elegant successes to point to, and we concluded that it's just as important to remember what's been accomplished as to identify what needs to be done. We decided that it would be essential to create good models that would make radical new approaches seem commonplace. The Future Sketch undertaking itself was one such example.

Buckminster Fuller once said, "You never change things by fighting the existing reality. To change something, build a new model that makes the existing model obsolete."

It's unusual for a small company full of carpenters, woodworkers, designers, and office people to take two days to consider the future together. There was, in fact, some skepticism and grumbling beforehand. The results, however, were satisfying to all.

Once completed, we didn't tend to think about the issues we uncovered during the Future Sketch on a daily basis, but the underlying principles remained present, guiding us quietly, like a rabbit scuttling in the underbrush. When I read through the resolutions we reached, today, I realize that many of the ideas and suggestions have been implemented, to a lesser or greater degree, in the eight years since.

The Island Plan

The Martha's Vineyard Commission was created in 1974 by an act of the Massachusetts Legislature in response to what legislators viewed as a threat of unchecked development on the island. It has broad regulatory and planning powers. The regulatory aspects, although controversial at times, have been essential to the maintenance of the Vineyard's character and livability. The planning aspect has been used less well, mostly, I assume, because the commissioners and staff feel that they must respond to the regulatory siege and rarely find time for proactive planning.

But in the fall of 2005 the commissioners, with new executive director Mark London, decided to undertake the preparation of a comprehensive island plan. They imagined this as a lengthy process that would engage the entire island—citizens, business, municipal officials, seasonal residents—in the process. I was invited to join the steering committee. As I attended my first few meetings, I began to think about what would make this different—in overall impact—from our Future Sketch or all the other previous Vineyard plans that were collecting dust on a variety of shelves.

In response to a request that steering committee members discuss why they'd agreed to serve, what they would like to see happen, and what the primary objectives should be, I wrote the following:

> I agreed to serve because I would like to encourage us to take a long term look at how we could create a hopeful, restorative community and economy. If we look at the next 25, 50, and 100 years—rather than just the next two, five, or 10—perhaps we find our way to solutions.
>
> I think it is possible to encourage appropriate development that will enhance preservation of community and character while increasing economic opportunity. In the post-Peak-Oil world economy to come, which may arrive sooner than later, we may want to understand how to make a vibrant, living local economy that produces as much of our food, energy, shelter, and other needs as possible. I hope we'll think hard about that.
>
> Finally, I would like to encourage something compelling and enduring that will capture the imaginations of all citizens and stakeholders—something beyond a planning document, something that assembles a portrait of what the Vineyard can be and designs an inspiring path toward that future.

The Island Plan examines nine different areas: natural environment, energy and waste, housing, water, livelihood and commerce, built environment, transportation, social environment, and governance, with a particular focus on the interdependencies. If successful, the plan will be an adaptable blueprint, of sorts, for durable community—a robust vision that cascades down to the actionable, measurable goals and strategies that we hope will benefit all of us who live here, full- and part-time, and all who visit. It will break new ground while it incorporates and learns from the best of the past and present. Have we done that? Not yet. Are we getting there? Maybe—we'll soon see.

The Long View

The Future Sketch was an important passage for the company. Perhaps its most immediate impact was to facilitate our thinking in generational terms about our work and our legacy. Our developing commitment to place and our policy of limiting our work to the Vineyard led to our efforts to think about the future of our region. It was a natural progression to begin to consider, in new ways, the future of our company. How can we enhance the durability and the longevity of our buildings? How can our buildings contribute to the enduring qualities of this place? How can our company become a lasting participant in the future of this community?

Danny Hillis, the inventor of massive parallel computing, recently designed an immense clock that will tick once a year, bong once a century, and chime once a millennium. Its purpose is to illustrate a different way of thinking about time. It is intended to work for ten thousand years, roughly the span of human civilization to date, once it is built on the high-desert mountaintop property in eastern Nevada that has been acquired by the Long Now Foundation for that purpose. In Stewart Brand's book about the project, *The Clock of the Long Now*, the author says,

> Civilization is revving itself into a pathologically short
> attention span. The trend might be coming from the
> acceleration of technology, the short-horizon perspective
> of market-driven economics, the next election perspec-

tive of democracies, or the distractions of personal multi-tasking. All are on the increase. Some sort of balancing corrective to the short-sightedness is needed—some mechanism or myth that encourages the long view and the taking of long-term responsibility, where "the long term" is measured at least in centuries.[1]

This is how we're thinking about our community, our business, and our buildings. This is how we're beginning to think about problem solving, too. Big problems don't often respond to short-term bursts of energy. Problems take on a different cast when we put them into a long-term perspective. Hillis points out that difficult problems become impossible if you think about them in two- or five-year terms, as we usually do, but they become easier if you think in fifty-year terms:

> This category of problems includes nearly all the great ones of our time: The growing disparities between haves and have-nots, widespread hunger, dwindling freshwater resources, ethnic conflict, global organized crime, loss of biodiversity, and so on. Such problems were slow to arrive, and they can only be solved at their own pace.[2]

The long-term approach breeds optimism and resolve. From the short-term vantage point, sometimes it looks like we've crossed a line—there's no way we could ever go back and no way we could take steps big enough to matter. Sprawl is a good example. How could we possibly reverse or change the haphazard cycles of urban and suburban growth of the past several decades?

If we think in sufficiently long time frames, we can see how cycles of development and restoration work. Take the Martha's Vineyard town of Chilmark, for example, where I lived for twenty-five years. A little more than a century ago the town had three thousand people and eight brick factories, and there was not a tree in sight from one end of town to the other. The voracious appetites of grazing sheep and burning brick kilns had turned forest to pasture. Today the population has declined by two-thirds, there is no industry, and the town is 90 percent wooded. It's an entirely different landscape—not better or worse necessarily, but certainly far more diverse. Chilmark is a living example of the extent to which landscapes and communities can change over time.

That change happened by chance. Others happen by choice. Making new landscapes and shaping new communities takes twenty-five, fifty, even a hundred years. Here on the Vineyard we can begin the process of restoration at the same time that we create a New Vineyard in accordance with the Island Plan—a New Vineyard perhaps made up of villages, farms, and wilderness like the old one, but certainly incorporating what we determine is best about technology and the modern economy. We can't do this by turning back the clock; instead, we must turn it forward. We need to imagine a way that is economically robust—Realtors need to continue to sell, builders need to continue to build, property rights must be respected, and everyday rhythms of life must be preserved while culture and character are, too. Can we imagine a future like that—a future that does not turn its back on technology but employs it to invent a place we can love and care for without loving it to death?

To do so will require a bold vision that can be appreciated, implemented, measured, and adjusted over decades and centuries. Its success will require a cooperative commitment shared by community stakeholders. This kind of vision may be rare, but it does exist. It's the vision of the cathedral builders. If effectively placed among a community of stakeholders, its power to shape the economic and cultural life of a region may be monumental.

Thinking like cathedral builders, whose work would not be completed in their lifetimes, has become our seventh cornerstone principle.

Some ancient cathedrals took centuries to build. Their builders had endless social, political, economic, technical, and climatic factors to contend with. The work continued as the cast of characters changed, the master builder died, wars were fought, and regimes changed. These remarkably complex undertakings somehow continued. The perceived rewards were great.

Regardless of the personal returns that accrued to each participant, cathedrals stand as important community anchors. The great ones evoke a sense of permanence and architectural grandeur, reminding us of a vision so strong it could be maintained over time.

In the case of a company, it's fair to ask why longevity and survival matter. Why not let the company die when it seems that it no longer has a purpose? To arrive at an answer we must ask other questions: What is our company? What is its purpose?

More than anything else, South Mountain Company is a community, a community whose purpose will never end. Its legal structure takes the form of an employee-owned cooperative corporation. But its motivation revolves around the web of relationships in its internal community and in the larger community of which it is a part. The people who are part of South Mountain and the people whom it affects have ongoing relationships with the company. These relationships overlap, and I don't imagine, for instance, that there will ever be a particular day when everyone in the company will be ready to retire. There will never be a moment when our clients' houses cease to need maintenance, alteration, or addition. We will never complete the learning that can allow us to make better buildings and build a better economy. It is highly unlikely that we will look around someday and say, "Hey, we did it. All is well. We committed to one another and to this island, and now we're all fine and it's fine, too. The job is done." Because these things won't happen, we are organized around the idea of maintaining and perpetuating our community for one another and for future generations.

Arie de Geus, former head of the Strategic Planning Group at Royal Dutch/Shell, is considered to be the person who originated the concept of the "learning organization." He agrees in *The Living Company* that a company is primarily a community and that its purposes are longevity and developing its potential. To produce both profitability (a means to those ends) and longevity, he says, we must attend to the processes that build community. He goes on:

> Founders and managers of long-lived companies, a hundred years or more in the past, did not link their values to a particular product, service, or line of work. They knew, or sensed, that the life mission of a work community was not to produce a particular product or service, but to survive: to perpetuate itself as a work community.[3]

One of the key elements of community creation at South Mountain is our policy of hiring future owners as opposed to "just" employees. We envision people who enter the company staying in the company and becoming owners. We don't know what they, as the perpetuators, will do or what they will produce, but the essence of our collective enterprise will survive in them.

Regions, towns, neighborhoods, and individuals are heavily impacted when a business closes its doors. Only forty years passed between the time my grandfather started his business and the time it began to be sold off and shuttled around. The community he had developed was left unprotected. Once we have succeeded at the job of creating community, our new job becomes its maintenance, enhancement, and perpetuation. When we build a business, we are building a legacy.

Peter Senge, author of *The Fifth Discipline*, the book that popularized the idea of the learning organization, writes about the difference between a company that is seen as a "machine to make money" and a company that is perceived as a "living being" with a heart and a mind:

> Seeing a company as a machine implies that it will run down unless it is re-built by management. Seeing

a company as a living being means that it is capable of regenerating itself, of continuity as an identifiable entity beyond its present members.[4]

When the employees own the company, it becomes that kind of living entity from early on, and it is, we hope, better prepared for the journey to come.

The Sabbatical

I thrive on the clamor of work. It feels good when people poke their heads in to ask me a question while the phone is ringing, a dozen e-mails need replies, and the to-do list is long. But I like it when the dust settles, too, like at dawn on the day I'm traveling somewhere. On those days, I usually come to the office to collect my computer and a few last-minute items. My desk is clean and spare (for a change), almost everything's done that needs to be, and I have extra time on my hands before I go (sometimes). I've fed the stray cat and made the coffee, and now I can wonder what I forgot to pack. I sit for a few minutes, thinking, feet up on the desk.

During one of those early-morning musings nearly ten years ago, I had a thought: When our youngest child, Sophie, went off to college, maybe Chris and I could take a year away, and I would take a year's sabbatical from work. I didn't know what we would do or whether I really meant it, but the idea stuck; it kept returning. As the time neared, it came into focus. It was clear to me that I wanted to write a book about business, but I had no idea what shape it would take. It also occurred to me that after many years of employee ownership, perhaps there was now potential for the people at South Mountain to emerge from beneath the constraints of my leadership and begin to grow into a new level of responsibility and independence. My absence might provide the space and opportunity.

It would be the first time in twenty-eight years I'd been away for more than a few weeks. Planning for the sabbatical within the company began to make us wonder what would happen to South Mountain when my working days were done, and it was the first time we seriously considered the "hit-by-a-bus" scenario. We bought a $1 million key-man life insurance policy to give some room for recovery in the event of my death. It was to be the beginning of a long march toward succession, an expression of intent by our small workplace community to endure beyond my tenure.

Being away from my work allowed me to write this book and allowed the company to do remarkable new work. It turned out that instead of a yearlong sabbatical, we took off two consecutive winters. I arrived in Vermont the first winter with milk crates full of books, a case of Jack Daniels with special JOHN ABRAMS SABBATICAL labels that was a going-away gift from my co-workers, and big questions about myself: Having been engaged in business so long, could I disengage, and sit, and focus, and write? If I could, would I like it? Could I leave the business alone enough that the kind of growth we were imagining would have room to happen? Would things go well without me, or would there be dissension and resentment? Should I just drink all the whiskey and not worry about it?

I began to read the books in the milk crates, and it turned out that I kept reading—solid—for nearly two months, gulping down pages like a thirsty man who had just found water. Gradually I buckled down to work and found myself running down a series of blind alleys, but each time, before backing out, I scavenged and collected useful material. Occasionally I found alleys that led through. I was able to focus, I was having fun (some days), and I wasn't thinking obsessively about the company.

My primary diversion from writing was skiing for an hour or two most days. The joy of skiing is the search—for fresh snow, for new lines, for feelings of grace. "Finding a line" is the act of planning a descent while within the act of descent. One snowy spring day in Stowe, Vermont, with my son Pinto, my grandson Kalib, and Kalib's friend Nate, I ducked off the Cliff Trail into tight trees. We caught a little north-facing pine-tree-filled pocket where the sun had been refused admission and the snow was still deep and soft. We hadn't known this glade was there. We were lucky and hit it right for a sweet run. There's something sublime about picking your way through thickly wooded glades or crossing a high traverse on a powder day, looking for that perfect line. The likelihood of that perfect line is slim because the variables are huge—the terrain, the snow quality, the temperature, the wind, how you're feeling, how you hit it—but when you get lucky and find the line, when each turn is smooth and you're reading the terrain and looking three turns ahead, never seeing the tips of your skis but only the path you're about to create, your mind picking the routes and your body making the adjustments, the pleasure of effortless flow mixes with the thrill of exploration. Each line is new and different and unique; it is being invented as you go.

Writing this book has been like that for me. Early on, I was lost in a blizzard. As I began to understand what I meant it to be and where I was headed, and I felt myself arriving somewhere, it started to come into alignment. I gradually got my legs beneath me and learned to maneuver—tentative turns at first, but with gathering speed and fluidity as I began to know the terrain and sense the outcomes.

It was good to be away.

Things were going well at South Mountain, but there was confusion and stress. Some employees felt overburdened and believed other employees weren't pulling their weight. Things fell through the cracks. The management system we had devised to cover my absence was flawed. Those troubles did not obscure the fact that when I returned in April, I came back to a better company than the one I'd left. There was tremendous pride and good feeling. Some people had truly stepped up, produced, and paved the way to new transitions.

The time between the two sabbaticals was devoted to picking up the pieces, gathering ourselves, making adjustments, and putting our heads together to prepare for round two. As we approached my second departure, the energy was palpable and the path was clear.

Writing about the company also gave me a chance to consider the company's future. Back on the Vineyard, an extraordinary group of dedicated and gifted people was building on the cornerstones, making the foundation for that future. The development and growth the first winter had been halting, slow, step by step. The second time through it was dramatically different, bold and decisive. We had replaced our larger management committee with a three-person group comprising the people who had taken on the most responsibility. This group navigated effectively.

My absence opened a floodgate, setting free a powerful stream of new management approaches. A greater sense of responsibility and a deeper understanding of collaboration spread throughout the company. A new South Mountain was under construction. I was excited to return and lend a hand.

My time away was a period of tremendous growth and change for the company. When I returned I was afraid we would settle back to where we were before. We haven't. We continue to decentralize and refine management, and to create new systems and practices to prepare us for the eventual transition from Generation One to Generation Two.

It took all of eighteen years for my co-owners to assume fully the burden of responsibility that my absence demanded. During those years, we developed a clearer sense of company values and a stronger set of relationships. We may spend another eighteen years, or far less—who can say?—making the actual transition from me, as leader, to whatever or whomever is next. That's okay. Our job is to ensure that the values that are now embedded are accompanied by the skill and the motivation to practice them over a long period of time, without my leadership, and to go beyond where I have led. My time away helped us identify what needed work so that we can tackle those areas gradually and thoroughly. Like cathedral builders.

Large organizations—corporations, governments, universities, professional sports teams—are expected to handle changing regimes and leadership. Small businesses are not; they are notoriously dependent on their founder. If we begin to reduce reliance on the founder and leader of a company slowly and steadily, over time, we may be able to manage organic transitions instead of having transitions play themselves out in sudden and unexpected ways. People who are new to the process have time to watch and learn. As my co-owner Mike Drezner said:

> A group of people of goodwill and character can learn new roles and make worthy decisions. They can become facilitators and leaders. Making them full participants is a part of the journey, the transition to a different way of thinking. During the sabbatical period there was intensive structural and psychological change. New committees were formed. New attitudes developed.

The sabbatical, and the planning and internal growth it stimulated, was not the beginning of a subtle exit strategy but rather an unvarnished attempt to begin the preservation and perpetuation of a valuable community and to take it beyond its founder. It would be false modesty to downplay my influence and importance to the company, but it would be equally shortsighted to overlook the role I play as an impediment to the assumption of responsibility by and the professional development of others.

A Legacy Gathering

In the fall of 2003, Marjorie Kelly, publisher of *Business Ethics* magazine and author of *The Divine Right of Capital*, gathered thirty people to spend an evening and a day discussing the issues of legacy and to launch the Legacy Project, which was intended to be an ongoing exploration of this subject. The fundamental question was: How can the values

embedded in a socially responsible business be maintained when it is
sold or when the founder retires?

Marjorie described the backdrop in a 2003 article in *Business Ethics:*

> It was April 11, 2000 when the legacy problem burst
> into view. That was the day the Ben and Jerry's board
> was forced by law to sell the premier socially oriented
> firm in America to multinational Unilever, against the
> wishes of CEO Ben Cohen. In the three years since
> 4-11, Ben and Jerry's has seen its social mission begin
> to seep away—Unilever has laid off one in five B&J
> employees, stopped donating 7.5 percent of profits to
> the Ben and Jerry Foundation, and hired a CEO Cohen
> did not approve of. It's been a wakeup call in socially
> responsible business circles, where preventing mission
> loss when a company changes hands has become the
> problem of the hour.[5]

She observed that we were entering a new era of socially responsible
business, one beyond the founders' era:

> Entrepreneurs have met the challenge of how to manage
> in socially responsible ways, but few even recognize the
> new challenge ahead: how to create the architectural
> forms that can hold social mission for generation after
> generation to come.[6]

The questions posed at the gathering were compelling to me because
they were so closely related to the questions we were grappling with at
South Mountain. Mostly, the discussion was about the kind of corporate entities we must create to encourage long-term social responsibility. Everyone there was familiar with the recent tendency of
socially responsible businesses to lose their independence, and all were

concerned that the important gains of the corporate social responsibility movement would be swallowed up and lost.

Leslie Christian of Portfolio 21 Investments in Portland, Oregon, described her work on a new corporate structure. She has created Upstream 21, a Berkshire Hathaway type of holding company that could be a guiding light for a new ethic. It began as a private company that could later go public, chartered with the purpose of serving the public good rather than maximizing return to shareholders. The ownership structure differentiates active from passive owners. Different share classes have different voting rights. People who work there and direct investors get one kind of share. If you leave or trade your shares, they become a different class of shares. According to Christian:

> A basic assumption about business is you can't responsibly invest without majority control. What would it be like to have a deep and trusting partnership without control? Control is a really old model. What are our deeper assumptions about how business has to operate?[7]

There were other inventive schemes proposed. There were also discussions about employee ownership transitions, and how difficult it is for people to make the cultural shift from being employees to being owners. After watching these transitions for more than two decades, and hearing reports from others, I've come to the conclusion that everyone is a leader, just as everyone is a designer, if they are brought to a seat at the table. The problem I see is the abrupt way in which the change usually takes place: The owner sells to the employees, and suddenly they're the owners. If the legacy begins as part of the early organizational planning, it can happen gradually, so that it's a continuum rather than an event. This allows time for training, for the development of decision-making and leadership skills, for the formation of social bonds, and for the emergence of collaborative management systems.

That's how it has happened at Carris Reels and that's what's happening now at Of Grape and Grain, the only locally owned wine and liquor store in Aspen, Colorado. It was started by Gary Plumley in 1975 and is a community fixture. At sixty-eight Plumley decided to restructure the business as an employee-owned cooperative after his wife read an article in a business magazine about Select Machine in Ohio.

Plumley did a valuation of the business and arrived at an agreeable figure. He was not interested in maximizing the value, but rather in finding the right place, the place that would work for him, for the employees, and for the business. He had a small group of committed longtime employees, much younger than he, and they agreed to make a down payment of one-third the valued price. They were each able to come up with $10,000 in cash, and a local bank financed the rest. The loan is being paid back from company revenues. When this loan is repaid, they will take on another chunk, until the employees own 100 percent. One of the employee-owners is Plumley, who continues to be a central part of the business, continues to benefit from ongoing profits, and is engaged in training the other three in all aspects of managing the business. Plumley plans to retire in five or six years.

Plumley's enthusiastic co-owners are in their thirties and forties. "Gary has taken it 30 years and we want to take it another 30," said Jonathan Chaplin, in a profile in the local *Aspen Times*. Plumley and his co-owners are passionate about wine. They inventory more than seven hundred labels. Not all are high end; at least sixty cost less than $10, an uncommonly large selection of inexpensive wine. They buy in quantity, work on their distributors to keep prices low, and minimize the markup. And, as Chaplin said, "We love turning people onto wines, whether it's a $6 bottle or a $600 bottle." They taste it all, and they travel to source lesser-known local wines from Europe and elsewhere.

They seem to like the new structure, too. As for Plumley, he finds it very satisfying, so far. He says the big question for him was whether four people could really run a business together; he's pretty certain now that the answer is yes. He feels the transition has been seamless for the customers. One thing has changed: Although they didn't expect it, after making loan payments they still had a dividend to distribute the first year, and sales, which used to be steady, have been growing every month. Plumley doesn't know what to attribute it to; he finds it puzzling.

I suggested that maybe his new co-owners are more invested in the business now that they own a piece of it. Could that be? "Oh, yeah, they're far more motivated, and this whole thing has created great PR in town, too."

That might be two reasons right there. And as Plumley and his co-owners build capacity, it may get better still.

Someone at the Legacy Project meeting noted that the reason most entrepreneurs form companies is not to *make* money. They form companies because everyone needs to work, and this is the kind of work they like to do. That's surely how Plumley's career path developed. As John Logue of the Ohio Employee Ownership Center said, "The primary legacy of employee ownership is the legacy of a retiring owner concerned about the economic security of people he worked with, the people who built the business." So let's put those two together. The entrepreneur starts a business and begins to build it. That's what entrepreneurs do. He or she brings in people to help, with the idea that they will become owners. When it's clear the business is going to be a success, arrangements are made for the gradual sale of the company to the employees. This is the path we have taken at South Mountain by chance rather than by design. We threw in the ingredients and stirred the soup. Only now have we come to understand the recipe.

Most small businesses that endure are family businesses passed from parent to child. As family structure changes and our society offers broader opportunities, however, fewer businesses are passed down from generation to generation. In craft-based businesses like ours, and the information businesses of the new economy, the employees *are* the business. The development of the business is synonymous with the evolution of the employees—our own unfolding, blooming, and ripening at work. The business is a community, and one of the essential reasons for its existence is to maintain the community it has created. Employee ownership holds within it the seeds of continuity. But we must plan for succession.

According to the Federal Reserve, 50,000 US businesses changed hands in 2001. That number rose to 350,000 in 2005 and is projected to increase to 750,000 by 2009. We baby boomers own millions of businesses, and the time has come, or is coming soon, for many of us to pass them on. A PricewaterhouseCoopers survey of owners of companies in the $5 to $150 million range indicated that 65 percent of them plan to leave their companies within ten years, two-thirds of those in the next five years. But very few had begun to work on succession plans. There seems to be all too little intergenerational thinking in US business today. There should be more, because these transitions take time.

SMC Ten-Year Plan

During my second sabbatical, Deirdre Bohan was the chair of our management committee. She continues to be (the management committee consists of Deirdre, me, Mike Drezner, and Jim Vercruysse as standing members and one rotating member of the owners' group, who serves for a six- to nine-month term).

In 2005, mostly at the urging of Deirdre and the rest of the management committee, I prepared SMC's first formal Year in Review. It included our company goals for 2006 and 2007. In 2006 we expanded the review to include goals not only for the upcoming year but also for the next five and ten. In 2007 we did the same, but this time we structured the report in terms of South Mountain's various departments and committees (eleven in all), with the one-year, five-year, and ten-year goals originating directly from these entities. The twenty-page 2007 report includes a number of tables and indicators as well as the goals and narrative.

This ongoing developing process has proven immensely valuable. Without it we wouldn't know (even if we're headed there) that we have a goal of being carbon-neutral by 2017, as I indicated in this book's introduction. In order to achieve that, it is our goal, by 2012, to know what we mean by *carbon-neutral*. It's not uncomplicated. There are many levels of possible compliance with this grand ideal.

The long-term planning we have begun is certain to grow more and more important in the complicated years to come. After two full decades of transitioning to shared ownership, we are now actively engaged in the exhilarating work of gradually shifting from Generation One to Generation Two.

Our 2007 Year in Review and Ten-Year Plan for South Mountain was completed just before I took some time off to work on this second edition. Working our way through that exercise remains an important way to reflect on where we've been (for certain) and where we're going (perhaps).

Here is the summary of where we see ourselves headed this year, in the next five years, and in ten years:

By the end of 2008
SMC will have dramatically shifted its emphasis, make-up, and operations from what it was 10 years before, having expanded from a company that had two major functions—Design and Construction—to a company that has six, having added Interiors, Renewable Energy and Window Sales, Lighting Design and Fabrication, and Teaching and Consulting Programs. We are more mature, stable, diverse, and prepared for the future than ever before.

The biggest differences we see at the end of 2007 from the end of 2006 are:
- Profits have increased dramatically, allowing us to do more of the things our mission calls for;

- Renewable energy promises to be a larger part of our mix than we previously imagined;
- Our new lighting design and manufacturing endeavor has come into focus and become more of a reality;
- Teaching and Consulting is beginning to show promise as a long-term potential profit center and driver of our mission.

Our overarching theme for 2008 is to continue to focus on our efforts to systematize and increase the effectiveness of our design and construction work, the bread and butter of the company. Big strides forward have been taken and it is essential to our future success that they continue. Our newer endeavors are on firmer footing because they are more contained, and because they began later in our evolution. In contrast, Design and Construction is large, complex, and has a long history, and therefore, if we are not thorough, vigilant, and change-oriented, it has the potential to suffer from calcification and inertia.

By the end of 2012

SMC will have established and fully integrated the several new endeavors we are currently developing, and they will have become a significant part of our workload and revenues. We will have made significant progress in our planning for transition to Generation Two leadership and our march toward the goal of becoming a carbon-neutral business (at least, by then, we hope to know what that truly means). Finally, we will have enlarged our contributions to the island community, and we will have moved from our current 32 employees and 16 owners to approximately 40 employees and approximately 26 owners.

By the end of 2017
SMC will be a strong, diverse carbon-neutral company of +/- 43 employees and +/- 30 owners deep into its Generation Two journey and prepared for John's retirement, which is likely to occur in the decade that follows. We will continue to be a leader in the post-peak-oil Vineyard economy and community, and we will have begun new endeavors that we have not even identified yet.

You notice the Generation Two theme. There is a new group of young employees whose task it will be to take us beyond what we, the first group of owners, has been able to accomplish. They are thoughtful, articulate, passionate, and irreverent.

As South Mountain progresses past my tenure, one issue sure to arise is that of identity. Small businesses tend to be identified not by their company name or brand, but by their leader. So it is with us, but the company has been gaining identity swiftly in recent years—for the last decade at least. Still, many identify it with John Abrams, and employees (and employee owners) often get asked, "Oh, so you work for John Abrams?" At a recent future owners' meeting one of them shared his great stock answer when confronted with that question: "No, I work for South Mountain Company, and so does he."

There you have it.

This "intergenerational yielding," as author Peter Barnes calls it, is a key to maintaining vitality. One of the difficulties with having such a stable workforce of long-term owners is the potential for cultural hardening of the arteries. The conservatism that comes with age can overtake our spirit of innovation, and the desire for security can cause us to become risk-averse. We, the owners and leaders of this company, must continue to welcome new leaders. We must look to younger people to do more than hold steady; the business must evolve if it is to continue to thrive. There must always be a fresh group to dare to innovate, and to carry on.

New Growth for New Endeavors

As I mentioned in chapter 4, we determined in 2003 that we had reached our optimum size. At the time, we had twenty-seven employees and $6 million in sales. The no-growth commitment did not last long. Today we have thirty-three employees and $8.4 million in sales. There is more growth ahead. Our plan predicts that in 2017 we will have forty-three employees, $9.5 million in sales, and thirty owners (a dramatic increase from the current seventeen).

What happened?

Two things. One was the realization, discussed above, that we need to bring in younger people to begin the transition to Generation Two. In addition, and after years of talking about it, we decided to begin new kinds of job creation that will make sense for aging carpenters as they get ready to stop running around on roofs and come in from the cold . . . but aren't yet ready to retire.

Two of these—South Mountain Renewables and Red Arrow Lamp— are well under way. Another—an educational and consulting arm—is beginning to percolate.

For thirty years we have provided solar, wind, and energy conservation to our design/build clients. Last year we began to offer these services to all Vineyard homes, businesses, and institutions. We are providing planning, design, installation, and service for small wind, solar electric, solar domestic hot water, and solar pool heating.

Renewable energy has entered a dramatic growth period. As a company, we think this is one of the most important things we can do. We have decided, for the foreseeable future, to pursue all opportunities for growth because of the importance of the endeavor. For now, it is thriving right out of the gate. The demand is great. We all seem to be waking up together to the understanding that, here in the twenty-first century, we must deploy renewable energy in as many ways, and as rapidly, as we can. We want to assure that, here on the island, we do this in the very best way for both our public and private clients.

Because load reduction (energy conservation) is the low-hanging fruit of decreasing dependence on fossil fuels, and the least expensive way to make progress, this is how we are conducting our service:

- When a potential client contacts us, we charge a predetermined fee to conduct a thorough energy audit of their property.
- We recommend efficiency improvements and renewable energy installation(s) for on-site energy production, and the client chooses which recommendations to implement.
- We do not recommend solar or wind installations without efficiency improvements first.
- Once decision making is complete, we handle all design, permitting, installation, and long-term maintenance.

Now that the energy conservation and renewables division is in full swing, we have begun to concentrate on Red Arrow Lamp, an effort to develop a line of elegant energy- and resource-efficient lamps and lighting fixtures designed and crafted by SMC.

Did you ever wish that you could find the perfect lamps and lighting fixtures? Did you ever sigh and say, "It just doesn't exist"? We have, over and over. In 1975, when we started designing and building houses, we also started designing and building in some of the lighting fixtures. Mostly, we liked what we built more than we liked what we could buy. We've done that ever since. It seemed a natural progression to turn this into a manufacturing effort that would fit the talents of aging carpenters and craftspeople. We figured, "Why not get serious about lighting and lamps, and develop of a line of them with a sense of sustainability in mind?"

Still deep in development, we have a long way to go. We have never made a product; we started in without knowing the first thing about it. We are learning how difficult and complex it is to actually create a product line—design, fabrication, naming, branding, labeling, testing, marketing, packaging, shipping, guarantees, customer service. All need analysis, distillation, and solutions. It requires a serious investment of time and money. To make it happen we have assembled a collaborative team with a variety of skills from within the company, and we use outside consultants when we run up against issues that exceed our limited knowledge. In March 2008 we completed our first floor lamp prototype—Red Arrow Lamp #0001. It's risky—will this ever pay for itself? It will be a while before we'll know.

Beyond lighting, we have begun to dip our toe into the deep water of education and consulting. I'll talk more about that in the final chapter.

The Cambium Network

My friend Jamie Wolf runs a design/build business in Connecticut that is similar to ours. He is part of the Cambium Network, a group of ten design/build companies across the country that have been meeting for more than a decade, once a year, for three days. The companies are spread out geographically, serve local territories, and don't compete with one another. For many years they would gather at one of the companies and spend their three days drilling deeply into that firm. The purpose was to uncover the secrets, the weaknesses, the obstacles, the difficulties—all that might stand in the way of achieving the owner's goals—as well as just plain helping one another and sharing stories, accumulated wisdom, practices, and discoveries. Their encounters have always been characterized by blunt honesty and unbridled sharing.

Sometimes they have gathered at more neutral locations and tackled important issues that affect all of them. Each year a different participating company organizes the proceedings. In 2006 it was Jamie's turn. He proposed to invite the group to Martha's Vineyard, in February (a bold beginning—the Vineyard can be mighty bleak then) and to invite our company to engage for the three days with the others and share our methods and our model. This was the first time an outside company had been involved. Jamie felt that exposure to us would be an eye-opener, especially because the other businesses are run by people with such diverse points of view—from progressives to conservatives to fundamentalist Christians. We would certainly be on the far left end of this spectrum, and we were a bit hesitant. Still, we agreed, because Jamie has been a great friend to our company. Mostly we thought we were doing Jamie a favor.

Nothing could have been farther from the truth. Several of us—the members of our management committee—spent about forty hours holed up with these business fanatics: lunches, dinners, and all-day sessions. It was a significant time investment, but it turned out, despite our initial misgivings, to be a pathbreaking, revealing experience.

As preparation for the session, Jamie had sent each member firm a copy of the first edition of this book. The views expressed here proved a bit radical for some of these businesspeople. But each had read it thoroughly, digested it, and thought deeply about it. I knew this was going to be different than I imagined five minutes after I walked into the hotel conference room the evening they arrived.

A man in his late fifties approached me. He introduced himself in a quiet voice. "I'm Pete Schrader," he said. "I'm very happy to be here and to meet you." We exchanged a few pleasantries and then he said, "I admire what you've done with the ownership of your company. It's hard to turn our companies over to our employees."

"It is," I said, "but it's a great group of deserving people and I have a long time to get the job done."

"Not me," said Pete. "I have Parkinson's disease and I need to get it done in the next five years."

That's the way it went.

The first day was devoted to one hour for each company—where they'd been for the past year, a review of their financials and momentous changes, comments from the others, and questions about progress on issues that had come up in past years. Nothing was sacred—all was revealed. The second day was devoted to us. They dug in—probed, parried, and queried. They dug deep, looking for the soft underbelly, the path to the fatal flaws. They found a firm foundation, but they uncovered plenty of grist for the mill. A long and fertile discussion concluded with a novel solution for the weakness that we had long held to be our most difficult and insoluble—how to forge a systematic connection between our design and construction operations. It was thrilling, to say the least.

During these first two days I heard viewpoints expressed that were sharply different from my own, over and over. But I never heard any bigotry, never heard any disrespect, and never once saw a big ego on display. This was soulful human communication at its best, designed to uplift, inspire, and improve the lives of everyone in the room. The next day they invited us to join them on their journey going forward, and we accepted. We are now a member company.

One of the reasons we signed up is that we see great potential in this group—potential to change the world as well as potential to change the individual companies within it. Improving one another's companies has been the group's focus. That's what offers constant value and makes the space that prepare the group—I think—to do even more.

Some of the group members, well to the right of us on the political spectrum, think differently from us in many ways. But wary as we were, we could only see splendidly open-minded people with stellar hearts bursting with compassion. Their commitment to learning, sharing, and supporting transcended—in an uncomplicated way—all the differences. It became clear how little those differences matter. How powerful is that? What can we harness that power to achieve? I'm convinced that we cannot even begin to imagine it all, at least I can't. It is an example of deeply shared core values overcoming differences. It's clear to me that the heart and soul of America transcends red and blue, and the Cambium Network is a shining example, a wonderful model.

I sent this story to my friend Bill Greider. He wrote back and said,

> One of my best moments occurred a year or so back at my 50th high school reunion (gasp). This is small-town Ohio, an affluent suburb of Cincinnati, very self-satisfied and very, very Republican. The event was surprisingly pleasant. Everyone mellows with age, even me.
>
> I was approached by an old nemesis—a very hardheaded right winger with whom I used to argue every question, from race to Social Security. Johnny approached in peace. "I thought you might be interested to know," he said, "that Oscar [brother] and I sold the family business to the employees." I was aghast. This was an old company, not large but profitable, the classic situation where none of the children were interested in keeping it going.
>
> I asked all the skeptical questions and, to my amazement, Johnny gave all the right answers. Oscar wanted to sell to a larger company that would doubtless have paid more, but John argued that this would doom the firm. Eventually, it would be hacked up. Their father's and grandfather's lifework destroyed.
>
> Besides, he said, these employees knew how to run things since many had been with them for decades. The two brothers signed a 10-year management contract (required by the bank) but after four years it

was obvious they weren't needed. So the bank agreed to cut them loose and the employees are managing themselves.

This ain't utopia. But it tells me we are preaching a doctrine that is deeply appealing to human nature, regardless of religion or politics or even social class. That's what you have experienced too, I think.

In February 2008 Deirdre and I attended our third meeting of the Cambium Network. It was held in Saratoga Springs, New York, and hosted by the Schrader Company in nearby Burnt Hills, owned by Pete Schrader. We were truly impressed at this small bedrock-American company. A group of sharp young people seemed well prepared to steward it onward. Pete seemed comfortable. They are thinking like cathedral builders and erecting their own.

Thinking Like Republicans

When Barry Goldwater lost the presidential election in 1964, a group of wealthy and influential Republicans decided to mount a long, patient effort to move the country to the right and wrest control of the US government from moderates and liberals. They coined the term *Moral Majority* and formed the Christian Coalition, whose leader Ralph Reed was once called "the right hand of god" by *Time* magazine. They appealed to young intellectuals with a conservative bent, took them under their wing, supported their work and research, and gathered them in work–live think tanks that created cadres of hardworking, close-knit political allies. It was brilliant, and it worked. Ronald Reagan's election in 1980 was a beginning of their success, the Republican Revolution of 1994 continued the journey, and George W. Bush's election in 2000 was perhaps the crowning achievement of this highly effective cathedral-building project.

On the Vineyard we are involved with a similar effort that has a very different purpose. A new program run by a family foundation, the Martha's Vineyard Vision Fellowship, supports the higher education of Vineyard high school grads and midcareer people who share a particular interest in some aspect of sustainability. The kids selected spend three seasons of each year dedicated to their education; each summer they complete internships at Vineyard nonprofits and progressive businesses. They are fully supported. Every week, all summer long, they get together and share a meal with one another and their mentors. The idea is that after their education is complete they will return—some of them—and help to build the kind of institutions and companies we need. This will be a cadre of like-minded individuals who care about the Vineyard and its future, who have bonds with one another, and who know how to work together. We are building a cultural force. This, too, is a long-term cathedral building project, a localized version, with a different point of view, of what the conservative edge of the Republican party did after 1964.

Cathedral building can be put to nearly any purpose we want.

JOHN ABRAMS

· 9 ·

Committing to the Business of Place

Children left un-attended will be given 2 shots of espresso and a free puppy.
—SIGN IN A COFFEE SHOP IN ASHEVILLE, NORTH CAROLINA

With ten seats crowded into the small cabin, Cape Air's Cessna 402 is built for neither comfort nor speed. Its twin engines putt like an old Evinrude outboard. Roughly fit aluminum is fastened with rows of rivets and screws, and the wear of years ripples across the wings—no shining true surfaces here, just sturdy no-frills construction and practicality.

I'm alone in the plane with the pilot; nobody else is heading from Boston to Martha's Vineyard on this sparkling clear April afternoon. This is the off-season. The "shoulder" season has not yet begun. We motor out toward the runway. The little Cessna scampers among the 747s and DC-9s like a Border Collie herding buffalo. The pilot briefs me and we take our place in line. USAir takes off. Delta follows. Continental. United. Our turn now. We leave the ground.

From above, Logan looks gritty with the debris and disorder of renovation and construction. Boston looks like a fully assembled puzzle, with pieces that fit together miraculously. We turn south. I'm mesmerized for a time by the great wind turbine on the tip of the Hull

Peninsula, gracefully powering small-town life, and by the juxtaposition of the simple turning of those blades with the complex operations of the airport, city, and Big Dig just behind us. We make our way to three thousand feet. The plane bounces and buffets on changing air currents like a mountain bike on dirt-road corduroy. The brilliant blue of oceans, inlets, lakes, and rivers mixes sweetly with the pastel greens, reds, and browns of fields, cranberry bogs, and woods.

As we approach Buzzards Bay, I see the Vineyard ahead and the Elizabeth Islands strung out to the west, beating a path to little Cuttyhunk, the outermost. Before we reach the Vineyard Sound, the pilot begins to drop altitude. We pass above Woods Hole at twenty-two hundred feet. The Vineyard shoreline ahead is crisp and complex, each crenellation recognizable. The North Shore bluffs are sullied by an occasional house. Then more houses come into view, scattered like chess pieces swept off a board. But mostly I see woods and fields and water. Those who fly over the Vineyard for the first time are often amazed at how undeveloped it seems, how much space is left untouched.

We're close to home and flying low. As we descend, a more detailed picture comes into view. The small towns at the island's edges are clustered around steeples on shore and masts in the harbors. The wooded middle is broken up by the gravel pit, the high school, the hockey rink, and the small industrial park. The airport is just ahead. We hit the ground, bounce back up, and settle down for good. The plane slides to a halt. I unfasten my belt, crouch and shuffle to the rear, duck to exit, and take the few steep steps down. Home again. Standing on this ground brings a special comfort.

It wasn't always that way. When we moved to the Vineyard in the 1970s—from the hills of Vermont and the mountains of British Columbia before that—it felt, at first, like an alien, one-dimensional landscape and a parochial culture. But, happily, our work has kept us here long enough for us to begin to know this place in a deeper way.

What Kind of Community?

As we came to each cornerstone and as our company became more connected to our community, I began to think differently about the products of our work. My affinity for old structures led me to wonder, as we made new ones, what their fate would be. Would the buildings endure and be used for centuries like the venerable barns I loved? Would the summer houses we made, like the hallowed old shingle-style houses of the Cape and Islands, become family compounds that would be enjoyed for generations by extended families? The aspiration of my twenties—to live in another time—evolved into a different quest: to craft buildings that were sturdy, timeless, and beloved, and to imagine how people would live in them and care for them. Emphasis shifted from past to future. Our houses began to have an eclectic character that linked each to the others. They did not mimic the old; in fact, they were intended to be buildings for tomorrow. It has been said that the first rule of intelligent tinkering is to save all the parts. Salvage materials and solar panels—we saved old sensibilities and mixed in new technologies.

Like a hound picking up a scent, I seemed to be homing in on a new way of thinking about the future of our buildings, which is less about the structures themselves and more about the places they will inhabit. I was becoming attached to the Vineyard, and as I began to sense that my future was tied to the island's, I became increasingly invested in its fate. We know enough to make buildings that will be around for our grandchildren's grandchildren, but we don't know what kind of world theirs will be. What kind of landscape will surround them? How will people make a living and how will they govern? How will their energy be supplied and how will they move around? Will they feel safe and secure, satisfied and fulfilled, and will they treat one another with kindness and civility? Wherever you may be, these questions are equally relevant. Our business inquiries were leading to a new understanding: that an essential aspect of commerce is building community. We had assumed, in the 1960s, that the choice was between accepting an existing community (or society) and creating a new one; now, in the late '70s, it was dawning on me that we could participate in designing the future of the community we'd joined, not just the buildings that would be a part of it.

What kind of community will it be? This much we can know: It won't be the vanished American past I had been so taken with. I think back to our endeavors of the '60s and early '70s, when we had distanced ourselves from the mainstream culture. Today, in 2008, I think we're still working on the same project, but with the refinements of age and new understandings, a sense of cultural integration rather than isolation, and, most important, a different relationship to time. Urgency has given way to determination, and our forays among the remains of the past have evolved into purposeful commercial endeavors with an eye to the future. Forty years later we're still working on the same cathedral.

The Texture of Community

In our early years we had a small fleet of character-rich and mechanically challenged vehicles, including a '55 Pontiac Stratostreak, a '65 International Harvester flatbed, and a Dodge panel truck that had previously been abused by the local utility. All needed constant attention. On more occasions than I wished I would find myself in Ken Dietz's radiator shop. When you said good-bye to Ken he always replied, "Fly low." Stay under the radar. Ken died years ago and there is no longer a radiator shop on the island, but Martha's Vineyard remains dependent on many small businesses like his.

Businesses of every sort are woven into the fabric of this community. Bait-and-tackle shops mix with upscale galleries and antiques stores. Tailors, truckers, plumbers, and pet groomers all have their places. There are a slew of Realtors, a boatload of builders, more bakeries than banks, too many T-shirt shops, and one cobbler. Farmers and fishermen still harvest from land and sea. Boatbuilders still hew to a line. These small family businesses are the ballast and texture of the community. They create a kind of gravity, grounding and stabilizing us, and glue, cementing us together.

But at the same time there is, for some, a sense of nonreality about the Vineyard. People sometimes ask why anyone would devote so much work and effort to a place that is widely perceived to be just a playground for the wealthy. While it surely is that for some, it is many other things as well. For me, four distinct elements further define the Vineyard: It is the place I know; it has "fifth migration" qualities; it is socially complex; and it is in fair condition.

The Place I Know

I have lived in fourteen different towns and cities in my life, but I have lived on Martha's Vineyard for well more than half of my fifty-eight years. Although I will always be a "washashore," my children grew up here (one was born here), my grandchildren are now growing up here, and I am beginning to comprehend this place, just a little, through long association.

As a kid I was fascinated by geography. I pored over relief maps and atlases, wondering about all the mysterious places, memorizing place-names and populations. In my late teens and early twenties I loved nothing more than being on the road. I still wonder what's around the next bend. So how did a wanderer like me get hooked on a tiny island? The Vineyard seems small and limited, but after thirty-three years I still find new dirt roads I've never been down, new trails to walk for the first time, and new vistas to take my breath away. I've come to think that maybe to know many places, we need to deeply know at least one.

Our relationship with the Vineyard is rich and complex. If Chris and I were to move soon, we might be able to have as thorough a relationship with one more place in our lifetime, if we were lucky. But that is not likely. Here, we've watched our children and their friends grow up, and we've watched the children have children. We see them in the streets, at the grocery store, and at the movies. This experience is neither replaceable nor replicable. Most of the people of South Mountain are as deeply connected to the Vineyard as I am. Some were born here. Others have thrown in their lot here. It's the place that we know.

Fifth-Migration Qualities

Author Peter Wolf says that Americans are in the fifth national migration of our country's history.[1] From 1600 to 1785 discontented Europeans and enslaved Africans settled here. From 1750 to 1890 the poorest Americans pushed westward. From 1820 to 1920 millions of job seekers moved into industrial cities during a century of urban concentration. Between 1930 and 1990 one hundred million people drove out of town and created the suburbs. The fifth migration, which began in the 1970s, is a dispersal—across the country, Wolf says, millions are streaming into communities distinguished by physical beauty, abundant recreation opportunities, clean air and water, and relatively few social problems. I would add to Wolf's list the following attractive qualities: tolerance, diversity, and educational opportunity.

The towns and cities that are the object of this fifth migration are the most desirable places to live. As the US economy has shifted from manufacturing to information and service, many cities, towns, and regions are welcoming the rapidly expanding "creative class." Sociologists Richard Florida, in *The Rise of the Creative Class*, and Paul Ray and Sherry Ruth Anderson, in *The Cultural Creatives*, hypothesize that this identifiable group now includes forty to fifty million Americans.[2] Florida defines the two parts of this new class. He says that the core of it includes scientists and engineers, university professors, poets and novelists, artists, craftspeople, entertainers, actors, designers, and architects, as well as the thought leadership of modern society, including nonfiction writers, editors, cultural figures, think-tank researchers, analysts, and other opinion makers. The other part includes "creative professionals" who work in a wide range of knowledge-intensive industries such as high-tech sectors, financial services, the legal and health-care professions, and business management. More and more businesses are locating in the places where these people (the resource that business needs most in this new economy) want to be. Centers of creativity are developing in such locations throughout urban, suburban, and rural America. Florida calls them "creative centers" and notes that they are thriving, but not for such traditional economic reasons as access to natural resources or transportation routes or tax breaks and business incentives. Rather, they are succeeding largely because people want to live there.

Along with being a resort community, Martha's Vineyard has all the qualities listed above. It is safe, beautiful, and culturally rich. It maintains strong characteristics of community. Many live here for that simple reason; some seasonal residents return year after year as much for the community as for the beauty. My friend Jamie vacations here each June with his family and says the first thing he does when he arrives is to get a local paper and catch up, because our community is more real to him than his own! "You face all the same issues we do, but there is a tangible sense that you can talk about them as a community and work together to do something about them at a scale that makes accomplishing something feel possible." Whether we can solve the issues we face as a community is always in question, but at least they get fully aired out.

The Vineyard has those fifth-migration qualities that make it an attractive place to be.

Social Complexity

It's interesting to discover that the Vineyard is also socially complex. A friend who grew up in a poor rural area says he's from a place "where most of the pickup trucks were up on cement blocks and the houses all had wheels." Before my family and I moved to Martha's Vineyard, we lived in several rural areas that fit that description—down-at-the-heels regions that had seen better days and saw little opportunity to restore what had once been vigorous rural economies driven by farming, fishing, ranching, or logging. The Vineyard is cleaner, almost whitewashed; it has lots of open space mixed with spruced-up towns, thanks to the thriving tourist economy that replaced the declining rural farming and fishing heritage. But this new economy, ironically, is helping an agricultural and craft-based revival occur as the demand for fresh food and authentic experience grows.

Although it looks pretty spiffy, it's not so rosy. The junk-cars-and-plastic-toys-in-the-yard look may be less prevalent, but it's just a matter of space. In most poor rural areas, there is room to spread out, so the stuff of peoples' lives is more visible. In resort communities with high land values, space is at a premium. The Vineyard can more aptly be compared to a city, which has poor neighborhoods dense with people and other, more sparsely populated areas where the well-to-do folks live and/or vacation. This is not a wealthy county. Of the other thirteen counties in Massachusetts, half have higher median incomes than the Vineyard, and none (except the farther-out island of Nantucket) is a more expensive place to live. The year-round population is not so affluent.

The social mix compares to that of cities as well. The high profile of some of the wealthy and celebrated can distort the picture. Along with them, there is a large service class that caters to their needs, there is considerable poverty, and the high real estate values make affordable housing scarce. The Vineyard has a middle class made up of small-business owners, tradespeople, professionals, and white-collar workers, although the housing crisis threatens even this group. There are ethnic enclaves (Native Americans, African Americans, and Brazilians),[3] a growing population of retirees, and a thriving arts scene. An influx of young families who depend on the information economy for livelihood, and therefore are not tethered to any particular place, has arrived. They are attracted by the fifth-migration qualities that the Vineyard shares with small cities like Portland, Oregon, and Portland, Maine, and hundreds of college towns, state capitals, and resort towns across the country.

The profile of seasonal residents is changing, too. We have built a number of houses for people who originally imagined them as summer residences, only to see them transformed into primary homes because the island offers such an appealing way of life. Many have sold the suburban house where they raised their families, rented or bought an apartment in the city, and now spend a larger part of each year living on the Vineyard. Some have begun to vote here, because their vote may have greater impact in local elections, which have such a direct impact on their adopted community and therefore on their lives.

What's happening to Martha's Vineyard may presage what's in store for significant parts of America as our economy and demographics shift. More places will develop their fifth-migration qualities as more people have enough financial resources and job freedom to relocate. But desirable places all share at least two vexing problems: outmigration forced by dramatic real estate appreciation and housing costs; and changes to the character of the community resulting from the influx of people who seek to enjoy qualities that their arrival increasingly imperils. We all know places that have suffered this fate.

I think of islands as laboratories, and the Vineyard is a good one for recognizing, testing, and working to enhance the connections among small business, the built environment, and community, and for realizing the potential of commerce, local government, and nonprofits to collaborate for the common good. The physical isolation may allow us to see things more clearly, because boundaries and limits are so well defined. Islands are semi-closed systems. When you get off the boat or the plane and set foot on the Vineyard, you know immediately that you are in a place with limitations. The social complexity combines in interesting ways with the fixed boundaries, creating conditions for innovative problem solving and community initiative.

Fair Condition

From an environmental perspective, the Vineyard is like the old '55 Pontiac Stratostreak I drove when we first arrived: in fair condition and decent running order. It has been capably preserved, always garaged, but not yet restored. It needs attention if it's to keep running.

Islanders have always been aware that our unique environmental qualities are strong suits, tied directly to the character of the community and our economic vitality. Some of our early seasonal residents were visionary conservationists. In the 1890s a Harvard geologist created Seven Gates Farm, putting seventeen hundred acres into a permanent trust that provided for just thirty homesites and no private landownership (those who have built houses there lease the land). It was carefully planned; each house had to touch a steel stake that he drove into the ground on its site. In those days Seven Gates was a long day's carriage ride from the ferry in Vineyard Haven. These properties (although you can't even own one) have become some of the most expensive on the island because they are in an uncommonly beautiful area with such well-protected surroundings. There are still a few unbuilt properties in the trust, and there, more than one hundred years later, you can still find the steel stakes; in fact you must, because your new house must touch that stake.

The island has a robust tradition of land conservation and stewardship. Private nonprofits have been buying and managing local land for decades. The Nature Conservancy, a major landowner, conducts long-term projects to restore ancient sand-plains environments. In 1986 island voters created the Martha's Vineyard Land Bank, an unusual public body (there are still only half a dozen in the nation) that collects a 2 percent transfer fee on real estate purchases, except for some which are exempted, like the first $300,000 for first-time homebuyers. Revenue has averaged roughly $9 million annually for the past five years. The funds are used to purchase, hold, and manage property for public access and environmentally appropriate use. The Land Bank now owns roughly two thousand acres, including many beach accesses, and is in the process of creating a necklace of properties that, over time, will make it possible to reach most of the island by foot, horse, or mountain bike without using roads. The organization is neither a sanctuary program nor a park system; rather, it is a middle ground in which conservation values are balanced with public enjoyment, and sophisticated management secures the land's permanent stability.

At the same time, people conservation has taken its place alongside land conservation as the community has united to solve the affordable housing crisis. We are beginning to understand that "continuity of generations" (as local ecologist Tom Chase calls it) is essential for keeping a place whole—it's what keeps stories and traditions alive, maintains a population with a good understanding of the land and the climate, and provides a window to the past and the door to the future.

Sprawl has not yet gotten out of hand. The villages still feel like villages. To keep it that way we must make good choices. In many cases we have; in others we haven't. For example, large-lot zoning initiatives adopted in the 1970s led to the unintended consequence of partial suburbanization of a rural landscape. Inadequate transportation planning and funding has led to serious traffic problems. But the Vineyard remains in fair condition. Restoration is conceivable.

Basil

Sometimes random incidents, apparently minor, become emblematic, helping us to see our communities and ourselves in a fresh light.

One day in 1975, while my partner Mitchell and I were in the process of building our first Vineyard house, we, with a helper, were raising a timber wall. The wall was too heavy for the three of us. We raised it to shoulder height but could go no farther; we could rest it there, but we hadn't the strength either to keep it moving up or to let it down easy. Stuck there, we considered counting to three, letting it go, and jumping clear. At that moment the telephone repairman arrived to fix our job-site phone. He saw what was up, slammed on the brakes, hopped out, and lent a shoulder. It was just enough—the wall rose past the pivot point and settled into place. Once it was secured, we breathed deeply, congratulated one another on our good fortune, and thanked our redeemer for his timely arrival and spirited participation.

We were new to the area then, and that was the first time I'd met Basil, the telephone repairman. I saw him over and over after that day. For years he never failed to say, "Hey, got any walls to raise?" For him, the opportunity to help us out of a jam was memorable; for us, he became an example of small-town camaraderie and a reminder that our business can be, to our community, what Basil was, at that moment, to us. Pitching in to help one another, and our town, and our region, makes us more alive and present. It makes us part of the stories of others.

Local Commitment

As South Mountain has developed and our Vineyard bonds have strengthened, we have made several commitments to ourselves regarding the work we will do and the work we will not. One of these—the commitment to work only on Martha's Vineyard—is central to this chapter. Its emergence led directly to our eighth cornerstone principle: committing to this island in order to promote local economic stability and to strengthen community. Here's how it happened.

In 1995 we expanded the company's reach. South Mountain became a partner in a new practice called ARC Design Group. I had met the other two partners, architect Bruce Coldham and systems engineer Marc Rosenbaum, years before. Our first work together was organizing conferences about green building as board members of the Northeast Sustainable Energy Association (NESEA). NESEA brings together renewable energy and green building advocates and practitioners from all over the Northeast. It has been a remarkable spawning ground for professional friendships, business associations, and collaborations—a true community of practice.

In 1993 South Mountain was asked to design the Wampanoag Tribal Center on the Vineyard, which was to be the first building the Wampanoags had built, as a tribe, in three hundred years. The project was beyond our capabilities, so I asked Marc and Bruce to collaborate with us. They did, and the partnership emerged, with the specific purpose of bringing integrated planning, architecture, engineering, and construction management to New England institutional, commercial, and multifamily residential projects in which the client had a particularly strong commitment to environmental sustainability. While South Mountain's residential practice on Martha's Vineyard remained our bread and butter, ARC Design completed several successful projects during the second half of the 1990s.

This was an opportunity to do work that fit our company values, with people we liked to work with—yet it had serious drawbacks. Aside from the travel and the divide it created within the company, I came to believe we couldn't do the job with the kind of depth and attention to detail to which we aspire.

Successful development work, in my view, relies on deep understanding of people and place. You have to be there. After a quarter century working on the Vineyard, our local knowledge is still increasing.

Even here, there is so much more to learn. Sometimes we still slog through the tangles of information like a short-legged dog in deep snow.

Tom Kelley, CEO of the industrial design firm Ideo, says in *The Art of Innovation*:

> Inspiration often comes from being close to the action. That's part of why geography, even in the internet age, counts. New ideas come from seeing, smelling, hearing—being there. . . . It's . . . why people still go to museums, to be inspired in the presence of original artwork, though a digital image may be easily available on their home computer screen. Asking questions of people who were there, who should know, often isn't enough. . . . It doesn't matter how many astute questions you ask. If you're not in the jungle, you're not going to know the tiger.[4]

Every region has distinct landscapes, microclimates, and local cultural practices that influence design and building practice. As we had more and more opportunities to work in other places, I was starting to be attracted to a different idea: What if we, as a business, decided to confine our work to the Vineyard, for the foreseeable future at least, to help make it the best place we can imagine, the kind of place we'd want our grandchildren's grandchildren to live in? If we imagined our eggs in that one basket, over many decades, our work might take on a different cast. We could commit to thinking like cathedral builders in our own small locale.

When I shared these thoughts with my co-owners, there was agreement, and our deliberations led to this cornerstone commitment, as a company, to limit our work to the island of Martha's Vineyard, with the exception of educational work beyond our shores. That covenant defines and guides us today. In the past, each off-island inquiry was a seduction that had to be evaluated. Now we are clear: If we can be educationally helpful in another community we will try to accommodate, but when it comes to actual design and building projects, we keep to the Vineyard. We're staying in our jungle.

Beyond Global to Local

After reading an article in the Hartford, Connecticut, newspaper about the closing of a local plumbing supply company, my friend Jamie Wolf was moved to write the following letter to the editor:

> Like the contractor in your story about the closing of Carlton Supply, I learned a lot sitting across the counter from Mike as he patiently explained the nuances of the plumbing in the old Lincoln Street two-family house I had just bought and was renovating. It was 1978 and I was one of the many who, in their 20s and early 30s, found the opportunity in Hartford's aging neighborhoods to own, and often improve, homes with architectural character in richly diverse areas. When I created

a business in remodeling I continued to benefit from relationships with people like Mike in businesses like Carlton Supply. Most of these businesses closed up in the economic slump of the early '90s or were driven out by the arrival of the big boxes. I'll never forget the day I called a local millwork company looking for an old house's big fat door trim. "What neighborhood's that in?" the fellow asked, and when I told him he replied, "We've got the cutter to mill that. We made the original." That was my lesson in the equity of local knowledge and irreplaceable community resources. I can't get that trim anymore; they're gone. The loss of Carlton Supply is one more such loss to the community. The next young urban homesteaders will have to figure it out for themselves. Alas for Hartford. The heart and wisdom offered by folks like Sid and Mike and Junior are the genius of the place. The city will more than miss them.[5]

Jamie's letter touches on many of the essential characteristics of a stable community economy: familiarity, local knowledge and production ("we made the original"), diverse small businesses, and the desire and responsibility to be helpful beyond selling a product or service. These valuable businesses, which are the heart of local economies, can be lost, just like species and forests and soil, if we don't protect them, honor them, nurture them, and maintain them.

Every community has businesses and institutions that would, if gone, fundamentally change the character of that place. I can think of many here. I cannot imagine the Vineyard without Trip Barnes's colorful trucking company (or Trip himself, for that matter, who presides with humor and passion at many of our charity auctions), or Reynolds, Rappaport & Kaplan, the legal firm that manages to do both public and private work and stands as a symbol of integrity. Life would be different without Gannon and Benjamin, the wonderful builder of wooden boats that routinely draws five hundred people to celebrate the launchings of its extraordinary vessels. There's no doubt we would live in a lesser place if not for the presence of Chilmark Chocolates, the public-spirited candy maker that provides a homey working atmosphere for those with disabilities, supports many local causes, and fattens us up joyously each holiday. How about our fiercely independent bookstore, The Bunch of Grapes, which author William Styron once called "the best bookstore in America"? Founded by Ann Nelson in 1975, the bookstore has now been passed on to her son John, and it maintains the selection, the personality, and the vitality it has always had.

There are new businesses, too, that have become institutions in a very short time. Whippoorwill Farm, the CSA (community supported agriculture) that provides fresh produce to hundreds of Vineyard families, was recently in danger of losing the leased land on which it is located. A groundswell of support swept across the island, and a number of people and organizations worked hard to raise the money needed. It was too much to raise, and the effort looked like it would be unsuccessful, but when a wealthy new seasonal resident, wanting to do something for the community he was beginning to adopt, saw how much it meant to people, he stepped in, bought the farm, and committed it to the CSA long-term.

Maintaining core businesses is critical, but it's only a beginning. As the South Mountain local commitment has developed, I have become curious about the potential of local economies to serve as an antidote to the negative consequences of globalization. As we probe into all things local, we must also look outward. Events beyond our shores will always have significant local effects; we need to understand them as they relate to relocalization or we are like ostriches with heads in the sand. As we struggle to understand and correct that which we cannot fully control, we can invest at once in that over which control is more direct: the process of localization.

Local enterprise has different aspirations· and different constraints. Worker-owned firms, social enterprises, community nonprofits, and community-owned corporations are tied to the communities in which they operate. They have greater accountability. And the people involved are part of the community. For these reasons such enterprises are more responsive to local social and environmental concerns, and they anchor jobs and reinvestment locally.

MV Livelihood and Commerce

Island vacationers and seasonal residents largely drive the Vineyard economy. While we need to keep this part of the economy robust and responsive, there is also a sense, among many, that there should be more balance, and that a more diverse and stronger year-round economy would be good for the island's residents, seasonal and year-round alike. The Livelihood and Commerce Work Group of the Island Plan set out to understand how the Vineyard might support the existing economy, imagine the next one, and help our economy to serve us all in the best possible ways.

The natural beauty and history of the island are matched by the great diversity of its community. The Vineyard is a refuge for many—the place where they can let their hair down and truly relax. The essential indicators of community remain strong and rich, but our economy needs to focus on the significant benefits of greater balance to remain strong in the face of upcoming challenges. Greater economic self-reliance can assure that—as climate change, peak oil, and globalization continue to influence our lives—our residents and visitors can count on authenticity, beauty, health, and a strong sense of community.

The economic approaches we encourage are:

- Supporting the existing visitor/seasonal-based economy.
- Increasing economic multipliers by fostering the circulation of money within the community.
- Reducing economic leakage by encouraging more island spending.
- Supporting local ownership so that those who

are conducting commerce are anchored in the
community.
- Substituting imports through local production, espe-
cially of such essentials as food and energy.
- Stimulating local investment.
- Increasing year-round jobs with living wages.
- Optimizing self-reliance, so that we become less
dependent on distant forces and events.
- Utilizing our historic character and geophysical attri-
butes more fully by promoting a greater diversity of
off-season activity.
- Creating a robust environment for lifetime learning.

In summary, we aspire to encourage a diverse and prosperous year-
round economy that enhances our community and environment,
respects our character and history, and understands that although we
are an island, we are also part of the larger world. We can imagine, and
develop, the economy we would like rather than accepting—without
question—the economy we have. But how will we move our economy
in this direction?

Subsidiarity and Federalism

First and foremost, we need to make a commitment to satisfy as many
needs as possible at the local level and to reduce reliance on imports.
If we do as much as possible as close to home as we can, we will create
a supply of good stable work, a reservoir of strong community engagement, and the economic multiplier effect that comes from money
being spent over and over in the same place.

A good frame of reference is the principle of subsidiarity, which
proposes that matters should be resolved, decisions made, and responsibilities accepted at the lowest possible level of organization, the level
closest to the people affected by the decision. The term is used mostly

in reference to governments and churches, but it extends comfortably to business and social organizations as well. It is simply a preference for the most local decision making and economic activity that is adequate and appropriate for a given task. If we apply this to any small town or region it means that the more food, energy, and other essentials we produce, the more investment we access locally, the more control we exercise over our economic institutions, and the more political decisions we make at the local level, the better our community life will be. Our community will be more responsive to its inhabitants and the inhabitants more responsible for its fate. It's just like in an employee-owned business—if the people who make the decisions are the people who will also bear the consequences of those decisions, perhaps better decisions—and a better economy—will result.

Making choices with the subsidiarity concept in mind allows us to benefit from the explosion of knowledge and products in the global economy, while at the same time working for vibrant and democratic community economies. Embracing subsidiarity is an argument not for minimal government or dogmatically small-scale enterprise, but rather for a society of appropriate scales in which we, as individuals, are influential in as many of the decisions that affect our lives as possible. The same reasons that make it desirable for people to own and control the companies they work in—because people should have the right to determine their own destiny, because those who do the work should share the bounty, and because being stakeholders makes people more effective and responsible decision makers—apply to economies as well.

Economist Michael Shuman, in his book *Going Local*, points out another virtue of subsidiarity. He says that local failures are usually smaller, less catastrophic, and easier to fix than those that occur on a larger scale. There may be more opportunity for influence, too, on the part of those affected by decisions, because it's harder for decision makers to hide from their mistakes when they're part of a community. As Shuman notes, however, this doesn't mean that local decisions are "necessarily efficient, fair, democratic, sensitive, creative, or disaster-proof."[6] But there is more incentive for responsibility and transparency when things are decided and conducted close to home.

Business philosopher Charles Handy uses the word *federalism* to express similar ideas.[7] Federalism, or the distribution of power between a central authority and constituent units, is a more familiar concept than subsidiarity, and an integral part of our country's governance structure. There is constant discussion about what is appropriately federal jurisdiction, what is under the purview of the states, and what is properly local. Adjustments are made. The concept of home rule, or the right of a town or city to enact laws that are primarily municipal and do not violate state law, is well understood.

Subsidiarity and federalism are not absolutes, and they do not work in one direction only. Martha's Vineyard has six different towns on one small island of less than a hundred square miles and a population of sixteen thousand. That means we have six town halls, six police departments, six school committees, six planning boards, six boards of health, and so on. Does this make sense? Mostly it doesn't, because issues, problems, and consequences cross town lines. If I pollute the water in my town, it will eventually have an effect on yours. The cars clogging our major intersections come from all six towns. In addition, the cumbersome nature of all this government costs too much and stretches citizen participation. Many of these entities would function better regionally than they do municipally. But people cling to the existing structure because it's the way it's always been, because they worry that the individual characteristics of the different towns would be lost with regionalization, and because of a concern about loss of control. Our lives are attached to the Vineyard, not just to a single town. Subsidiarity works both ways.

Wearing Many Hats

Young people in the United States grow up with a political system that bargains back and forth about minor adjustments and never considers an actual overhaul. Swing a little left, swing a little right, one step forward, two steps back. In our huge, increasingly diverse nation, small changes seem to have little impact, and the big issues don't get tackled in significant ways. Participation in political life is low. That could be changing with the election of 2008, which is surely the most exciting in my lifetime.

In the absence of big changes in a big place, perhaps big changes in many small places can substitute. One avenue toward such change is the collaboration of three types of interdependent entities: (1) democratic, place-based small businesses; (2) local governmental agencies; and (3) charitable nonprofits that are dedicated to specific geographic regions. All three can bring different attitudes, modes of working, and funding sources. The intersection is dependent on strong community interest among the three and an involved, engaged citizenry.

Small businesses committed to a locale have a natural interest in creating a better business climate. The people in those companies, the employees, want a better place to live and raise their families. Businesses can act quickly and decisively, and they are able, if so motivated, to share the profits they earn.

Well-run local government can provide a broader platform through which to connect a particular business or undertaking to the citizenry. Government generally has a longer view and slower pace than business.

Private nonprofits, like church and ecumenical associations, social service agencies, conservation organizations, housing groups, support groups, environmental groups, and a host of issue-oriented alliances and coalitions, can afford an even longer view, filling the gaps where government is unable to act. They facilitate volunteerism and effective citizenship. As we live longer and healthier lives, more and more of us have the time and inclination to participate in helping to solve our social problems.

There is a nascent "fourth sector" as well, which consists of organizations that merge for-profit activity with nonprofit mission. These organizations fall somewhere between traditional companies and charities. I suppose South Mountain could be counted as one.

In small communities people often wear many hats and work on several sides of the table simultaneously. This can lead to conflicts of interest, long-standing feuds, and small-mindedness, but it also can lead to wonderful synergies. Small towns where people know one another in different contexts have built-in safeguards—family connections, business associations, and the ever-active rumor mill—that help maintain balance. When you can't hide, there's more incentive to behave. People learn whom they trust, whom they can work with. The wearing of many hats creates a more informed citizenry and greater possibilities for shared cooperation among business, government, and nonprofits. The three sectors can weave together their different perspectives and abilities to energize positive change.

At SMC one year, we counted among our thirty employees the chair of the regional planning commission, the vice chair of the regional housing authority, two board members (including the chair) of the Island Affordable Housing Fund, one town conservation commission member, two members of town zoning boards of appeal, and many other civic and local government participants. These individuals bring the community into the company and the company into the community.

Local Enterprise and Ownership

To serve different purposes appropriately, we need big organizations and small organizations and everything in between. But current thinking is so committed to big that small gets left in the dust, even when it can do the job best. Take agriculture, for example. Today's agribusiness makes large quantities of food that must be shipped over long distances. A large percentage spoils before it ever reaches a shelf. In terms of freshness, nutritional value, and freedom from chemicals, the quality is low. The number of middlemen is large. Energy input is high. Fertilizers, preservatives, additives, and pesticides are pervasive. Small farms have declined and small-town life has eroded as agriculture has become increasingly corporate.

But communities are positively affected when companies like Stonyfield Farm create demand for high-quality organic agricultural products. Gary Hirshberg of Stonyfield says that his company, in building a market for organic yogurt and other dairy products, has caused more than one hundred dairy farms in New England to convert to organic farming methods by providing encouragement, assistance, and a steady market at good prices. These organic farms are thriving while traditional small farms are collapsing.

The Island Grown Initiative, a tremendously active local nonprofit that works with farmers to create new infrastructure and expand opportunities, is part of a vibrant resurgence of Vineyard agriculture that has tremendous potential for growth. Similar efforts are under way in many areas, even in cities. Some believe that local food is one of the most important political movements in today's world. It is a reaction to the "total economy" that makes everything wherever it can be most cheaply made, regardless of the effects, and moves it to where it can be sold at the highest price. Bill McKibben, the author of *Deep Economy*, says,

> Small farmers spent twenty years spreading the idea of "organic" food. They were persuasive: by the turn of the century, sales were growing 20 percent a year. Which was enough to attract the attention of the big growers, who quickly took over the business. But "Local" will be harder to co-opt, because Del Monte and its ilk simply can't grow different food in every market; if they tried, their economies of scale would disappear. "Local" steps far enough outside current conventional economics to represent a real challenge.[8]

Energy production, likewise, is an opportunity for appropriate small-scale production. As we all too gradually switch to conservation and renewables, and as hydrogen becomes a more likely prospect as a future energy source, the decentralized nature of new technologies has been responsible for a new industry of "energy service" companies (ESCOs) that began as conservation service providers and are now becoming small-scale producers. Michael Shuman again: "Judicious uses of land to produce food and solar energy to produce electricity demonstrate how community business can transform natural assets into a profitable product that serves local needs."[9]

As wind power has become more economical, and its worldwide potential better understood, new proposals are emerging—sparking controversy, creating dialogue, and, in many cases, finding acceptance. Europeans are leading the way, but as American communities find out about the benefits, we are seeing more and more of this promising technology. An important benefit of wind is that it can coexist on land and water with other typical uses. It does not use up anything. Wind energy is compatible with agriculture; the two endeavors can share the same land. If agriculture and energy move toward decentralization and localization, two of our most basic needs could gradually be met by local producers, leading us toward a healthier economy.

To make airplanes and steel we need large organizations, but most products, even high technology, do not require large enterprise. Chapter 5 described the Emilia-Romagna region of northern Italy, where small, locally owned firms involved in flexible manufacturing networks make an array of high-tech products for regionwide benefit. Networks such as Mondragon, as well as individual companies like Carris Reels and countless others, likewise demonstrate that worker ownership can be more than just a different way of doing business—it can be a strong part of community revitalization and economic relocalization.

Those who invest without a local interest in a business care mostly about financial return, whereas community members will often invest for nonmonetary return. Employee ownership and community ownership make an enterprise nearly invulnerable to outside takeover. Shuman says,

> If enough of us create our own corporations based on
> new visions of social responsibility, and if we choose

to buy and invest only in these firms, other corporations will either adapt or die. If we create even a small
number of self-reliant communities in which every
resident has a decent job that produces basic necessi-
ties for one and all, other communities will visit, learn,
and follow. We have far more power than we realize.[10]

Local business and industry need support, encouragement, incentives, and controls. Fortunately, despite whatever encroachments
have been made by dispassionate big business (each new Wal-Mart
ultimately puts an astonishing number of local businesses under), we
still have our local economies. We don't need to take them back from
global corporations; we already have them, in whatever condition
they're in—good, fair, or poor. We can move them forward from here.
And if we can keep local institutions and businesses—like Carlton
Supply in Hartford—alive, we will keep the continuity of generations
alive and maintain the richness of our communities.

If we patronize local businesses when we have the opportunity,
start more, support efforts to restore small agricultural capability, and
develop new renewable energy sources, perhaps we can, in time, through
localization, find more balance within the global economy. In Jeffrey
Hollender's *What Matters Most*, he quotes Judy Wicks of the White Dog
Café in Philadelphia, a treasured community institution that has been
committed to local community and economic development for decades.
While Wicks "applauds those who are working to tame globalization and
reform the corporation," he notes, she is focused on "trying to engineer
a more fundamental shift toward local economies as an alternative to
corporate globalization. We're interested in a corporate model oriented
around small businesses, small farmers, small buyers, small sellers."[11]

Some may see this as unrealistic. Maybe, but I'm with Judy. It's an
admirable goal to try to restore commerce to a more local orientation,
serving people more equitably, positively, and directly. While reform
efforts must intensify to curb corporate excesses worldwide and to

harness globalization, there is much to do in our own backyards. The two efforts are complementary.

At South Mountain we treasure the opportunity to limit our primary endeavors to this complex little island that we've come to know well. It's still a fine place to live and work. Committing to the business of place is an unconditional investment in the people and economy of a single locale. We've tossed our hat in the ring here and tied our future to the future of the Vineyard. We're eager to see what comes next and pleased to be able to take part in the evolution of this place. We're staying close to home.

Mad River

In the Mad River Valley of Vermont, Betsy Pratt, the owner of the beloved ski area Mad River Glen, was ready to retire and sell in the mid-1990s. Locals were worried that the character of the storied place would change under new ownership, and Betsy wanted to sell to skiers. Someone suggested a cooperative, so that the skiers and townspeople to whom the area means so much could maintain and operate it as they wished. A local group organized and began to sell shares for $1,500. They were unable to raise the full amount, so Pratt gave them an interest-free loan for five years, and the group bought the area in 1995. The debt has since been paid and the price of the shares has risen. No one can own more than four shares, and there is no profit sharing—the profits all go back into the area. It's another example of an investment in community. Mad River is an essential part of the valley, and the employees, townspeople, and users are at the helm.

There are nineteen hundred owners of Mad River Glen. It takes a two-thirds vote to get anything done. The storied single chairlift that was hailed as an "engineering feat" when it first opened in 1949 has run ever since but recently reached the limits of its service. There was debate about replacement. It would cost less to install a new double chair than a new single, but that was not what the shareholders wanted. There is now a new electric-driven single chairlift in place of the diesel-powered chair that ran for fifty-eight years.

Last year I rode up the Forerunner double chair in Stowe, Vermont, twenty-five miles up the road from Mad River. I was sharing the lift with an old skier like me, and we started talking ski areas. He turned out to be a sourpuss, almost curmudgeonly. He said, "The stupidest thing I've ever heard of is replacing that single chair in Mad River with another single. Shoulda put a double in."

"Well, " I replied, "I guess they must have done the right thing. There are nineteen hundred owners and that's what they wanted."

"They're a buncha idiots," he growled. "Just think, if we were in Mad River right now we wouldn't even be able to ride up together and have this conversation."

That would have been just fine with me.

The Mad River shareholders are committed to maintaining the qualities that compelled their allegiance to the ski area. They've made an interesting corollary discovery: They have come to realize that their organization, which formed simply to maintain an important community institution, has the ability to tackle other issues important to their region. They have created a new framework for local problem solving and community building. The Mad River cooperative owns and operates a ski area for community benefit, but it could just as well be a community-owned wind farm, or solar power station, or composting facility, or anything else the community might need.

BRIAN VANDEN BRINK

· 10 ·

A Company to Keep

What if you slept? And what if, in your sleep, you dreamed? And
what if, in your dream, you went to heaven and plucked a strange
and beautiful flower? And what if, when you awoke, you had the
flower in your hand? Ah, what then?
—Samuel Taylor Coleridge

First, master your instrument. Then, forget all that shit and play!
—Charlie Parker

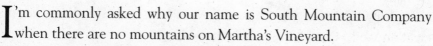

I'm commonly asked why our name is South Mountain Company
when there are no mountains on Martha's Vineyard.

When we started out in New York State, we worked out of a shop we
built on South Mountain Road. Chris carefully handpainted the name
on the door of our old flatbed truck. When we got to the Vineyard,
we didn't want to bother to repaint, so we kept the name. Years later,
I tried to change it, but people in the company reacted so negatively I
never tried again. I suppose the name is endearing because it reminds
us of our irregular beginnings. Perhaps it's also comforting that something—anything—stays the same, given the constantly changing
nature of our business.

Tachi Kiuchi and Bill Sherman, in *What We Learned in the Rainforest*,
say, "We don't believe change has to seem draconian to be fundamental.

It's hard to build a tree but easy to plant a seed. Building a tree is draconian, desperate, and ineffective. Planting a seed is fundamental, serene, and easy."[1]

Having planted the seeds of shared ownership, democracy, and cathedral building, we can only guess at the shape of the trees that will result. What will the next generation of owners do?

The questions at hand are these: Can small business, supported by strong underlying principles and shared ownership, help make better lives and better communities? To go farther, and perhaps too far, can business conducted this way help us be kinder to ourselves and to one another, to the planet, and especially to our children? Is it a stretch to say that the more fully we are fulfilled in our work, the more fully we can love both our children and our community? And that the more fulfilled we are, the more we can help build a future that's sane and just? If I overreach, it is only my enthusiasm for the possibility that is to blame.

The arc of this book is an attempt to find answers to these questions by tracking back through the experiences I've had as part of South Mountain Company, and by considering this experience in the context of the work and thinking of others. This process has led to many hunches and conjectures and some new understandings, but no clear answers yet, as far as I can tell.

My good friend Lee Halprin says about writing:

> A lot of writing does not show that it knows the slightness of its knowledge. I think it is good to consider how one feels about the relation between what one can say and what one knows and between what one knows and what one doesn't, and between what is known and what isn't, and between what's knowable and what isn't. I think it's good to think hard enough about this for the thought to somehow color one's writing, somehow to seep into it.[2]

That feels particularly right to me, but hard, too, to uphold. I've tried to remember the slightness of my own knowledge as I have written, and tried to separate what I think I know from what I'm certain I don't.

Here's what I'm thinking now.

What I think I know is that the process of telling this story has helped me to know more about where we have been and where we are headed, in the same way that my colleagues at South Mountain continue to help me know more, every day, about the community we build and the company we keep.

I thought, when I started writing, that I wanted to tell a complete story about something we had started, grown into, and become. I see now that the story is not about what South Mountain has become as much as it is about what we have begun. There are things that we have learned to do, that we can do, right now, reasonably well. We can make good houses. We can develop other enterprise that extends our primary endeavors. We can develop effective relationships with those who are connected to our business. We can support a community of employees and employee-owners, giving them the opportunity to make good livings. We can offer, to one another, ownership and a voice in the conduct of our work. We can contribute to the well-being of our community and create small successes that enhance it. We can carefully consider those decisions that affect the evolution of our enterprise. We can infuse our work with a cooperative spirit that feels better than competition. We are beginning to have the capacity to think long-term. We're off to a good start. But there is much more to do, and much more to know.

I think I know that the ongoing attempt to balance multiple bottom lines has been, and continues to be, a worthy, enriching endeavor.

I think I know, too, that our craftsmanship, in all things, is the central thread that makes visible and tangible the underlying principles that guide us. Surrounded by the things we make, we are constantly reminded of the expressions and collaborations from which they resulted. Our doors warp, windows stick, tiles crack, floors shrink, finishes blemish. We fix these so that what we produce is the best it can be. The aspiration is genuine. Craft is a guiding star.

I think I know that the idea of community entrepreneurialism has taken hold within this company. As we move from our decades-long concentration on affordable housing to a more active role in renewable energy and relocalizing the economy, there is new excitement.

I think I know, because the tenor is so pervasive, that there is a developing notion of legacy in the company that hints at a bright future. We will endure.

Finally, I know that we belong here on Martha's Vineyard. Not because it's special. Not because it's different. We belong here simply because we are here, because we've been here, because we know that we will stay here. There is virtue, poet Gary Snyder says, in "staying put." That may be enough to know for now.

These are the things that I think I know.

I don't know yet, nor do I know whether I will ever know, to what degree we can build on the foundations we have created and to what degree we can improve our skills. Neither do I know to what extent our experience can help other business entities walk the path toward economic democracy, community entrepreneurialism, and environmental stewardship. I don't know whether, in time, many more people will share ownership and control of the companies they work in, although I sense there is significant movement in this direction. I don't know for certain whether local economies will experience significant resurgence or whether the forces of globalization will overwhelm this young movement.

In *The Soul of Capitalism*, William Greider writes:

> The idea of reinventing American capitalism sounds far-fetched. I can report, nevertheless, that many Americans are already at work on the idea in various scattered ways. They are experimenting in localized

settings—tinkering with the ways in which the system operates—and are convinced that alternatives are possible, not utopian schemes but self-interested and practical changes that can serve broader purposes. This approach seems quite remote from the current preoccupations of big politics and big business, but this is where the society's deepest reforms usually have originated in the American past. The future may begin among ordinary people, far distant from established power, who are brave enough to see themselves as pioneers.[3]

My father has never wavered in his firm belief that if you work hard enough at changing the world, the world will surely change. It's easy to throw up our hands and turn back in the face of the great obstacles we face. There seem to be two opposing points of view that trump all other distinctions and have nothing to do with politics or race or gender or religion. One group embraces cynicism, and thinks it's not worth trying to change anything, because it's never going to happen. That's just the way it is. Just maintain; that's the best we can do. The people in that group are generally quite certain about their point of view.

Others are less so. Those of us in this camp see the bright side, recognize the good things that happen, the times when history has surprised us all. We believe that humans may still be moving inexorably toward the fulfillment of our positive potential.

Nobody knows which way we will go. But where do we want to spend our time? As Paul Loeb says in *The Impossible Will Take a Little While*, "On the side of cynicism, even if they're right, who wants to win that argument? If I'm going to stick with somebody, I'd rather stick with people who have a sense of possibility and hope . . . that's the side I want to be on."[4] That's the side I'm on. I feel hopeful about the effort, although I can't know what the outcome will be.

What has happened at South Mountain during the past few decades has led to some surprising outcomes that, had we followed a different itinerary, we would not have achieved. The fact that we can do some good things with some degree of success and satisfaction is testimony to the spirit of a group of people who have ownership, voice, recourse, and tools. The fact that we, as a group, have the freedom to determine how much or how little we wish to grow empowers us to self-consciously, in the best sense of the word, create the setting for our endeavors.

I recognize, however, that things won't necessarily go the way I wish. Our business fortunes could go sour—the fact that everyone has received a paycheck without fail for thirty-three years, and that the company has earned a profit every year since we began to keep records, could change in a heartbeat. People could lose hope if things become too hard or take too long or become too divisive along the way. It could turn out that the line that I think doesn't exist—the one beyond which all hope is lost—does, in fact, exist for our island community, and that we will cross it. Any of those could happen, or other unfortunate things I haven't thought of yet.

But let's say none of that happens. These first few decades have been a beginning. Let's say that we can manage another few decades, and another few after that, and maybe more. Given all that has happened in just the first few decades, I have to guess that we can achieve more in the years to come. If we look at the alternatives to going where we're going, it seems particularly sensible—not visionary, not risky, not wacky, and not trivial, but just sensible—to try to continue down this path. Perhaps to take it farther.

Franchising South Mountain

In 2003 a group of University of Oregon architecture students were doing a studio project on the Vineyard for their spring term. They visited us. One of the students, after touring our facilities, asked, "If this business and your design/build approach is so successful, why aren't companies doing this all over?"

There are some, but not so many. What I've come to find out, though, since the release of the first edition of this book, is that there are more than I thought, and that there are many, many more who want to do it but aren't sure how to go about it. There's a hunger out there for making work more meaningful and rewarding.

Given that, maybe we at South Mountain could assemble our expertise in ways that would be useful, in ways that could satisfy some of that hunger. The products and services we could offer include the following:

- Integrated design/build skills and methods.
- Building science, green building, and renewable energy expertise.
- Complex building systems and methods.
- Affordable housing and community entrepreneurism skills.
- Owner's manual formats and templates.
- Workplace democracy and decision making.
- Meeting facilitation and consensus decision-making training.
- Employee ownership conversion and long-term legacy and succession assistance.
- Methods of evaluating corporate social responsibility and balancing profits with service.
- Strategies for gaining confidence of clients and community.
- Compensation, benefits, pensions, and personnel issues.
- Employee evaluations.
- Business systems that support these many practices.
- Strategic plans and business plans.

- A coordinated, self-regulating, electronic information exchange medium, like Great Harvest's.

Along with these we could offer a healthy dose of hope, supportive guidance, and the benefit of learning from the many mistakes we've made along the way. It might save others the difficulty of laboring too long before recognizing the obvious, as we often have.

Organizational consultant Robert Leaver says that most people think about power as a pie to be divided—if I give you a piece, I have less left for me. Leaver asserts that power is infinite, however, and that if I give some to you, there is now more of it. Isn't knowledge the same? If I share knowledge with you, we both have it. And if we combine our knowledge, new knowledge results. That's precisely what Great Harvest Bread Company does: share and build knowledge. Here's how you can make the best bread in the world, they say. We'll give you the information. Then you can do it your way.

In our line of work, there's no question that people must do it their way, because local conditions vary so widely. We can't try to teach you what to design and build, because what works in our area and for our clientele may not work for yours. We could, however, teach processes that could be translated into practice and product.

"Yeah, sure," we sometimes hear. "You can do it on Martha's Vineyard, but . . ."

The model we have created can be replicated in most parts of the United States, anyplace where there is some level of prosperity: all cities, most suburban areas, state capitals, college towns, areas where people like to vacation—anyplace, in fact, where people want to live. It probably cannot be replicated where people don't want to live. In those places, nothing else is working, either. The New England states, the West Coast, the Rockies, Minnesota and Wisconsin, the Ozarks, the Carolinas, and the mid-Atlantic states are full of such enterprises. Do these enterprises also serve diverse social purposes? Do they share ownership and cultivate workplace democracy? Do they have an absolute commitment to their locale? Mostly not, in my experience. Would they like to? I think in many cases the answer is yes, but the culture does not support these approaches.

My thinking is to franchise in the old sense of the word: "to make or set free." The preparation of the information we have in order to make it useful for others would involve substantial work. If we did that work, maybe we could set it free, and perhaps free others to find new ways to enhance their work and enliven their communities.

I don't imagine that South Mountain will ever offer franchises in the true sense of the word. The "franchisees" would be more like part of a loosely amalgamated business network. We could learn from one another. We are at the beginning of something that we think will endure, and we may be just far along enough to share it with others. We have begun to treat educational and consulting activity as a new profit center, meaning that it is an area in which we're beginning to invest time and effort, an area that has both income and expense (at this stage the latter exceeds the former).

Each of the past two years I have taught a two-day business class at the Yestermorrow Design/Build School in Waitsfield, Vermont. It has given me the opportunity to assemble some materials and ideas, and it has helped me to gauge what might be useful to others. Both years I have been fortunate to have a diverse and lively group of business-people, from all kinds of small businesses, looking for just the kind of guidance and assistance I'm suggesting. They have offered valuable feedback. The "Employee Ownership Transition Process" (appendix 2) was suggested by the first-year class.

One of the participants, a builder, wrote me after the class. He said,

> Creating beautiful and livable homes is not sufficient
> for me. I feel the call . . . to contribute to a broader
> social good. I have never paid much attention to the
> business side of what I have been doing, and the not-
> yet-fully-recovered Marxist in me has allowed me to

justify that neglect. Having encountered your work, I now can see the broad ranging benefits that derive from smart business management. And . . . I find myself inspired to proudly and purposefully take on the mantle of successful small business manager.[5]

He requested further mentoring. Others have as well. Together they may constitute the early "franchisees."

We are in the process of offering a three-day workshop called "Drawing and Building Eyebrow Dormers" by master carpenter and SMC owner Billy Dillon. It's an exercise in drafting, model building, and complex roof geometry. It is our first test run here on the Vineyard. It feels to us that there are many underutilized facilities here in the off-season, and we might be able to expand our effort over time to offer a full complement of small-business and design/build study opportunities.

We'll see. As I said earlier, you can't count the apples in a seed; you can only plant the seed, cultivate and nurture, and see what grows.

New Job

My career has had a distinct pattern. I learn how to do something and gain reasonable skills and experience, and then someone else comes along who can do it better, while I move on to something else. I was a competent cabinetmaker and furniture maker, but we now have people who can run circles around the highest levels I was ever able to achieve. The same goes for carpentry; my skills and talents have been surpassed by orders of magnitude. I used to design the houses we built and spent years learning to do a credible job. Now others do that. I used to be the person who found the oddball tiles, old stained glass, or soulful furnishings that would make a project special. Now Deirdre, who runs our interior design department, is out on the prowl turning up new stuff and working with artisans as I used to do. For many years

I have overseen all aspects of the business; my sabbatical meant others had to take on more management responsibility, and they do it well.

My job has begun to change again. As always, it's not without sadness. But from each endeavor some part stays with me and informs the new things I do. The great reward is that I get to watch and help others do these things I care about, and I get to see them done with skill, enthusiasm, and concentration.

According to the history, those parts of my job that move into the hands of others will be handled better and better. Others will grow into the areas that I am growing into now, and eventually beyond. It will happen in due time, as we're ready and able. It will happen at a pace that works for us. It will not happen without bumps in the road. We continue to be a work in progress, a foundation on which we layer our accumulated experience. We sustain the journey, always practicing and adjusting, tearing and mending, folding and unfolding, building the road as we travel, shaping our future. This company's failures and weaknesses stand side by side with its successes and fulfillments.

It's the company we nourish, the company we test and challenge, the company we hope will endure and continue to enjoy the opportunities conferred upon us by this place. This is the company whose care is entrusted to us, and whose success requires our relentless dedication. This is the company we will keep.

The process of making this book has turned out to be surprisingly like that of making a house. You design the book and then you build it. You have to conceptualize it (design it), write it (build it), edit (move the walls that don't work), and acknowledge (honor the many relationships that combined to make it happen). Then you have to let it go.

Partly this project is an outpouring of gratitude for the things that have gone our way, the people whose paths we've crossed, the pure dumb luck that has allowed us to practice the craft we love, and the splendid group of colleagues and fellow owners who have been company on this journey, which has been, for me, more fun than I could possibly have imagined. And partly the purpose is the hope that a few of our chance discoveries will be helpful to others.

As I come to the end I feel like I'm standing on deck, looking over the rail, watching the water as our ship cuts through, hugging the edge of a channel. Our balancing act—the thorough but thorny attempt to harmonize financial success with social progress and environmental responsibility—requires that we steer clear of the crowded middle.

I am enjoying this moment in time, as I near completion of this particular journey. I am humbled by the generosity of all those who have shared the journey, from the most recent meeting with our future owners way back to the early days on the Vineyard when we were just getting started, and farther back still, to the image I hold of my grandfather steaming into New York's harbor in 1899. The observations and stories I've offered tell who and what we are now, as it appears to me. Most likely others who have been in the thick of it would tell it differently.

If the discoveries from the beginnings of our journey inform yours, I hope you will share your findings and further enlighten ours. Together, perhaps, we can share the very best of what we learn, and the love that comes from the learning, with our children, and theirs, as they invent a future we can't even imagine.

ACKNOWLEDGMENTS

We think of writing a book as a solitary enterprise. The author, alone with a collection of ideas, tries to convey them to others in a compelling way. The experience of making this book, at least, has been different from that, and as highly collaborative, in a way, as anything I have ever done. No part was done alone.

The book is a product of countless shared experiences. The people mentioned in the text, and hundreds of others who are not, have contributed to the undertaking. These acknowledgments are my opportunity to thank some of them—the ones who have specifically, and generously, helped me with this project. But a host of others have contributed in ways they probably do not know and in ways I cannot fully identify. This so-called solitary enterprise seems more to me like a shared journey, akin to building a house.

The journey has been important to me as part of my work, but as part of my life, too. And nothing is more important to me in life than my family—my wife, Chris, my kids, Pinto (and his partner Jessica) and Sophie, my grandchildren, Kalib, Silas, and Axel—they bring me unremitting joy.

My parents, Marilyn and Herb Abrams, have supported me in so many ways they can't be counted or measured or even, I'm sure, fully recalled. They have been rock solid, always there for me, and my father's work ethic, optimism, and sense of commitment have been instrumental in shaping my own. My sister Nancy helped me out of the starting blocks: Each day she taught me everything she learned in school, when I was three (and she has since brought husband, Richard Eilbert, and my niece, Natasha, into the fold).

I treasure them all.

Three people have been essential mentors to me in writing this book and more: Jamie Wolf, Lee Halprin, and my wife, Chris Hudson Abrams.

I have been engaged in a discussion with Jamie about business and community for two decades. It started when we met as co-conspirators at the Northeast Sustainable Energy Association in the late 1980s. We organized conferences together, struggled to help build a good nonprofit into something even better, and enjoyed each other's company. Jamie runs a design/build remodeling company, and we came to find that we shared many ideas about business . . . and life. Our ongoing discussion has been mostly by e-mail. Every so often we get tired of the electronic back-and-forth and pick up the phone or find a way to meet. One way or another the discussion goes on. It always challenges me to think harder. Jamie has been an avid, critical, and supportive reader as I've been writing. I'm grateful for the company and the help. I look forward to continuing this inquiry and this friendship together.

Lee goes back a long way in my life, to the beginning of our time on the Vineyard. He is a relentlessly caring friend and mentor who never lets me get away with anything if he can help it. Over the years, at regular intervals, I have had enough nerve to give writings to Lee for review. They come back smothered in red. Sometimes there is a note at the end as long as the piece itself. A superb editor who probes and queries, suggests and soothes, digs way deep, and never minces words, he has helped me learn to write a little, as he has helped me with so many other things.

When I was in the early stages of this project I gave him my book proposal to read. Then, after I had written a few chapters, I passed them to him and he read them, as always, with care. He made me think differently, in so many ways, and changed the course of this project. If—and I know this is a big if—knowing what I don't know has somehow seeped into my writing to some small degree, it is because of Lee.

Along with teaching me more about life and humanity and love than anyone else, Chris is one of the best bullshit detectors on the planet. It's a good thing, I think, for each of us to have one of these in our lives. She has carefully read my writing and looked for those parts that don't ring true. If you find a lot of BS in this book, some small part may be because Chris missed it, but more likely it's because I didn't listen. But she always does.

She also managed to put up with my absolute self-absorption during periods of time when I was consumed by my writing. We've been together since 1969, when we were just twenty years old, so we've been on this entire journey together. In a way, we grew up together. If not for her, I doubt any of this would have happened the way it did, or even at all.

The generosity, wisdom, and goodness of these three people just knocks me out.

There are other people who have been essential to this project. Several stand out.

I met Bill Greider when we were both speaking at the Vermont Employee Ownership Center annual conference. I had appreciated his writing and social commentary for years, but at the bar that night, swapping tales, I had the sense that I was in the presence of a great raconteur whose wisdom was legion. He told me that night that he'd had "a low-grade obsession with employee ownership for the past twenty-five years." I liked that. We talked a few times after that. When I crossed paths with him later at a meeting in Boston, I asked him if he would consider writing the foreword to this book. He graciously agreed. Later, when the manuscript was complete, I sent it to him. He read it and wrote me a remarkably thoughtful letter. Along with plenty of encouraging words, it contained a suggestion for how to make the book better—one single, clear, but large idea. I took him up on it and restructured several sections. It's a better book because of him.

I was skeptical when I learned that Woody Tasch, the chairman of the board of Chelsea Green and the founder of Investor's Circle, wanted to be the developmental editor for this book. He had never edited a book before, and, besides, I knew him to be a very busy guy.

Would he be good at it? Would he be available? I agreed to give it a try. He was tremendously valuable: teasing out meanings, analyzing structures, and offering alternatives with great skill. He once substituted the four-letter word *lieu* for eleven words of my prose without changing the meaning of the sentence. I'm grateful to Woody for being there. He did a splendid job. It has been a fine collaboration. And now there's another: Shay Totten, Chelsea Green's editorial director, who has been the developmental editor for the second edition. While I was holed up in Vermont working on this latest go-round, Shay came to visit. We talked about the book and its structure, and I was immediately at ease. Shay knows his stuff. He gets me. He gets my book. He makes it better. He wastes no time. He has been an absolute pleasure to work with.

Kevin Ireton, the editor in chief of *Fine Homebuilding*, started helping with this project ten years ago, when I wrote an essay for his magazine. At the time I didn't know what an editor actually did. He taught me, by doing so, that an editor has only one objective: to help you say what you want to say, better than you can say it yourself. Kevin is a great editor, a clear thinker, and a treasured friend.

Mike Drezner is one of my co-owners. I wanted one person in the company to read the manuscript before it was published. He was my choice, because for twenty years Mike has been a piece of the bedrock of this company. He plays many significant roles. He has been a particularly good partner for me. We're very different from each other in ways that are complementary. We agree about a lot. We disagree about a lot. When we disagree, we learn from each other. I also want to give a special nod to two other co-owners, Deirdre Bohan and Phil Forest, who stepped forward and became, with Michael, the management committee when I took my sabbatical. They did a tremendous job, and they are an important part of the future of this company. Jim Vercruysse replaced Phil on our management committee when Phil became consumed with the start-up of our new renewable energy division, and Jim has been a great working partner as well.

Other people read parts of the manuscript along the way and were immensely helpful: my father, Herb Abrams, and friends Jonathan Orpin, Nina Keller, Jeff Halprin, and Carol Evans.

Nick Weinstock, an accomplished author and the son of wonderful longtime clients, helped me create the book proposal. Somehow he generously fit my stuff into his remarkably busy life. He helped me understand that I could do this.

I sent my proposal to only one publisher, Chelsea Green. I had an intuitive sense that Chelsea Green had commonalities with South Mountain, and that their values foreshadowed a successful collaboration. Margo Baldwin, Chelsea Green's publisher, accepted the proposal, apparently without hesitation. She called and said, "These are the precise issues we are grappling with in our company. I want the book." I'm grateful for her confidence—she's been with it all the way from the start. I am immensely appreciative that Margo believed in the book enough that she suggested a second edition—and that she and Chelsea Green have invested again. I'm a great believer in the work of Margo Baldwin and Chelsea Green Publishing.

The first time around, Marcy Brant was the editor at Chelsea Green saddled with the responsibility of overseeing and shepherding this project, and dealing with me. She did so with huge grace and skill. She missed nothing. She and the others at Chelsea Green were a joy to work with. My frequent questions—as a rank amateur—must have been annoying, but I never got that sense. I was in very good hands at Chelsea Green. I still am. There are new people—Peg O'Donnell, Jessica Saturley, Jonathan Teller-Elsberg, Allison Lennox, Bill Bokermann, Emily Foote, and others—who are unceasingly helpful.

Peter Holm and his assistant Daria Hoak, at Sterling Hill Productions, did a superb job with something very important to me—the design of the original hardcover. Nancy Ringer did a great job with the copyediting—she made insightful suggestions. Laura Jorstad did a superb job copyediting the manuscript for this edition, as did Helen Walden proofreading the pages.

Just before I sent the proposal to Chelsea Green, I sent it to three agents. One of them, Upton Brady, responded positively, but his response came after I had decided to send it to Chelsea Green, and after Margo had called and indicated that she wanted the book. Upton agreed to take it, also, and in his letter he said he thought it would be perfect for a small, independent publisher in Vermont: Chelsea Green! I had already agreed to go with Chelsea Green, so I had no need of an agent, but Upton was very helpful in several ways, and I appreciated his confidence. He passed away recently, and I read his wonderful obituary in *The New York Times* with sadness.

Lucine Kasbarian, of Progressive Book Publicity, worked tirelessly to promote this book. I am tremendously grateful for her deep commitment (to so many things) and her elegant exuberance as she pursues her goals.

I also wish to thank the photographers who took photos that appear in this book, especially Brian Vanden Brink and Randi Baird, and I particularly want to mention Betsy Smith, my office assistant here at South Mountain, for the tremendous help she has been to me in this project—organizing and managing the photos, transcribing my endless underlinings from books and magazines, assembling the reading list— you name it, she did it. She's the best.

The real heroes in this story are the people of South Mountain—my colleagues, co-owners, and co-workers. I am deeply appreciative of all that each of them has been and done. I want to include each name, because each person has different meaning to the company, and to me personally. First, my co-owners: Pinto Abrams (my son), Derrill Bazzy, Deirdre Bohan, Peter D'Angelo, Bill Dillon, Mike Drezner, Phil Forest, Pete Ives, Ken Leuchtenmacher, Peg MacKenzie, Tim Mathiesen, Peter Rodegast, Jim Vercruysse, and Laurel Wilkinson. Because of all these wonderful partners I was able to take the sabbaticals I took, and I was able to write this book. It's amazing to me to think that one of them, Pete Ives, has been here thirty years, just two fewer than I have! And he's still the dean of Vineyard surfers.

Next, the other South Mountain employees and, hopefully, future owners: Aaron Beck, Rocco Bellebuono, Matt Bendle, Ryan Bushey, Jean DaSilva, Curtis Friedman, Taylor Ives, Bob Julier, Jon Lange, Rob Meyers, Siobhan Mullin, Steve O'Brien, Greg Small, Betsy Smith, Don-E Turnell, and Jill Walsh.

To the three former owners who are no longer here—Kane Bennett, Steve Sinnett, and Vicki Sperry—I want to say thanks for paving the way. From the beginning, Steve has been immensely important as both a friend and a co-worker.

I want to thank all our former employees, too: Eric Bates, Lou Botta, Ben Cameron, Isaac Canney, Marc Carroll, Meredith Dillon, Steve Donovan, Woody Douglas, Tim Eddy, Sean George, Greg Hise, Bruce Ignacio, Judy Jardin, Patty Leland, Patrick Lindsay, Primo Lombardi, Chris MacLeod, Chadd Meerbergen, Scott Mullin, Dana Petersen, Carl Pratt, Carlos Ramirez, Nancy Rodgers, Eric Ropke, Tara Simmons, Heikki Soikkeli, Alicia Spence, Phil Strother, Dennis Thulin, Justin Tourigney, Marco Turoff, and Suzanne Williamson. I include even those few we parted with uncomfortably because I'm certain I could have done something to make it go better.

And the kids (many of whom are no longer kids) who have worked summers over the years—some have gone on to great things, while others are still going there. They are Sophie Abrams (my daughter), Vamp Campbell, Nat Cohen, Mark Couet, Milo D'Antonio, Darin Evans, Insley Julier, Tim Laursen, Scott Lazes, Chuck Leger, Eben Light, Wesley Look, Sam Miller, Skye Morse, Jack Reynolds, Jake Ryan, Stuart Rodegast, Danny Sagan, John Stanwood, Josh Vag, Taza Vercruysse, and Noah Yaffe. Danny started when he was fourteen, in 1980, when we built his parents' house. He worked for many years after and he's now an architect and design/builder in Vermont. Noah worked with us for years, too, and he also went on to architecture school and recently began to practice in New York.

None of South Mountain's accomplishments would be possible without the folks at Indigo Farm and the many superb subcontractors, suppliers, and associates of all kinds who have been such essential parts of our work through the years. Their work is woven inextricably into the fabric of ours.

I'm most appreciative to those who were gracious enough to be interviewed for this book and shared their expertise, their stories, and their wisdom. Doug Beavers, Cecile Betit, Bill Carris, Mike Comer, Mike Ferretti, Greg Graham, Don Jamison, Rob Johnston, John Logue, Steve Magowan, Karin McGrath, Jim Megson, Gary Plumley, the guys at Red House Builders, and Mark Stewart. I hope none of you have been misrepresented.

There are scores of others who have played essential roles in my learning and my journey. I'll single out a few—some from long ago, some more recent, a few who have passed away: Merle Adams, Clarissa Allen, Nat and Pam Benjamin, Madeline Blakeley, Dick Bluestein, Stewart Brand, Terry Brennan, Phil Brougham, Tom Chase, Bruce Coldham, Sanford Evans, Smokey Fuller, Lorie and Richard Hamermesh, Glen Harcourt, Terry and Jerry Hass, Fritz Hewitt, Ralph and Olivia Jenney, Marjorie Kelly, Rob Kendall, Matthew Kiefer, Jerry and Nancy Kohlberg, Bob Kuehn, Rick Lazes, Jim Leach, Robert Leaver, Richard Leonard, Tom Lesser, Ed Levin, Tony Lewis and Margie Marshall, Brian and Anne Mazar, Gino Mazzaferro, Dennis and Nancy McHone, Peter Pitegoff, Christina Platt, Mitchell Posin, Job Potter, Ron Rappaport, Marc Rosenbaum, John Ryan, Eli and Frimi Sagan, Jerry Tulis, Roy and Diana Vagelos, Kingsley Van Wagner, Kate Warner, Davis and Betsy Weinstock, Allen White, Alex and Jerelyn Wilson, my cohousing co-conspirators Paul and Sylvie Farrington and Philippe Jordi and Randi Baird (and the rest at Island Cohousing), all the friends and colleagues I have worked with at Island Affordable Housing Fund, Island Housing Trust, the Livelihood and Commerce Work Group, the Northeast Sustainable Energy Association, the Cambium Network, and so many other local and not-so-local organizations, and my in-laws, Martha McGuffie and Perry Hudson, who helped us get started long ago on South Mountain Road.

Finally, I want to express my gratitude to all the readers who have communicated with me since the publication of the first edition. Each time I hear what the book has meant to one of you, and how you have used what I have offered, it makes it that much more worthwhile. It makes me want to do more. You are the inspiration for this second edition.

Now what? Just sit here and try to think whom I may have forgotten? That list would likely be long.

You can contact me at jabrams@vineyard.net. The South Mountain Web site is at www.southmountain.com. The *Companies We Keep* Web site and blog can be found there too.

South Mountain Employee Ownership Particulars

Mission, Goals, and Principles

Mission
- To enrich our community through our work.

Goals
- To make places that draw from past intelligence and anticipate future needs;
- To craft buildings and settings that will be loved and admired for generations;
- To further our understanding of employee ownership and workplace democracy;
- To create affordable housing opportunities that help to . preserve community;
- To extend the use of renewable energy in our work and our region;
- To develop new business opportunities that extend our primary endeavors;
- To practice the best level of environmental steward-ship we can;
- To share what we learn;
- To continue our work for generations.

Guiding Principles
Our mission and goals are living expressions of our will as a company. They spring directly from these guiding principles:

- Create enduring and respectful relationships;
- Encourage individual creativity, health, and fulfillment in the workplace;
- Ensure opportunity for all;
- Honor craft and those who practice it;
- Embrace new ideas with a bold and flexible approach;
- Use reclaimed, renewable, and energy-efficient materials and systems as much as we can;
- Accept only projects that are consistent with our values;
- Practice design/build to create buildings, landscapes, and neighborhoods;
- Produce lasting value for our clients;
- Grow only with purpose;
- Use our financial resources to support our mission and our goals;
- Limit our endeavors to Martha's Vineyard, except educational work;
- Cultivate a spirit of cooperation, teamwork, and fun!

Ownership

Generally

Ownership at SMC is a privilege, an expectation, and, to some degree, a responsibility. This does not mean that all employees will necessarily become Owners. Our policies regarding ownership, in addition to the basic structure and governing rules contained in our bylaws, are outlined below. More detailed information about our ownership history and structure can be found in the SMC Ownership Discussion on our Web site (www.southmountain.com).

Becoming an Owner

(A) PROCESS

1. Employees are evaluated for ownership suitability and educated about the meaning of ownership during their first five years of employment. The process is conducted by the Personnel Committee, and consists of, at a minimum, at least one evaluation and educational session with all future employees, followed by a report to the Board, which is responsible for the final decision regarding acceptance. During this process, the Personnel Committee will prepare employees for ownership, including, if necessary, recommendations for individual improvements.

2. The intention is that it will be clear, when each individual reaches eligibility, whether the individual is ready to accept the responsibility and whether the current Owners are ready to accept the individual as a new Owner.

(B) ELIGIBILITY

Ownership eligibility begins once an individual has worked a minimum of five years full-time employment or equivalent. Additionally, there are four essential criteria that prospective Owners are expected to meet:

1. The intention to work at South Mountain for the foreseeable future; not an absolute commitment for a certain number of years, but the expectation of long-term employment;

2. An ability to work well and cooperatively in whatever job the employee does. Evaluations should demonstrate exemplary work and cooperation, or steady improvement where necessary, and a nondefensive attitude that allows criticism and self-criticism;

3. A commitment to understanding and honoring the issues that are central to the company's values: quality work, ethical

business conduct, environmental responsibility, and concern for other people; in other words, we expect that a new owner will be a good representative of the company;

4. A commitment that, while an owner, the individual will make SMC their primary work.

(C) New Owner Fee

1. *Purpose:* This fee is for the purchase of a share of SMC ownership. It is described in the bylaws as the "membership fee."

2. *Procedure:* The fee may be paid (on May 1 or November 1) in cash, or payments may be spread, at no interest, over a period of time not to exceed 36 months. The new Owner takes on all responsibilities and receives all benefits of ownership once 50 percent of the fee has been paid. When the fee is paid, it is deposited into the SMC cash fund. At the same time, the amount is credited to the new owner's internal capital account.

3. *Amount:* Beginning with the initial 1987 restructuring, the fee was set at $3,500. Originally there was a 10 percent yearly escalation, but in 1993 the Board agreed to reduce this to 2 percent per year to keep the amount more affordable. It was considered from the start that this fee should be substantial (of real value to the company), but affordable. We have kept it, as Michael Drezner says, "to the cost of a good used car." The current fee schedule is as follows:

May 1, 2008	$12,438.00
November 1, 2008	$12,562.00
May 1, 2009	$12,688.00
November 1, 2009	$12,815.00

Responsibilities of Ownership

(A) Attend and Participate in Board Meetings

Owners are expected to digest all material in Board meeting packets and attend all Board meetings. This requires an understanding of SMC operations and mission. A new Owner must begin to understand what it means to act in the best interests of the company, and should take an active role in charting the course of the company.

(B) Understand SMC Governance

An Owner should be familiar with SMC bylaws, and should know how governance and internal capital accounts work.

(C) Represent SMC

In a way, each owner is a community ambassador for SMC. We hope that all of us will conduct ourselves in ways that are consistent with the values of the company, as expressed in our bylaws, mission, goals, and guiding principles.

(D) Management Committee Service

The SMC Management Committee consists of four standing members and one rotating member who serves for a period of six to nine months. All Owners are expected to serve as part of the rotation.

Benefits of Ownership

(A) One Vote (or Voice) on Policy Matters

Ownership is an opportunity, as well as a responsibility, to impact the policy matters that decide the direction and destiny of SMC and determine the quality of each individual's work-life. Each Owner has one voice in the consensus process and one vote on matters that are put to a vote.

(B) Ownership Position

This is an intangible that may mean more to some than others, but the ability to consider and call oneself an Owner is an important benefit. Owners don't just work here—they own it.

(C) EQUITY SHARING/INTERNAL CAPITAL ACCOUNTS (ICAs)

1. *Generally:* One of the important aspects of the system SMC has adopted is building equity through ownership. All Owners share equity in the form of internal capital accounts, which are discussed in Article III of the bylaws. These are accountings of each person's accumulated equity. They are paper accounts (not cash accounts) that are backed up by the company's net worth, and specifically, by the company's reserve fund. (The primary purpose of the SMC reserve fund is to provide funds to assure that our equity commitments can be met. The Board is committed to maintaining the balance of the reserve fund at a minimum of 50 percent of total equity owed.)

2. *Establishment and Growth of Account:* Equity accounts begin with the membership fee that each owner pays. They grow at the end of each profitable year. A percentage of each year's net profits (collective net income less 50 percent of the accounting net income) is distributed (on paper) among the Owners, based on hours worked (patronage) during that calendar year. This is separate and distinct from the cash profit sharing that is extended to all employees each year in the form of wage bonuses. No interest is earned by the equity accounts.

3. *Dividends:* The Board may decide to distribute all or part of the patronage as dividends in any given year. These may or may not be cash, but at least 20 percent must be cash (according to the IRS). The entire annual dividend is taxable income to each individual, even the noncash portion. The Board distributes dividends only in high-profit years when there is a tax advantage to the company, and the Board distributes 40 percent in cash to at least cover the increased income tax liability generated from the cash distribution, so as to not cause a financial hardship to the individual Owners. The part of the dividend that is not paid in cash goes into the Internal Capital Accounts, and, when distributed as cash at a later date, is nontaxable.

4. *Reserve Fund:* In 1999 a Reserve Fund was established to back up the equity and to use to pay out departing owners. The Fund has been built using corporate earnings, and the money is invested in socially responsible stocks and bonds. The Board has committed to always maintaining this account with at least 50 percent of total equity. Money from the Fund can only be used to pay out departing owners unless all Owners consent to using all or any of the Fund for other purposes.

5. *Distributions While Employed:* The Board has established the following guidelines for distributions from individual equity accounts while members are still employed:

   (a) Up to $30,000 per year can be distributed, up to $15,000 total per person, on a first-come, first-served basis;

   (b) Distribution is at 60 percent of value (recipient can take a tax deduction on the remainder);

   (c) There are no restrictions on use except it is not intended that these funds be used for investment purposes.

6. *Payout upon Age 62:* All Owners may begin to collect equity upon reaching the age of 62. They are eligible to remain Owners as long as they are employed (full-time, three-quarter time, or part-time with Board approval) and until they have drawn their equity down below the amount of the then-current membership fee. This allows older people to continue their ownership rather than being forced to retire by a need or desire to begin collecting equity.

7. *Payout upon Ownership Termination*

   (a) *Adjustment for Share of Reserve Fund Earnings:* Upon termination of ownership, the member's equity account balance will be adjusted (using a formula specified in the bylaws) to include a prorated amount of the appreciation of the company's reserve fund. If there is no appreciation in the reserve fund, there will be no adjustment to the member's equity account.

(b) *Payout Procedure:* After the close of the fiscal year in which a member's ownership is terminated, the value of that member's equity account will be paid out in equal payments spread over a period of 10 years. If an individual wishes an accelerated payout of their account, they must make their request in writing to the Personnel Committee, who will make a proposal pending the Board's approval. In such cases, the account will be valued as follows:

immediate payout:	60.0 percent
three-year payout:	72.5 percent
five-year payout:	79.5 percent
seven-year payout:	86.5 percent

An Owner who is planning to retire or depart can end ownership as of April 30 (end of fiscal year) of the year in which the departure will occur. If a departing Owner has any special requests regarding equity payout, they must be submitted in writing to the Personnel Committee. If any requests do not fit precisely with our policies, Personnel will make a recommendation to be acted on by the full Board.

Part-Time Ownership

The Board agrees that to limit ownership to full-time workers may be to lose valuable wisdom. Moreover, there are no additional costs for Owners who work less; they share less of the profits (in both ways). Therefore, three-quarter-time and full-time employees may continue their ownership by right. Part-time ownership (less than three-quarter-time) must be approved by the Board (see Benefits).

Termination of Ownership

Nobody may maintain ownership and share profits beyond the termination of employment. At termination or retirement, an Owner's share must be sold back to the corporation.

Governance

Generally

Decisions are made by the Board of Directors, which consists of the Owners. All Owners are employees; there are no outside Owners or Board members. Each Board member has one vote, but we generally work by consensus. In 21 years we have had to take only three votes. When we vote, a 75 percent supermajority is required for passage of a proposal.

Our management system is relatively traditional but perhaps more open and decentralized than some. There is a spirit of inquiry and experimentation. All are encouraged to make decisions and accept responsibility for those decisions. All are encouraged to question the decisions of others. Taking risks and making mistakes are everyday events.

The President and CEO has overall responsibility for operations and is directly responsible to the Board, but much of the management is in the hands of a variety of committees. The Management Committee, which includes the President and CEO, manages the company. At present, there are a number of distinct areas of the company, each consisting of a team of employees: business office, design group, woodworking shop, product sales and renewable energy, and carpentry crews (there are currently three carpentry crews and one small job/repair crew). In addition, there are currently eight other standing committees (Personnel, Design, Production, Education, Charitable Contributions, Lighting, Housing, and Waste.

Our governance system is a democracy that has clear divisions of responsibilities and authorities. The group of Owners has the ultimate authority but it delegates much of the trust and authority to management. There is a well-defined mechanism for discussion, debate, and change.

Board of Directors
(A) MEMBERS/OWNERS

 John Abrams (President)
 Pinto Abrams
 Derrill Bazzy
 Deirdre Bohan (Vice President)
 Peter D'Angelo
 Billy Dillon
 Michael Drezner
 Phil Forest
 Peter Ives (Clerk)
 Ken Leuchtenmacher
 Peg MacKenzie
 Tim Mathiesen (Treasurer)
 Peter Rodegast
 Jim Vercruysse
 Laurel Wilkinson

(B) RESPONSIBILITIES

The Board has responsibility for policy decisions that determine the course of the company and its future, such as:

- New Owners;
- Compensation and benefits;
- Direction of future projects and work;
- New ventures, initiatives, and projects;
- Investments;
- Major financial decisions, including profit sharing, major purchases, and expansions;
- Involvement in community projects;
- Major donations;
- Governance and bylaw changes.

(C) DECISION MAKING

1. *Process:* Management prepares the Board to make the above decisions and in most cases recommends direction and courses of action for the Board's consideration. Before each bi-monthly board meeting an agenda and a package of supporting material is distributed to the Owners so they are prepared to discuss and deliberate.

2. *Board v. Management Decisions:* There are times when it is not clear whether a decision should go to the Board or not. The best test of this is how we all feel and what's reasonable. Sometimes a Board member will say, "Why weren't we consulted about this?" A discussion will follow and we will reach a conclusion together so we know how to treat similar situations in the future. This way informal adjustments and new understandings are crafted over time. Everyone understands that it is important to balance participation and efficiency. Everyone understands that there is no map to guide us, and that we need to be comfortable with trial and error, always being ready to alter the process as needed. Everyone understands that we are a "work-in-progress."

3. *Decisions Involving Relatives:* Whenever there are issues of hiring, termination, or ownership that involve close relatives (spouses, siblings, parents, children) of an individual Owner, the Owner will have an opportunity to express his or her views about the issue, will recuse himself or herself from deliberations, and will have an opportunity to be involved in the decision making (whether it be by consensus or vote). This applies to deliberations in both Personnel Committee and Board meetings.

4. *Difficult Decisions:* The process we commonly use with difficult decisions is to make a decision, sleep on it, and then revisit it at a subsequent special or regular meeting. Any Board member should call for this procedure when he or she feels it is warranted.

(D) Meetings

1. *Open Meeting Policy:* Board meetings are open to non–Board members if they wish to attend. Board minutes and attachments are available to anyone interested.

2. *Attendance:* All Board members should attend all Board meetings whenever possible. Board members who miss meetings must expect, of course, that important decisions may be made in their absence.

3. *Company Meetings:* The Board attempts to schedule two to three company meetings per year that all employees are expected to attend.

4. *Agendas and Minutes:* All SMC meetings (including Board meetings and committee meetings) will abide by the following procedures:

   • Agendas will be distributed before meetings;
   • Minutes will be distributed within 24 hours of meetings, if possible;
   • Minutes will note assigned tasks, with doers and deadlines where applicable;
   • Agendas and minutes will be distributed by e-mail, with paper copies only as necessary.

APPENDIX TWO
Employee Ownership Transition Process

Organizing a worker-owned business, or restructuring an existing one, is daunting. It brings up endless questions, and not all have easy answers. There is no single set of rules to guide the process, and this is a dynamic, growing movement; therefore, new approaches and understandings are constantly being created. The following is an attempt to outline a possible agenda to help you move through the process, and provide you and your company some helpful resources.

1. First and foremost, you the owner(s) (or a group of people in the case of a new start-up) must have an interest in examining the possibilities, the benefits, the drawbacks, and the obstacles of a democratic workplace, and have at least a philosophical commitment to it.

2. Given that, identify a few key employees to work with in the exploratory phase. In an existing business, if it is not possible to identify some such people, or at least one or two, this might not be the right thing, or the right time.

3. Remember, there are no right answers, and there is no business exactly like yours. This is an inquiry to discover how *your business* might transition to a new form, and whether it is an appropriate direction.

4. Read whatever you can (or whatever appeals to you) from the "Reading List" below and spend some time on the Web sites listed in the last section. Distill the nuggets—the ones that seem to apply to your sensibility and your situation. Talk with your key employees about the readings—what have you (all) learned that may be useful?

5. At this point it is important to hire a consultant with employee ownership knowledge and experience to help you navigate (a few are listed at the end of this document). The consultant can help you undertake an internal examination and do a preliminary feasibility assessment and risk analysis. Dig deep. When short on knowledge, use common sense to work through as far as you can. These are some of the questions you'll need to answer:

- What does the owner(s) want? When?
- What do the key employees want?
- Where do the needs intersect? Where are there tensions?
- What is your initial sense of the value of the company?
- What does the future of the company look like?
- How committed are the key employees to the future of the company?
- How committed is the owner(s) to taking this step?
- How will the purchase be financed?
- How much can the business afford to pay out to the owner(s)?
- What form of ownership seems most appropriate to current company realities:
- Cooperative corporation?
- Employee stock option plan/cooperative hybrid?
- Limited employee stock option plan?
- Simple expanded partnership (for those not ready for—or inclined to—employee ownership)?
- Other?
- How will decisions be made?
- What will be policy decisions and what will be management decisions?
- What kind of ownership training will be needed?
- What kind of management training will need to occur

to prepare for the owner(s)'s departure (if this is part of the plan)?

6. If the results of this inquiry are generally positive and indicate that it may make sense to move forward, summarize all findings and draw conclusions about the following:
   • Here's where we think we're at right now.
   • Here are the remaining questions we have.

7. It can be very valuable, at this stage (or earlier), to talk with a few other employee-owned companies, of roughly your size, about your findings, and your specific questions, and get their reactions.

8. With consultant's assistance, and with the assistance of an accountant and attorney:
   • Conduct a company valuation analysis and prepare a financial buyout scheme.
   • Prepare corporate bylaws.
   • Prepare a formal business plan.
   • Prepare an offering statement and legal agenda for reorganization.

9. At this point you should be prepared to initiate the restructuring and birth the new company.

10. Go through the steps. Live happily ever after (maybe). Adjust as necessary.

Employee Ownership Reading List

Note: The three books and two articles marked with an asterisk * together comprise a good overview of the subject.

*Adams, Frank T., and Gary B. Hansen. *Putting Democracy to Work: A Practical Guide for Starting and Managing Worker Owned Businesses*. San Francisco: Berrett-Koehler Publishers, 1992. The primary focus is worker cooperatives.

Bell, Daniel. *Bringing Your Employees into the Business: An Employee Ownership Handbook for Small Business*. Kent, Ohio: Kent Popular Press, 1988.

Ellerman, David P. "Notes on the Co-op/ESOP Debate." Somerville, Mass.: Industrial Cooperative Association, 1983.

Gates, Jeff. *The Ownership Solution: Toward a Shared Capitalism for the 21st Century.* Reading, Mass.: Addison-Wesley Press, 1998.

Kamoroff, Bernard, and Jim Beatty. *We Own It: Starting and Managing Coops, Collectives, and Employee Owned Ventures.* Laytonville, Calif.: Bell Springs Publishing, 1982. A bit outdated, but useful.

Industrial Cooperative Association, Inc. "The Internal Capital Account System." 1982.

*Logue, John, Richard Glass, Wendy Patton, Alex Teodosio, and Karen Thomas. The Worker Ownership Institute. *Participatory Employee Ownership: How It Works.* Kent, Ohio: Kent State University, 1998. A well-organized analysis and how-to book.

Logue, John, and Jacquelyn Yates. *The Real World of Employee Ownership.* Ithaca, N.Y./ London: ILR Press, 2001.

*Logue, John. "The 1042 Roll-Over Cooperative in Practice: A Case Study of How Select Machine Became a Co-op." Ohio Employee Ownership Center. Kent, Ohio: Kent State University, 2006. An excellent article about the nuts and bolts of an employee-owned cooperative restructuring via an important IRS tool.

*Pitegoff, Peter. "Worker Ownership in Enron's Wake—Revisiting a Community Development Tactic." *Journal of Small & Emerging Business Law,* Vol. 8, pp. 239–259, 2004. An up-to-date analysis of the state of employee ownership.

*Rosen, Cory, John Case, and Martin Staubus. *Equity—Why Employee Ownership Is Good for Business.* Boston: Harvard Business School Press, 2005. The big picture, primarily about ESOPs.

Rosen, Cory, and Karen Young, editors. *Understanding Employee Ownership.* Ithaca, N.Y.: ILR Press, 1991.

Whyte, William Foote, and Kathleen King Whyte. *Making Mondragon: The Growth and Dynamics of the Worker Cooperative Complex.* Ithaca, N.Y.: ILR Press, 1991. Good history and background about the world's most successful organization of cooperatives.

Employee Ownership Consultants and Useful Web Sites

The ICA Group
1 Harvard Street, Suite 200
Brookline, MA 02146
(617) 232-8765
www.ica-group.org
contact: Jim Megson
jmegson@ica-group.org

Ownership Associates
122 Mt. Auburn Street
Cambridge, MA 02138

(617) 868-4600
www.ownershipassociates.com
contact: Christopher Mackin
oa@ownershipassociates.com

National Center for Employee Ownership
(510) 208-1300
www.nceo.org
nceo@nceo.org

Ohio Employee Ownership Center
113 McGilvery Hall, Kent State University
Kent, OH 44242
(330) 672-3028
www.kent.edu/oeoc
contact: John Logue
jlogue@kent.edu

Vermont Employee Ownership Center
31 Main Street
Burlington, VT 05042
(802) 861-6611
www.veoc.org
contact: Jon Crystal
Jon.Crystal@VEOC.org

US Federation of Worker Cooperatives
P.O. Box 170701
San Francisco CA 94117-0701
(415) 379-9201
info@usworker.coop
www.usworker.coop

Southern Appalachian Center for Cooperative Ownership
125 Wall Street, Suite D
Asheville, NC 28801
(828) 232-0632
contact: Frank Adams
joehill@mindspring.com

Beyster Institute
1241 Cave Street
La Jolla, CA 92038
(858) 822-6000
www.beysterinstitute.org
beysterinstitute@beysterinstitute.ucsd.edu

Stephen Magowan, Attorney
Steiker, Fischer, Edwards & Greenapple, PC
156 College Street, 3rd Floor
Burlington, VT 05406
(802) 860-4077
smagowan@sfeglaw.com
www.sfeglaw.com
*Also with offices in Philadelphia, Pennsylvania; Morristown,
New Jersey; and Providence, Rhode Island.*

Mark Stewart, Attorney
Shumaker, Loop & Kendrick, LLP
1000 Jackson
Toledo OH 43624
(419) 321-1456
www.slk-law.com
mstewart@slk-law.com
*Also with offices in Tampa, Florida; Columbus, Ohio; and Charlotte,
North Carolina.*

James Dean, Attorney
Dean, Dunn & Phillips LLC
4155 East Jewell Avenue, Suite 703
Denver, CO 80222
(303) 756-6744
www.lawatddp.com
jim@lawatddp.com

Jerry Tulis, CPA
Tulis Miller and Company
313 Congress Street, 4th Floor
Boston, MA 02210
(617) 946-9118
jerry@tulismiller.com

Cooperative Development Institute
1 Sugarloaf Street
South Deerfield, MA 01373
(413) 665-1271
info@cdi.coop
www.cdi.coop

Canadian Worker Co-op Federation
#104, 402—30th Avenue
Calgary, AB T2E 2E3
(403) 276-8250
Hazel Corcoran, Executive Director
www.canadianworker.coop

ESOP Association Canada
www.esop-canada.com/ESOPCanada

Meeting Facilitation and Consensus Decision Making

Good meetings are a joy. Poor meetings are tragic. Many of us, in our lives, spend significant time in meetings, but we are not taught how to lead them well or how to effectively participate in them. The prevailing method for conducting meetings, Robert's Rules of Order, comes from military roots and relies on rigid structure, rules of conduct, and strict adherence to the rule of the majority. Often nearly half the people at a meeting disagree with a decision that has been reached. In many cases, by using a more open process that encourages dialogue and participation, we can arrive at decisions that are supported, at least to some degree, by everyone affected.

I have facilitated hundreds of meetings. This doesn't mean I'm particularly good at it or have special expertise, but my experience has given me great respect for the practice. I work in a company that operates by consensus, I live in a cohousing neighborhood that is governed by consensus, and I have chaired several nonprofits that operated by consensus. I find consensus decision making to be an effective, just, and highly collaborative way to make decisions, develop initiatives, and solve problems.

It's clear to me that a workplace is a better place when employees truly work in teams, but again, the most familiar team models we have are those that are created to win wars and games. We have a commander or a coach who gives orders, and the soldiers or the players use those instructions to defeat the opponent. Mediator Bill Ury says, "People are realizing that adversarial, win–lose attitudes in an increasingly interdependent world, where I depend on you and you depend on me, just don't work anymore. Using those tactics is like asking, 'Who's winning this marriage?'"

Who's winning this company? Wrong question.

Facilitation and consensus are two powerful tools for building the kind of nonhierarchical teams that can produce the best possible collaborative thinking. I am not suggesting leaderless teams and open-ended processes with no controls. Quite the opposite. I'm suggesting well-led processes that invite, engage, and expand capability.

To talk about facilitation and consensus we need to know what they are. I'll take them one at a time.

Facilitation

To create as a team we must meet as a team. Too many meetings are unsuccessful: too long, unfocused, petty, unproductive, led by domineering or disagreeable individuals, meandering, time wasting, boring, contentious. Such meetings leave participants dreading the next one.

A facilitator is an individual with a particular skill who accepts responsibility for helping the group move through an agenda in the time available and make necessary decisions and plans for implementation in order to accomplish common goals.

Unfortunately, meetings are usually facilitated by default, by whoever is in charge, without recognition of the meaning of the job.

Facilitation is part art and part science. There is a growing body of knowledge and resources about the practice, and there are several ways to learn the skill. It is being consciously practiced more and more in business, government, and the nonprofit world. There are also many natural facilitators—leaders who don't think about facilitation but practice it as their standard mode of conducting meetings. But mostly it's a skill we have to learn, like drawing.

Especially with large groups, facilitating can be scary—it's a big responsibility. It requires moment-to-moment awareness, being awake and active, and thinking on your feet. It's like dancing. If your mind wanders, you lose the rhythm and stumble. It's more like jazz than classical music, and it's exhausting.

And just as musicians have off nights, facilitators can have off meetings. I've had plenty.

The responsibility of the facilitator is to the group and its work rather than to the individuals within the group. The group gives the facilitator additional rights to accompany the increased responsibility.

A facilitator encourages the expression of various viewpoints—the more important the decision, the more important it is to have all pertinent information (facts, feelings, and opinions) on the table. A facilitator keeps the group focused on the agenda item and task at hand.

Perhaps the most common misconception about facilitation is that the facilitator is supposed to make sure that everyone gets to say what they want. That is the opposite extreme of not letting anyone speak at all. Facilitation is the art of finding the middle ground—the place where as many people as possible get to express themselves as completely as possible within the bounds of what the group is willing to listen to and what time permits.

Facilitation is not about encounter. It is about learning a form of group guidance that produces accommodation.

The facilitator is responsible for protecting ideas and individuals from attack, suggesting processes for following the agenda, and devising other approaches if the process bogs down.

Listening and summarizing are the primary skills of facilitation. The facilitator listens for the whole group and each person in it. As facilitator, you listen for the group's purpose, and the power of your listening focuses and energizes the group.

I have conducted facilitation training at both South Mountain Company and Island Cohousing, and in both organizations we now have a number of skilled facilitators. I have noticed that once they are trained to facilitate, people become better meeting participants as well as better meeting leaders. They understand the process in a new and more complete way.

Consensus

In my view, the highest goal of facilitation is to produce consensus. Consensus is a process of synthesizing the wisdom of all participants into the best decision possible at the time. It is not unanimous agreement, and in fact, participants may consent to a decision that they disagree with, but that they recognize meets the needs of the group or the situation. The root of consensus is consent, which means to give permission to. When you consent to a decision, you are giving your permission for the group to go ahead with it.

Consensus is about accommodation, but, more important, it's about nobody having to accept that to which they are vehemently opposed. The cooperative nature of consensus yields a different mind-set from the competitive nature of majority voting. Key attributes of successful participation include humility, willingness to listen to others and see their perspectives, and willingness to share ideas without insisting they are the best ones.

Some describe consensus as a transformational process. When we use the accumulation of several people's ideas and weld them together, the final product is better than what anyone could have devised on his or her own. The idea of consensus is not to eliminate conflict but to transform it.

At South Mountain Company we have used consensus decision making for two decades to run our business. At Island Cohousing, where I live, we have used consensus decision making for four years of development and eight years of living.

Consensus decision making can be divided into five parts or stages:

1. Expression of an initial idea.
2. Discussion of the idea.
3. Synthesis of reactions and creation of a proposal.
4. Testing of the proposal within the group, and modification if necessary.
5. Implementation and evaluation of the decision.

The fundamental difference between consensus and majority vote is that in a consensus process a single person can block a decision. Consensus empowers each individual in a way that majority voting does not. Majority voting can accomplish decision making quickly, but it also can strain relationships and sense of community. In achieving a majority of votes, expediency can become more important than relationship. What one individual thinks may not matter unless that individual has sufficient power. Consensus often requires more creativity, and it often results in more complete solutions.

Because consensus can become paralyzed by one difficult, powerful, or dysfunctional individual, I advocate a backup voting mechanism to be used when consensus cannot be reached after a specified amount of discussion. In the organizations with which I am most familiar, this mechanism has been essential but rarely used. Aside from its practical utility, its existence assures more adherence to the consensus process—when someone is being stubbornly disagreeable, they know they're likely to be outvoted if they don't find a way to compromise.

At both South Mountain Company and Island Cohousing the backup voting mechanism requires a 75 percent supermajority.

Occasions do arise in which individuals are consistently argumentative for the sake of argument. They often characterize their behavior as "playing the devil's advocate." I once heard a facilitator respond to someone who was "just being the devil's advocate" as follows: "Thanks for your sentiments, but I think the devil has all the help he needs."

Consensus is a conservative process. Because it takes a new consensus to replace an existing decision, decisions tend to stand once made. Some people are uncomfortable with this conservatism because it can be hard to change a decision. To address this, some consensus proposals include a review period or a sunset clause. Requiring that the decision be renewed after some time has passed can encourage a group to experiment with new ideas without fear of being locked into a risky or unfamiliar path. It also provides an easy mechanism for incorporating new learning, over time.

One way to ensure that group time is not spent reconsidering previously made decisions when only one person—or a few—wants to do so is to require that reopening a consensus decision have a minimum number of supporters, say 10 or 20 percent of the group.

There are some issues for which consensus may not be an effective process. A classic example is style issues or color or design choices. Choosing the color scheme for corporate headquarters may not be the best decision to put to a group consensus process, because there is no best choice between blue or green; they are simply personal preferences. In these cases, using a weighted voting system on a number of choices may be a more effective way to get the job done.

Degrees of Consent

Consent does not mean agreement. The goal of consensus is to come to a decision that everyone will give permission to, at least for a while. Supporters of a decision usually include true supporters of that position, those who don't really care either way, and those who don't fully support the position but don't wish to stand in the way.

Blocking is appropriate only if a participant strongly believes that a proposed decision is going to be bad for the whole group or to violate the mission of the group. If a participant blocks a group decision because of his or her personal values, that individual is essentially demanding that the whole group subscribe to his or her values. It is the facilitator's job to be clear about this and to remind participants of the powerful responsibilities that come with the ability to block decisions.

There are ways of objecting to a proposal without blocking consensus:

- Nonsupport—I don't agree with this decision but I will go along with it.
- Reservations—I think this decision is a mistake because _____, but I'll live with it.

- Call for a later review—I would like this decision
  reviewed after _____.

Decision-Making Reflections

I am sometimes asked whether it is perilous for the employees to make
the decisions for a business. What do they know? Isn't it inefficient
and potentially paralyzing for decisions to be made by consensus by
a diverse group? Shouldn't we leave the decision making to skilled
management?

I speak primarily from my particular experience. South Mountain's
governance system is a democracy with clear divisions of responsibility
and authority. Much of the authority to act is delegated to management. This delegation comes easily, because this was the established
mode of operation before the ownership of the company was shared.
The difference is that there is now a clear mechanism for discussion,
debate, and change. The comfortable delegation of authority may be
one of the advantages of a company converting to worker ownership
and control, and consensus decision making, rather than starting that
way. Once the entrepreneurial leap of starting a new business has been
achieved, adoption of consensus-based decision making becomes a
part of the maturation process. In our case, consensus decision making
has only broadened our view; it has not watered down our decisions or
derailed our ability to make them in any discernible way.

To our own I can add the experience of one of the largest companies in the world, Shell Oil, which finds consensus to be an effective
form of decision making, as author Arie de Geus explains in *The Living
Company:*

> From the top of the Shell Group down there is no tradi-
> tional mechanism to resolve conflict. . . . One way or
> another, the members of the Committee of Managing

> Directors (CMD) and the two boards of directors have
> to agree among themselves on solutions that are accept-
> able to all. In practice, there . . . is no good way to force
> through a decision to which one or more of the members
> are actively opposed. The minimum that is required is
> a quasi-unanimity. . . . Quasi-unanimity does not mean
> that everybody agrees with the proposal. It means that
> no one is so violently opposed that he will show a veto
> card. The chairman has no other power than his persua-
> sion; he has no casting vote or final decision.[1]

De Geus goes on to say that distribution of power can be frustrating,
but it brings more actively engaged minds into the decision-making
process. It may lead to better action and more complete organizational
learning because implementation is an integral part of the decision,
rather than something separate that is imposed later. The people whose
cooperation is necessary are right in the thick of it.

Over the years, as we came to recognize and define South Mountain
values, we were also learning more about decision making. Gradually
we were gaining understanding of the fact that ideas placed before us
were meant to be discussed, shaped further, and accepted or rejected
as a group. Each was fair game for adjustment, change, putting on the
back burner, or scrapping, so there was no need to fight for or against
new proposals; we had only to consider, to listen, to muse, to articulate. Dialogue produced satisfaction; argument did not. Each of us
must learn this differently. As the most entrepreneurial of the group
and the former lone decision maker, I must learn not to push too hard.
Others must learn not to cast themselves as powerless victims. We all
have to learn to trust one another. As we continue to work at these
things, we have begun to enjoy the conversation, I think, and in-your-
corner persuasion has given way to collaborative examination. We can
now effectively take a stand for what we believe in, as individuals who
are members of a group of owners, as a group that is the steward of the
company, and as a company that is part of a larger community.

I don't pretend to cast any of these gains as done deals. We will continue to struggle with these issues of responsibility, accountability, quality, fear, ownership, and direction.

Although both South Mountain Company and Island Cohousing are democratic organizations that rely on participation and consensus decision making, they are obviously different, as South Mountain is a business and Island Cohousing is a neighborhood. But there is another difference, less obvious but fundamental: South Mountain is a culture of expertise; decisions are made and actions taken by those who have the ability and experience. Others recognize that and place their trust in that approach, even though they may have the power to do otherwise. There's a strong sense of responsibility to essentials like clients, the bottom line, and company reputation. Island Cohousing, on the other hand, is a neighborhood, and neighborhoods are not about expertise; they're about neighborliness. At Island Cohousing I hope that we are gradually developing a culture of respect for the neighborhood itself, as well as for one another. Evolving traditions and standards and a sense of neighborhood history will, I hope, drive this cultural evolution.

One of the truly rewarding aspects of my work has been the long-term process of learning about and practicing facilitation and consensus decision making. Years of experience lead to confidence. When I begin a meeting these days, I generally know that we will reach agreement as needed. The exciting part is what I don't know—what the agreement(s) will be. Surprising conclusions and dramatic divergences from starting points are common when a community of interest engages in a well-conducted process of collaborative decision making.

Facilitation and Consensus Resources

Many resources that consider facilitation and consensus decision making in greater depth are available. I list only a few below. Much of the information in this appendix originally came from the work of Rob Sandelin, whose teachings I have found to be particularly useful and instructive, and much of the inspiration has come from Robert Leaver of New Commons in Providence, Rhode Island, my favorite facilitator.

A Facilitator's Guide to Effective Consensus Meetings, by Rob Sandelin (available at www. ic.org/nica/book/Cover.htm).

What Is Consensus? by Rob Sandelin (available at www.ic.org/nica/Process/Consensusbasics. htm).

Conversations That Matter . . . Convening, Facilitating, Collaborating (Volume 6 of The New Commons Papers, available at www.newcommons.com).

Getting to Yes, by Roger Fisher, William Ury, and Bruce Patton (Penguin Books, 1991).

The Third Side, by William Ury (Penguin Books, 1999).

The Makings of a Good Meeting, by Kevin Wolf (available at www.dcn.davis.ca.us/go/kjwolf).

NOTES

Introduction

1. Vaclav Hamel, *Disturbing the Peace: A Conversation with Karel Hvizdala,* English translation by Paul Wilson (New York,Vintage, 1991), 110.
2. Peter Barnes, *Climate Solutions* (White River Junction, Vt: Chelsea Green Publishing, 2008), 69–70.
3. Gretchen Spreitzer, "Giving Peace a Chance: Organizational Leadership, Empowerment, and Peace," *Journal of Organizational Behavior* (November 2007), Wiley Publishers.

Chapter 1

1. Bernard Kamaroff, *Small Time Operator* (Laytonville, Calif.: Bell Springs, 1991).
2. Mitchell is still farming, with his wife, Clarissa, on land that has been in her family for centuries.
3. Economist Schumpeter (1883–1950) felt that companies had to be organized for innovation and constant change, which he termed "creative destruction."
4. Marjorie Kelly, *The Divine Right of Capital: Dethroning the Corporate Aristocracy* (San Francisco: Berrett-Koehler, 2001), 110.
5. This phrase appeared in *A Voice Crying in the Wilderness: Notes from a Secret Journal,* the last book by this anarchist novelist, essayist, and environmental protector. It was published in 1989, the year Ed Abbey died.
6. Charles Handy, *The Hungry Spirit* (New York: Broadway Books, 1999), 121.

Chapter 2

1. William Greider, *The Soul of Capitalism* (New York: Simon & Schuster, 2003), 13.
2. Kelly, *The Divine Right of Capital,* xvi
3. Ibid., 186.
4. John Logue and Jacquelyn Yates, *The Real World of Employee Ownership* (Ithaca, N.Y./London: ILR Press, 2001), xiii.
5. These quotes come from the minutes of a series of meetings held in spring 1986.
6. Pitegoff, Peter. "Worker Ownership in Enron's Wake—Revisiting a Community Development Tactic." *Journal of Small & Emerging Business Law,* Vol. 8, pp. 239–259, 2004.
7. Cory Rosen, John Case, and Martin Staubus, *Equity: Why Employee Ownership Is Good for Business* (Boston:: Harvard Business School Press, 2005), 8.
8. Rosen, Case, and Staubus, *Equity,* 166.
9. Ibid.
10. Logue and Yates, *The Real World of Employee Ownership,* 73.
11. Carol Beatty and Harvey Schacter, *Employee Ownership: The New Source of Competitive Advantage* (Etobicoke, Ontario: Wiley, 2001).
12. Pitegoff, "Worker Ownership in Enron's Wake."
13. Arie de Geus, *The Living Company: Habits for Survival in a Turbulent Business Environment* (Boston: Harvard Business School Press, 2002), 108.
14. From a 2008 conversation with Jim Megson.
15. From Bill Carris's "Long Term Plan for the Carris Community of Companies," written in 1994.
16. Ibid

17. From a 2008 conversation with Cecile Betit. Cecile has published a number of studies and papers about Carris Reels. Some of these are: "Carris Companies' Long and Winding Road to Employee Ownership and Values-Based Governance" in the winter 2000 issue of *Journal of Organizational Excellence;* "Carris Companies' Practice of Employee Governance," in the summer 2002 issue of *Journal of Corporate Citizenship;* and "Working Toward Transparency and Accountability" in the winter 2002 issue of the same journal. I believe (and I hope) that she is working on a book about Carris Reels.

18. From a 2008 conversation with Cecile Betit.

19. From a 2008 conversation with Karin McGrath.

20. From a 2008 conversation with Karin McGrath.

21. From a 2008 conversation with Karin McGrath.

22. From a 2008 e-mail from Cecile Betit.

23. From a 2008 conversation with Karin McGrath.

24. From a 2008 conversation with Bill Carris.

25. From a 2008 conversation with Bill Carris.

26. Pitegoff, "Worker Ownership in Enron's Wake."

27. From a 2008 document e-mailed to me by Jim Megson, and adapted by me.

28. From a 2008 e-mail from Mark Stewart.

29. From a 2007 article by Mark Stewart, "The Employee Cooperative as a Plan for Business Succession," *Cooperative Accountant* (2007).

30. Ricardo Lotti, Peter Mensing, and Davide Valenti, "A Cooperative Solution," *Strategy + Business* (autumn 2007), www.strategy-business.com.

31. Corey Rosen, et al., *Equity,* 10.

32. Ibid., 11.

33. Greider, *The Soul of Capitalism,* 271–272.

Chapter 3

1. Sharon Daloz Parks, *Leadership Can Be Taught: A Bold Approach for a Complex World* (Boston: Harvard Business Press, 2005). This is a book about Heifetz's extraordinary method for teaching leadership.

2. I've lost track of where I originally read this.

3. Kelly, *The Divine Right of Capital,* 152

4. Logue and Yates, *The Real World of Employee Ownership,* 14.

5. Charles Handy, *The Elephant and the Flea: Reflections of a Reluctant Capitalist* (Boston: Harvard Business School Press, 2001), 129.

6. Jeff Gates, *Democracy at Risk: Rescuing Main Street from Wall Street* (Cambridge, Mass.: Perseus, 2001), iii.

Chapter 4

1. Herman E. Daly, *Beyond Growth: The Economics of Sustainable Development* (Boston: Beacon Press, 1996), 167.

2. Jamie S. Walters, *Big Vision, Small Business: The Four Keys to Finding Success and Satisfaction as a Lifestyle Entrepreneur* (San Francisco: Ivy Sea, 2001), 58.

3. Yvon Chouinard, *Let My People Go Surfing: The Education of a Reluctant Businessman* (New York: Penguin Group, 2005), 162–163.

4. Ibid., 164.

5. Bo Burlingham, *Small Giants: Companies That Choose to Be Great Instead of Big* (New York: Portfolio, 2005), xvi.

6. Handy, *The Hungry Spirit*, 106–107.
7. Burlingham, *Small Giants*, 5.
8. Gunter Pauli, *Upsizing* (Sheffield, UK: Greenleaf, 1998), 121.
9. Handy, *The Hungry Spirit*, 107–108.
10. Sarah Susanka, *The Not So Big House* (Newtown, Conn.: Taunton, 1998), 5.
11. It is beyond the scope of this book to consider large enterprise, but, ironically, Fritz Schumaker's classic *Small Is Beautiful* has a very thoughtful analysis of how large businesses can work well, and in 1973 Schumacher fully anticipated the problems of the global economy and recommended local control and oversight of large businesses. See chapter 19, "New Patterns of Ownership."
12. Information about the Rule of 150 was assembled from three places: *The Tipping Point: How Little Things Can Make a Big Difference* (Boston: Little, Brown, 2000), by Malcolm Gladwell; the Web site CommonSenseAdvice.com, run by a woman with the poetic name Lyric Duveyoung; and the W. L. Gore Web site, www.gore.com.
13. Gladwell, *The Tipping Point*, 180.
14. Greider, *The Soul of Capitalism*, 88.
15. From a 2008 e-mail from Dave Smathers.
16. Virginia Postrel, *The Substance of Style* (New York: HarperCollins, 2003), 10.
17. Dave Thomas and Michael Seid, *Franchising for Dummies* (New York: Hungry Minds, 2000), 104.
18. Tom McMakin, *Bread and Butter: What a Bunch of Bakers Taught Me About Business and Happiness* (New York: St. Martin's, 2001), 52.
19. Ibid., 63.
20. Ibid., 57.

Chapter 5

1. John Elkington, *Cannibals with Forks: The Triple Bottom Line of 21st Century Business* (Stoney Creek, Conn.: New Society Publishers, 1998).
2. Wayne Norman and Chris MacDonald, "Getting to the Bottom of 'Triple Bottom Line,'" *Business Ethics Quarterly* (March 2003).
3. At this point on the Vineyard, there seem to be more skunks than dogs and people combined. They have no natural predators here that I know off. Pedal to the metal is the only form of control.
4. These statements come from company minutes from February 1993.
5. Peter M. Senge popularized the term in his seminal book about organizations, *The Fifth Displine: The Art and Practice of the Learning Organization* (New York: Doubleday/ Currency, 1990).
6. Paul Wachtel, *The Poverty of Affluence* (New York: Free Press, 1983), 284.
7. Alfie Kohn, *No Contest: The Case Against Competition—Why We Lose in Our Race to Win* (New York: Houghton Mifflin, 1992), 48.
8. Ibid., 49.
9. Ibid., 22.
10. Ibid., 8.
11. Jeffrey Hollender and Stephen Fenichell, *What Matters Most: How a Small Group of Pioneers Is Teaching Social Responsibility to Big Business* (New York: Basic Books, 2004), 264.
12. Robert Putnam, *Making Democracy Work: Civic Traditions in Modern Italy* (Princeton, N.J.: Princeton University Press, 1993), 160.

13. James C. Collins and Jerry I. Porras, *Built to Last: Successful Habits of Visionary Companies* (New York: Harper Business, 1997), 228.

Chapter 6

1. In small business, it's much the same. According to the US census of 2000, for every hundred small businesses, only two make goods like food, clothing, machinery, and toys. Roughly eight are involved in construction. For comparison, two clean offices; seven lease us our apartments or sell us our homes; four provide personal services like wedding planning, dating services, and dry cleaning; three cut our hair or give us manicures; and two amuse us at recreational sites.
2. Alan Weisman, *The World Without Us* (New York: Thomas Dunne Books, 2007).
3. Stewart Brand, *How Buildings Learn* (New York: Viking, 1994), 166.
4. Ibid., 167.

Chapter 7

1. This quote came from an Island Affordable Housing Fund brochure for the "Raising the Roof" campaign. For details, contact the Island Affordable Housing Fund, P.O. Box 4769, Vineyard Haven, MA 02568.
2. Good sources for further information about cohousing are the Cohousing Association of the United States Web site (www.cohousing.org) and the following two books: Kathryn McCamant and Charles Durrett, *Cohousing: A Contemporary Approach to Housing Ourselves* (Berkeley, Calif.: Ten Speed Press, 1994); and Chris Hanson, *The Cohousing Handbook: Building a Place for Community* (Vancouver, B.C.: Hartley & Marks, 1996).
3. For more information about composting toilets see David DelPorto and Carol Steinfeld, *The Composting Toilet System Book* (Concord, Mass.: Center for Ecological Pollution Prevention, 2000).
4. He was making the interesting combination of *dysfunctional* and *feng shui*. Feng shui is part of an ancient Chinese philosophy of nature. It is mainly concerned with understanding the relationships between nature and ourselves so that we might live in harmony within our environment, both indoors and out.
5. "Jenney Lane Opponents Are Wrong," *Vineyard Gazette*, April 2, 2004.
6. For more information see www.capewind.org, or the excellent book about the project by Wendy Williams and Robert Whitcomb, *Cape Wind* (New York: Public Affairs Books, 2007).

Chapter 8

1. Stewart Brand, *The Clock of the Long Now: Time and Responsibility—The Ideas Behind the World's Slowest Computer* (New York: Basic Books, 1999), 2.
2. Ibid., 157.
3. de Geus, *The Living Company*, 108.
4. Senge, *The Fifth Discipline*.
5. Marjorie Kelly, "The Legacy Problem: Why Social Mission Gets Squeezed Out of Firms When They're Sold, and What to Do About It," *Business Ethics* 17, no. 2 (summer 2003).
6. Ibid.
7. Leslie Christian at the Legacy Project gathering, Minneapolis, 2002.

Chapter 9

1. Peter Wolf, *Hot Towns: The Future of the Fastest Growing Communities in America* (New Brunswick, N.J.: Rutgers University Press, 1999), 1.
2. Richard Florida, *The Rise of the Creative Class: And How It's Transforming Work, Leisure, Community and Everyday Life* (New York: Basic Books, 2002), 6.
3. These three groups have remarkable stories. The oldest, of course, is the Wampanoag tribe, members of which have lived on the Vineyard for thousands of years. Their descendants still make up the majority of the population of our westernmost town, Aquinnah. Federally recognized as a tribe in 1987, the Wampanoags are now a signifi-cant economic force and continue to be an important cultural entity, even more so as they revive lost aspects of their heritage.

    The African American population originated in the 1850s, when Oak Bluffs became a favorite resort area for middle- and upper-class blacks after a Methodist sect started summering here.

    The Brazilians arrived more recently, but their impact has been swift and far reaching. For a number of years they were quietly ensconced in menial hospitality industry jobs and barely visible. As their population has grown (it is now estimated to be three to four thousand), they have become an important presence in the life of the community. They have started businesses and built churches. Their children are in the schools. My friend Charley, the psychologist at one of our elementary schools, felt like he couldn't talk to the parents of many of his students, so he spent a summer in Brazil studying Portuguese intensively.
4. Tom Kelley, *The Art of Innovation* (New York: Doubleday, 2001), 31.
5. The letter was published in the *Hartford Courant* in 2002.
6. Michael H. Shuman, *Going Local: Creating Self-Reliant Communities in a Global Age* (New York: Routledge, 2000), 128.
7. Handy, *The Hungry Spirit*, 176.
8. Bill McKibben, *Deep Economy: The Wealth of Communities and the Durable Future* (New York: Henry Holt, 2007), 88.
9. Shuman, *Going Local*, 59.
10. Ibid., 202.
11. Jeffrey Hollender and Stephen Fenichell, *What Matters Most: How a Small Group of Pioneers Is Teaching Social Responsibility to Big Business, and Why Big Business Is Listening* (New York: Basic Books, 2004), 265.

Chapter 10

1. Tachi Kiuchi and Bill Sherman, *What We Learned in the Rainforest: Business Lessons from Nature* (San Francisco: Berrett-Koehler, 2002), viii.
2. Lee wrote this in his edits of an early draft of this book. We can be certain that his comments did not indicate that my writing made clear my awareness of the slightness of my knowledge.
3. Greider, *The Soul of Capitalism*, 22.
4. Paul Loeb, *The Impossible Will Take a Little While* (New York, Basic Books, 2004), 347.
5. From a letter from Joseph Carry.

Appendix 3

1. de Geus, *The Living Company*, 191.

READING LIST

This is a short list of books that have changed how I think, followed by a long list of other books that have been important to me in my work, listed in several categories.

The Books That Have Changed How I Think

This "changed how I think" list starts with Jack Kerouac's *Dharma Bums,* which I read when I was seventeen. Before that, I'm not sure *how* I thought, or what. This is not a list of books that have shaped my life—that one would be different and go back farther—but books that have instantly changed how I think and work (and live, I guess) when I read them. Not all are profound; some are simply how-to books that are the best of their kind (for me).

Dharma Bums, Jack Kerouac, 1958. The character Japhy Ryder showed me that convention need not be an impediment—we can simply ignore it and seek our own path.

Whole Earth Catalog, Stewart Brand, 1968. We went back to the land, but without the essential tools. Here they were—presented for our use in an amazingly practical but insightful way, along with an essentially new way to inquire about and think about the world. A towering accomplishment. To this day I continue to learn from Stewart's eclectic and unbridled thinking. Recently there have been several books published that trace the many ways that Stewart, the *Catalogs,* and the magazines that grew out of them (*Co-Evolution Quarterly* and *Whole Earth Review*) have influenced contemporary business and environmentalism.

The Grapes of Wrath, John Steinbeck, 1939. Holed up in a cabin fourteen miles from Selma, Oregon, in winter 1970, working in the woods with the McMichael family and making do, Chris, Smokey, Mitchell, Judy, and I read this book aloud every day at 5 PM. Before long we were talking like Okies.

The Way of Life, Lao-tzu, fourth century BCE. My intentional spiritual quest was short but intense, as I devoured everything I could find about Eastern religions. This is the one that stands out. I've had a copy ever since, and I read through it every few years.

From the Ground Up, John Cole and Charles Wing, 1976. This is, quite simply, the best how-to book ever written about house building, even now, after thirty-two years.

Small Time Operator, Bernard Kamaroff, 1976. This practical, irreverent how-to book taught me useful lessons while giving me the sense that serious business doesn't have to be all that serious. It's the business equivalent of *From the Ground Up.*

We Own It, Bernard Kamaroff, 1982. This was my first brush with the idea of employee ownership. It would prove to be a fateful meeting.

Small Is Beautiful, Fritz Schumacher, 1973. The subtitle—*Economics as if People Mattered*—is at the heart of what this classic is about. The influence of this book, with its profoundly different take on economics, has been widespread, and it connected deeply with my late-adolescence early-business thinking.

A Pattern Language, Christopher Alexander, 1977. This bible for environmental design takes us from towns to trellis to trim, and provides a magnificent framework for harmonious designing and building. I have given many copies to clients, and when I pull out my dog-eared copy I'm always astonished by the depth of the inquiry.

Nine Nations of North America, Joel Garreau, 1981. This book introduced me to the concept of regionalism and put words to the collection of feelings Chris and I were left with from our years of wandering North America. It provides a backdrop for my interest in relocalization.

No Contest, Alfie Kohn, 1986. Kohn has been described as the country's leading critic of competition (although he says there's not much competition for the title). Reading this book was a memorable affirmation for me, and helped me with both child rearing and business.

The Fifth Discipline, Peter Senge, 1990. How companies and organizations learn (and don't). The indispensable guide to organizational behavior.

Ecology of Commerce, Paul Hawken, 1993. Hawken's ringing endorsement of replacing the industrial world as presently constituted with responsible human-centered enterprises got the corporate world's attention, and mine, too.

Another Turn of the Crank, Wendell Berry, 1995. For me Berry is the clearest, most honest American cultural thinker and critic today. A powerful sense of the meaning of place runs through his writings. He says, "Before we can know who we are we need to know where we are."

Hope, Human and Wild, Bill McKibben, 1995. After writing *The End of Nature*, with its dismal premise, McKibben decided to look for the hopeful antidote. He found three: his own backyard in the Adirondacks, the province of Kerala in southern India, and the city of Curitiba in Brazil. More powerful by far than the nightmare scenario.

The Art of the Long View, Peter Schwartz, 1991. Rather than trying to predict the future (it's futile), Schwartz advocates preparing for it, whichever way it goes.

Built to Last, by Jim Collins and Jerry Porras, 1994, and *Good to Great*, by Jim Collins, 2001. The habits of successful companies and what distinguishes the good ones from the great ones.

Shackleton's Way, Margot Morrell and Stephanie Capparell, 2001. Because of the way he led his men out of disaster when they were stranded in Antartica for nearly two years, explorer Sir Ernest Shackleton has become a model for great leadership. I like his style.

The Divine Right of Capital, Marjorie Kelly, 2001. The former publisher of *Business Ethics* makes a great case for the democratization of capital. She compares the overthrow of the divine right of kings (in favor of democratic government) to the need to undo the "divine right of corporations" and distribute wealth to those who make it.

The Soul of Capitalism, William Greider, 2003. How to change capitalism so it truly works for all. Greider is my favorite thinker on economics, social policy, and current affairs.

The Company We Keep, John Abrams, 2005. This book, of course, changed me by the experience of creating it, not by what it says.

Employee Ownership and Workplace Democracy

Adams, Frank T., and Gary B. Hansen. *Putting Democracy to Work: A Practical Guide for Starting and Managing Worker Owned Businesses.*

Beatty, Carol, and Harvey Schachter. *Employee Ownership: The New Source of Competitive Advantage.*

Bell, Daniel. *Bringing Your Employees into the Business: An Employee Ownership Handbook for Small Business.*

Ellerman, David P. "Notes on the Co-op/ESOP Debate." Industrial Cooperative Association, 1983.

Gates, Jeff. *The Ownership Solution: Toward a Shared Capitalism for the 21st Century.*

Kamoroff, Bernard, and Jim Beatty. *We Own It: Starting and Managing Coops, Collectives, and Employee Owned Ventures.*

Kelso, Louis O., and Patricia Hetter Keslo. *Democracy and Economic Power: Extending the ESOP Revolution.*

Logue, John, Richard Glass, Wendy Patton, Alex Teodosio, and Karen Thomas. The Worker Ownership Institute. *Participatory Employee Ownership: How It Works.* Kent, Ohio: Kent State University, 1998. A well-organized analysis and how-to book.

Logue, John, and Jacquelyn Yates. *The Real World of Employee Ownership.*

Logue, John. "The 1042 Roll-Over Cooperative in Practice: A Case Study of How Select Machine Became a Co-op" (available from the Ohio Employee Ownership Center).

Morrison, Roy. *We Build the Road as We Travel.*

Pitegoff, Peter. "Worker Ownership in Enron's Wake—Revisiting a Community Development Tactic." *Journal of Small & Emerging Business Law*, Vol. 8, pp. 239–259, 2004.

Quarrey, Michael, Joseph Blasi, and Corey Rosen. *Taking Stock: Employee Ownership at Work.*

Rosen, Cory, John Case, and Martin Staubus. *Equity: Why Employee Ownership Is Good for Business.*

Rosen, Cory, and Karen Young, editors. *Understanding Employee Ownership.*

Whyte, William Foote, Tove Helland Hammer, Christopher B. Meek, Reed Nelson, and Robert N. Stern. *Worker Participation and Ownership: Cooperative Strategies for Strengthening Local Economies.*

Whyte, William Foote, and Kathleen King Whyte. *Making Mondragon: The Growth and Dynamics of the Worker Cooperative Complex.*

Meeting Facilitation and Consensus Decision Making

Kaner, Sam. *Facilitator's Guide to Participatory Decision-Making.*

Leaver, Robert. "Getting Results from Meetings" (rleaver@newcommons.com).

Rosenberg, Marshall B. *Nonviolent Communication: A Language of Life.*

Schwarz, Roger. *The Skilled Facilitator.*

Susskind, Lawrence E., and Jefferey L.Cruikshank. *Breaking Robert's Rules: The New Way to Run Your Meeting, Build Consensus, and Get Results.*

Ury, William. *The Third Side: Why We Fight and How We Can Stop.*

Wolf, Kevin. "The Makings of a Good Meeting" (kjwolf@den.davis.ca.us).

Good Business and Economics

Abrams, John. *The Company We Keep.*

Barnes, Peter. *Who Owns the Sky? Our Common Assets and the Future of Capitalism.*

Block, Peter. *Stewardship: Choosing Service Over Self-Interest.*

Burlingham, Bo. *Small Giants: Companies That Choose to Be Great Instead of Big.*

Chouinard, Yvon. *Let My People Go Surfing: The Education of a Reluctant Businessman.*

Cohen, Don, and Laurence Prusak. *In Good Company: How Social Capital Makes Organizations Work.*

Collins, Jim, and Jerry Porras. *Built to Last.*

Collins, Jim. *Good to Great: Why Some Companies Make the Leap . . . And Others Don't.*

Collins, Jim. *Good to Great and the Social Sectors.*

Csikszentmihalyi, Mihaly. *Good Business: Leadership, Flow, and the Making of Meaning.*

Daly, Herman E. *Beyond Growth: The Economics of Sustainable Development.*

Daly, Herman E., and John B. Cobb Jr. *For the Common Good: Redirecting the Economy Toward Community, the Environment, and a Sustainable Future.*

De Geus, Arie. *The Living Company: Habits for Survival in a Turbulent Business Environment.*

DePree, Max. *Leadership Jazz.*

Dolan, Paul. *True to Our Roots: Fermenting a Business Revolution.*

Drucker, Peter F. *Post-Capitalist Society.*

Gardner, Howard, Mihaly Csikszentmihalyi, and William Damon. *Good Work: When Excellence and Ethics Meet.*

Greider, William. *The Soul of Capitalism.*

Gunther, Marc. *Faith and Fortune: The Quiet Revolution to Reform American Business.*

Handy, Charles. *The Elephant and the Flea: Reflections of a Reluctant Capitalist.*

Handy, Charles. *The Hungry Spirit.*

Hawken, Paul. *The Ecology of Commerce.*

Hawken, Paul. *Growing a Business.*

Hawken, Paul, Amory Lovins, and L. Hunter Lovins. *Natural Capitalism.*

Hollender, Jeffrey, and Stephen Fenichell. *What Matters Most: How a Small Group of Pioneers Is Teaching Social Responsibility to Big Business, and Why Big Business Is Listening.*

Jacobs, Jane. *The Nature of Economies.*

Kamaroff, Bernard. *Small Time Operator.*

Kelly, Marjorie. *The Divine Right of Capital: Dethroning the Corporate Aristocracy.*

Kiuchi, Tachi, and Bill Sherman. *What We Learned in the Rainforest: Business Lessons from Nature.*

Komisar, Randy. *The Monk and the Riddle: The Art of Creating a Life While Making a Living.*

Korten, David C. *The Great Turning.*

Korten, David C. *The Post Corporate World: Life After Capitalism.*

McMakin, Tom. *Bread and Butter: What a Bunch of Bakers Taught Me About Business and Happiness.*

Parks, Sharon Daloz. *Leadership Can Be Taught.*

Senge, Peter. *The Fifth Discipline.*

Senge, Peter, C. Otto Scharmer, Joseph Jaworski, and Betty Sue Flowers. *Presence: An Exploration of Profound Change in People, Organizations, and Society.*

Schumacher, E. F. *Small Is Beautiful: Economics as if People Mattered.*

Walters, Jamie S. *Big Vision, Small Business: The Four Keys to Finding Success and Satisfaction as a Lifestyle Entrepreneur.*

Design, Place, and Local Economies

Alexander, Christopher. *The Nature of Order.*

Alexander, Christopher. *A Pattern Language.*

Benyus, Jannine M. *Biomimicry: Innovation Inspired by Nature.*

Berry, Wendell. *In the Presence of Fear: Three Essays for a Changed World.*

Berry, Wendell. *The Unsettling of America: Culture and Agriculture.*

Brand, Stewart. *How Buildings Learn.*

Cole, John, and Charles Wing. *From the Ground Up.*

Cramer, James P. *Design Plus Enterprise: Seeking a New Reality in Architecture.*

Cronon, William. *Changes in the Land: Indians, Colonists, and the Ecology of New England.*

Duany, Andres, et al. *Suburban Nation: The Rise of Sprawl and the Decline of the American Dream.*

Hale, Jonathan. *The Old Way of Seeing: How Architecture Lost Its Magic (And How to Get It Back).*

Hayden, Dolores. *Redesigning the American Dream: The Future of Housing, Work, and Family Life.*

Hiss, Tony. *The Experience of Place: A Completely New Way of Looking at and Dealing with Our Radically Changing Cities and Countryside.*

Jacobs, Jane. *Cities and the Wealth of Nations: Principles of Economic Life.*

Jacobs, Jane. *The Death and Life of Great American Cities.*

Jenkins, Robin. *The Road to Alto.*

Jensen, Derrick, and George Draffan. *Strangely Like War: The Global Assault on Forests.*

Kelley, Tom, with Jonathan Littman. *The Art of Innovation.*

Kunstler, James Howard. *The Geography of Nowhere: The Rise and Declines of America's Man-Made Landscape.*

Marshall, Alexander C. *How Cities Work: Suburbs, Sprawl and the Roads Not Taken.*

McCamant, Kathryn, and Charles Durrett; second edition with Ellen Hertzman. *Cohousing: A Contemporary Approach to Housing Ourselves.*

McDonough, William, and Michael Braungart. *Cradle to Cradle: Remaking the Way We Make Things.*

Metz, Don. *Confessions of a Country Architect.*

McKibben, Bill. *Wandering Home: A Long Walk Across American's Most Hopeful Landscape: Vermont's Champlain Valley and New York's Adirondacks.*

Mitchell, Stacy. *Big-Box Swindle: The True Cost of Mega-Retailers and the Fight for America's Independent Businesses.*

Moe, Richard, and Carter Wilkie. *Changing Places: Rebuilding Community in the Age of Sprawl.*

Mumford, Lewis. *Sticks and Stones: A Study of American Architecture and Civilization.*

Sherman, Joe. *Fast Lane on a Dirt Road: A Contemporary History of Vermont.*

Shuman, Michael H. *Going Local: Creating Self-Reliant Communities in a Global Age.*

Shuman, Michael H. *The Small-Mart Revolution: How Local Businesses Are Beating the Global Competition.*

Weschler, Lawrence. *Seeing Is Forgetting the Name of the Thing One Sees: A Life of Contemporary Artist Robert Irwin.*

Wilson, Alex. *Your Green Home: A Guide to Planning a Healthy, Environmentally Friendly New Home.*

Wolf, Peter. *Hot Towns: The Future of the Fastest Growing Communities in America.*

Ecology and Climate Change

Barnes, Peter. *Climate Solutions.*
Brower, David, with Steve Chapple. *Let the Monuments Talk, Let the Rivers Run.*
Brown, Lester R. *Eco-Economy: Building an Economy for the Earth.*
Brown, Lester R. *Plan B 2.0: Rescuing a Planet Under Stress and a Civilization in Trouble.*
Kirk, Andrew. *Counterculture Green: The Whole Earth Catalog and American Environmentalism.*
Kunstler, James Howard. *The Long Emergency: Surviving the Converging Catastrophes of the Twenty-First Century.*
McKibben, Bill. *Deep Economy: The Wealth of Communities and the Durable Future.*
McKibben, Bill. *Hope, Human and Wild.*
Roberts, Paul. *The End of Oil.*
Shellenberger, Michael, and Ted Nordhaus. "The Death of Environmentalism."
Shellenberger, Michael, and Ted Nordhaus. *Breakthrough: From the Death of Environmentalism to the Politics of Possibility.*
Stevens, William K. *Miracle Under the Oaks: The Revival of Nature in America.*
Wilson, Edward O. *The Future of Life.*

Social Policy, History, and Current Affairs

Alperovitz, Gar. *America Beyond Capitalism: Reclaiming Our Wealth, Our Liberty, and Our Democracy.*
Alperovitz, Gar, Thad Williamson, and David Imbroscio. *Making a Place for Community: Local Democracy in a Global Era.*
Boorstin, Daniel J. *The Americans: The National Experience.*
De Tocqueville, Alexis. *Democracy in America.*
Florida, Richard. *The Rise of the Creative Class: And How It's Transforming Work, Leisure, Community and Everyday Life.*
Frank, Thomas. *What's the Matter with Kansas? How Conservatives Won the Heart of America.*
Gates, Jeff. *Democracy at Risk: Rescuing Main Street from Wall Street.*
Hartman, Thom. *What Would Jefferson Do? A Return to Democracy.*
Micklethwait, John, and Adrian Wooldridge. *The Company—A Short History of a Revolutionary Idea.*
Ray, Paul, and Sherry Ray Anderson. *The Cultural Creatives: How 50 Million People Are Changing the World.*
Temin, Peter. *Engines of Enterprise: An Economic History of New England.*
Unger, Roberto Mangabeira, and Cornel West. *The Future of American Progressivism: An Initiative for Political and Economic Reform.*
Zinn, Howard. *A People's History of the United States, 1492–Present.*

Other

Bernstein, Peter L. *Against the Gods—The Remarkable Story of Risk.*
Berry, Wendell. *Another Turn of the Crank.*
Berry, Wendell. *The Way of Ignorance and Other Essays.*

Brand, Stewart. *The Clock of the Long Now: Time and Responsibility—The Ideas Behind the World's Slowest Computer.*

Brand, Stewart. *Whole Earth Catalog.*

Garreau, Joel. *Nine Nations of North America.*

Garreau, Joel. *Radical Evolution: The Promise and Peril of Enhancing Our Minds, Our Bodies—and What It Means to Be Human.*

Gladwell, Malcolm. *The Tipping Point: How Little Things Can Make a Big Difference.*

Hafner, Katie. *The Well: A Story of Love, Death, and Real Life in the Seminal Online Community.*

Hawken, Paul. *Blessed Unrest: How the Largest Movement in the World Came into Being.*

Kohn, Alfie. *No Contest: The Case Against Competition—Why We Lose in Our Race to Win.*

Klein, Naomi. *No Logo.*

Lao-tzu. *The Way of Life.*

Loeb, Paul Rogat. *The Impossible Will Take a Little While: A Citizen's Guide to Hope in a Time of Fear.*

Morrell, Margot, and Stephanie Capparell. *Shackelton's Way.*

Mortenson, Greg, and David Oliver Relin. *Three Cups of Tea: One Man's Mission to Promote Peace . . . One School at a Time.*

Schwartz, Peter, *The Art of the Long View.*

Sterling, Bruce. *Shaping Things.*

Turner, Fred. *From Counterculture to Cyberculture: Stewart Brand, the Whole Earth Network, and the Rise of Digital Utopianism.*

Williams, Wendy, and Robert Whitcomb. *Cape Wind: Money, Celebrity, Class, Politics, and the Battle for Our Energy Future on Nantucket Sound.*

INDEX

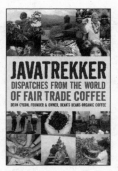